The INDIANA Book

of Records, Firsts, AND

Fascinating Facts

The INDIANA Book

of Records, Firsts, AND

Fascinating Facts

FRED D. CAVINDER

Indiana University Press

BLOOMINGTON

Library of Congress Cataloging in Publication Data

Cavinder, Fred D., 1931-
The Indiana book of records, firsts, and fascinating facts.
Includes index.
1. Indiana--History--Miscellanea. I. Title.
F526.5.C38   1985   977.2'002   84-43155
ISBN 0-253-14001-3
ISBN 0-253-28320-5 (pbk.)
1 2 3 4 5 89 88 87 86 85

CONTENTS

PREFACE

Gathering records about Hoosiers is something like evaluating the work of Penelope, who wove and unraveled while awaiting the return of Ulysses; there is no telling when the job is really done. There are two reasons for this. One is that the people of Indiana are prolific at setting standards and are in the forefront in almost every field; they have been since the state was formed. Right now it is likely that someone in Indiana is setting a new record.

A reader of Indiana publications once noted what could be a second reason; he said journalists claim as a Hoosier anyone who flew over the state in an aircraft. This, of course, is not true; to be classified as a Hoosier, one must *land* somewhere in the state at least once.

But the world *is* full of Hoosiers and former Hoosiers doing things. It is merely that many people fail to realize Indiana's omnipresence. An accomplishment anywhere may involve a Hoosier.

Not long ago an Indiana literary expert ranked bestselling books on the basis of the author's native state; Indiana surpassed all other homelands, including New York. Joseph Kane, in his *Famous First Facts*, has 52 entries for Indiana, instances in which activities by Hoosiers led the way for the nation. To be sure, getting rid of garbage trucks in favor of garbage disposals has doubtful leadership importance, but there is no doubt Jasper was the first town in the U.S. to do it.

Muncie was once chosen by sociologists Robert S. and Helen Merrell Lynd as the most typical town in the nation; a dubious honor, as it turned out; but everyone came to know this Hoosier community through the book *Middletown* (1924) and the followup study *Middletown in Transition* (1937). Franklin made *Life* magazine because of its typical rural-population-come-to-town atmosphere on

Saturday night. In the modern age, an Indiana native son helped launch the space age and an Indiana university leads the nation in the production of astronauts.

So there is no dearth of firsts, records, and prestige for Indiana. The difficulty is in finding all the accomplishments and determining if they are one of a kind, the best, worst, smallest, largest, first, or foremost. Hoosiers, besides being record-setters, are keen collectors not only of facts but also of fancies, trivia as well as tabulations, and they love histrionics as much as history.

You can't fault the legend of Abraham Walters, Jr., and Old Goldin', the deer, for drama, but does the incident belong in the record books? Walters was a pioneer great hunter in Steuben County and Old Goldin' was an elusive buck large enough to qualify for a Paul Bunyan herd. One day the paths of Walters and the deer crossed at Lake Withington. The hunter shot the beast and rushed forward to slit its throat; we can assume from what followed that this didn't finish the deer, but infuriated him. The two struggled in a death grip all night, in and out of the water and from shore to shore of the lake. At dawn Walters triumphed; the deer was dead.

Whether Old Goldin' was the largest buck ever wrestled to death in Indiana is anybody's guess. It's a good bet Walters and his progeny would say yes.

Dr. William Trafton of Evansville won national acclaim around 1824 when he found a cure for milk sickness, an ailment linked to consuming milk and dairy products from animals which had eaten certain plants; but the accomplishment pales in a scientific age of some 150 years later.

Although we know that Wanatah (meaning "kept knee deep in mud") was named for an Indian chief noted for his laziness, no documents verify whether he was the laziest Indian in Indiana. Nor do we know if Knute Rockne is *the* most famous football coach, although it is likely that he is. Whether *Desiderata* by Max Ehrmann of Terre Haute was *the* most popular piece of prose in the 1960s and early 1970s is debatable.

Such are the problems of records-searching.

In its truest meaning, a record indicates a mark set in competition, but the nature of humans to applaud superlatives and note extremes has broadened its application. We speak of weather records without wishing our place to be the coldest, hottest, or snowiest (we only revel in the crown later, when nostalgia makes it seem worthier). We also speak of records in crop production, which are often not so much a matter of competition among farmers of mixed ability as they are the result of mother nature and the world of chemistry. Any person who is the first or the only one to commit some act, or who goes where none have gone before, rates at least handshakes and sometimes parades.

There are some evaluations that obviously border on the impossible. Maybe some Indiana chicken somewhere has laid an egg farther underground than 185 feet. But this kind of "record" is something seldom tabulated. So the chickens of Ramsey, Ind., who made their home in caves of an abandoned limestone quarry, get the nod as the state's deepest hens until some deeper clucks come along.

Although difficult to verify, those kinds of trivial doings sometimes fascinate people more than activities that really matter in a historical perspective. For that matter, historical perspective isn't always crystal clear. Take the case of Elwood Haynes and Charles Black.

Black drove a motorized buggy-like automobile around Indianapolis in 1891. Haynes tested an automobile at Kokomo July 4, 1894. Since Black's "automobile" was ignited by a kerosene torch (and couldn't be driven on a windy day) and Haynes's was clutch-operated and spark-ignited, Haynes wins as the inventor of the car in Indiana. There is some question as to whether Black was first in Indianapolis.

Who is the Indiana record-holder of the two, then? Luckily, both can qualify. Black must be the first licensed driver because he got a permit to drive at Indianapolis city hall and he also had the historic misfortune to have an accident: a dubious first.

Haynes retains title to Hoosier inventor of the first successful "car" as we know it. Certainly the crowd was with him. Going back to Kokomo in his invention, Haynes and Elmer Apperson, who was with him, met some boys and girls on bicycles. They scattered like frightened chickens at the approach of the mechanical monster, so it must have been a new-fangled automobile.

Probably the most difficult category of records is sports. With or without steroids, new athletic accomplishments seem to be incessant; keeping abreast of them is difficult for the newspaper sports pages and almost impossible for the encyclopedist. It is not that sports bests aren't records in the classical sense, but that there is no central point for their collection. State-wide-high school sports records seldom are kept by any official body except at the tournament level. In this volume we have tried to present as many current records in sports as possible.

We have included records which would have gained little notice without the influence of Norris and Ross McWhirter of Great Britain. Their listings of stunts such as the time-honored task of seeing how many people can get into a phone booth sparked an avalanche of record attempts. The *Guinness Book of World Records* now tends to downplay such shenanigans because of the physical danger and because of unreliable verification procedures.

Listing of known stunts in Indiana in no way implies that they are sanctioned, recommended, or worthwhile. You can get injured ramming cigars into your mouth or food into your stomach and the rewards are not all that great. However, since, like mountains, they are there, they are part of the Hoosier menu of activities.

The natural and near-natural extremes in Indiana (weather, crops, geography, etc.) are not competitive records, but are almost idioms of conversation and incapable of being ignored. Certainly the state didn't plan on Deam Oak Memorial being the smallest park in Indiana, but it worked out that way.

There is a category of events that, if not records, should be. Maybe, for instance, there has been a sillier law pondered by the Indiana General Assembly than the bill introduced many years ago which sought to legally change the value of arithmetic pi, the figure used in calculating the dimensions of circles. But even if there is, the pi bill should be noted as some sort of high or low point in ludicrous legislation. And there are other happenings in the same class.

Is being "first" a record? Being first establishes a category of one. Even if thousands later join the parade, they all must fall in line behind the leader. It seems that someone like Virgil Grissom, the first Hoosier into space, deserves a place among record-holders at least as much as the man who can be bumped from his niche in history by a later competitor. Grissom's position, however, can never be topped or equalled.

So, we have records of competition, records of happenstance, records on activities undertaken to better another stunt or start a new category, firsts in the state (and nation and world) and events that clearly stand apart in the Indiana panorama: records, firsts, and fascinating facts.

Entries are supported by published accounts or witnesses. I saw James Mahler, long-time Indiana University instructor in photography, take the first sequence photographs without artificial lighting on the camera. Envy helps make it clear; I was one of his students locked into single photographs with the bulky Speed Graphic press cameras and flash bulbs commonly used in 1953.

Most entries are verifiable. Some are not. It is possible, for instance, that a Hoosier will claim his actions are without precedent and wear the crown simply because he escapes challenge. So be it. And there are a few historical facts that we accept as Hoosier faith.

But for the most part, Indiana records are subjected to the kind of rigorous peer review possible only by Hoosiers who take pride in their role and accomplishments in the nation and who hold scorn for pretenders.

More than record-setters are necessary. Compilers are vital. The number who have helped in this collection may constitute a record itself. Special thanks must go to the Indiana Division and the Microfilm Division of the Indiana

State Library, the keepers of the files at *The Indianapolis Star*, colleges and universities, many historical society museums, and sundry associations and statistics keepers.

This is certainly not the end of it. Sports records are subject to annual, sometimes daily, attack. Striving to be the best is an inbred Hoosier characteristic which threatens all kings of the hill. Indiana always goes for it. Of all the planes you see overhead in a year, one is sure to contain a Hoosier or a former Hoosier en route to a new accomplishment. If not, then perhaps that's a record.

The INDIANA Book

of Records, Firsts, AND

Fascinating Facts

A

ACCIDENTS AND DISASTERS

THE *worst commercial airline crash* in Indiana was September 9, 1969, when a DC-9 piloted by Capt. James M. Elrod of Plainfield collided with a Piper Cherokee 140 about 14 miles southeast of Indianapolis, killing all passengers and crew on both planes, a total of 83. The DC-9 was Allegheny Airlines Flight 853 carrying 78 passengers. The small plane was piloted by Robert W. Carey, Indianapolis, a student on a solo exercise.

THE *first automobile fatality* in Indiana, according to state police records, was John Rynearson of Frankfort, who lost control of his car while he was shifting gears August 2, 1905. The car jumped a 15-foot embankment and Rynearson died of a broken neck.

SURELY THE STRANGEST *traffic accident* in Indiana occurred February 20, 1940, seven miles from Rochester, when an unidentified motorist struck an elephant. The elephant was identified; it was Mollie, who had wandered away after being intentionally set free to escape a fire which wiped out the Cole Brothers Circus.

SINCE records have been kept, the *smallest number of highway fatalities* in Indiana was in 1906 when only 3 deaths involving cars were recorded.

THE *first train wreck* of consequence in Indiana was on the Lafayette and Indianapolis Railroad 8 miles east of Lafayette October 31, 1864, when a train carrying Union soldiers home crashed on Dead Man's curve. Although many were killed, the exact number of victims is uncertain.

THE *worst train wreck* occurred at Ivanhoe, near Gary; 85 died and 179 were hurt when an empty troop train rammed the rear of a section of cars of the Hagenback-Wallace Circus train June 22, 1918. A gas unit exploded in the circus train. No Indiana train wreck has had more casualties. The circus train was en route to Hammond, where it was to play the next day. It had pulled part way into a switching line because of a hot box. Among the victims were Miss Louise Cottrell of London, a bareback rider; Arthur Derrick, Belgian strong man; a Miss Jewell, a lion tamer, and Miss Jennie Todd, an aerialist.

THE *worst wreck on the Ohio River* was near Patriot, Switzerland County, about 11:30 p.m. on December 4, 1868, when the steamboats *United States* and *America* crashed on a curve. An estimated 45 passengers, plus a crew of 25, were lost from the *United States* and two aboard the *America* perished. The loss of the *United States* was greater because oil on board the packet exploded. The *United States* was bound downriver from Cincinnati, the *America* upstream from Louisville.

THE *biggest explosion* involving a populated area in Indian was that at Fontanet in Vigo County October 15, 1907, when a powder mill blew up. All homes in the town were damaged, 40 persons were killed, and 1,500 were injured. The blast caused some damage at Brazil, Terre Haute, and Crawfordsville. The Indiana National Guard was called in to help the townspeople, 1,100 of whom were made homeless.

THE *worst indoor explosion* in Indiana was October 31, 1963, in the Indiana State Fairgrounds Coliseum in Indianapolis when propane gas was ignited under seats during a performance of "Holiday on Ice," killing 73 and injuring about 400. One of the injured died later, bringing the toll to 74. The blast came during the finale of the initial performance of the ice show. Investigation showed that leaking gas was responsible for the explosion and a grand jury returned indictments against seven state and city fire officials, representatives of the coliseum, and the firm which supplied the bottled gas.

THE *worst mining disaster* in Indiana occured at 10:30 a.m. February 20, 1925, when an explosion in City Coal Company mine at Sullivan resulted in 52 deaths.

THE *worst disaster in an Indiana nursing home* was December 18, 1964, when 20 elderly persons died in a fire at the McGaw Nursing Home at Fountaintown in bitterly cold weather.

ALTHOUGH the *flood of 1913* was vast, in terms of casualties it takes second place to the *flood of 1937*. In 1937, 77 died and flood damage reached $24,735,000. There is no firm fatality figure for the 1913 flood, but it is estimated that 60 were killed.

ANIMALS

BOBBIE, a collie lost by its owners at Wolcott in 1923, made the *longest recorded journey by a dog* from Indiana. After six months the collie turned up at the home of its owners in Silverton, Ore., after traveling more than 2,000 miles. The trip was verified by those who saw the dog en route and it set a world record.

THE *lowest chickens* known are the 25,000 installed in caves left from limestone quarry work at Ramsey, starting in April 1954. A. J. Martin, owner of the hatchery, found the constant temperature of 60 degrees and lack of disturbance 185 feet underground beneficial to the chickens. Water was piped into the caves to drip constantly into drinking containers, fans maintained sufficient air flow, and 40-watt bulbs provided the illumination for 14 hours each day. The underground chicken house was lighted only by 7 1/2-watt bulbs for the remaining 10 hours, so the birds could get some rest from laying. Martin said egg production was 20 to 25 percent higher than that of above-ground hens in the summer months when temperatures up on the surface were hot.

BEECHER ARLINDA ELLEN, a holstein, holds the world record for *milk production* from one lactation, which is 365 days, of 55,661 pounds. Owned by Mr. and Mrs. Harold Beecher of Rochester, she set the mark in 1975. The cow, born in 1969, was put to sleep March 5, 1984.

LANDOWNER and cattleman Edward C. Sumner introduced *bullfighting* to Indiana before the Civil War by staging contests at his place, Sugar Grove, near Earl Park, in which one bull fought another bull. A few contests also were held after the Civil War. Sumner was considered by some to be Indiana's first sports promoter.

THE *first registered cattle* brought to Indiana were believed to have been shorthorns added by Chris Whitehead to his farm near Brookville in 1838. The herd included a 2-year-old roan bull called Eryx 1982.

THE *largest steer* in Indiana, certainly the largest preserved steer, is a cross-bred Hereford named Ben, who weighed 4,720 pounds when he had to be destroyed in 1911 because of breaking his leg in a slip on ice. Ben, raised on a farm north of Kokomo by the Murphy brothers, survives in taxidermy form to be wondered at in an exhibition in Highland Park in southwest Kokomo. Born in January 1902, the steer is believed to have been the largest calf in the world, weighing 1,800 pounds at the age of 18 months. When he was 4 years old he tipped the scales at 4,000 pounds, and he had reached his 4,720-pound weight when he had his accident in February, 1910. He stood 6 feet, 4 inches tall at the forequarter, had a girth of 13 feet, 8 inches, and was either 16 feet, 8 inches long from tip of tail to end of nose, or 16 feet, 2 inches long, depending on what documents are used. Another visuality oddity was his left horn, twisted at a rakish angle. During his life, Ben was exhibited at circuses and sideshows and received numerous ribbons for his remarkable size and fine lines. Because of his mixed ancestry, Ben was never a registered steer.

THE greatest Hoosier *sire of harness racers* probably was Blue Bill of Rush County, who sired 60 record-making trotters. His daughters produced 173 well-known trotters. The horse was buried on the Wilson farm near Andersonville.

THE Washington Park Zoo at Michigan City, with a population of about 300 animals of all kinds, is the *largest raiser of Bengal tigers* in Indiana and among the largest in the nation. Since Wessel Bannwart, a native of Michigan City, took over direction of the zoo in 1966, a total of 95 cubs have been born there and sold to other zoos. The dynasty began with Guinevere, who came from the wild, and Beowolf, who was purchased in Arizona. There have been as many as six tigers to a litter. When rearing of the tigers began, their birth in zoos was somewhat unusual, but the breeding of tigers in captivity has increased greatly.

THE *largest zoo* in the state is Mesker Park Zoo at Evansville, which has 67 acres and includes five ponds. The animal population is about 500.

THE *first sighting of a cattle egret* in the state was May 1, 1964, five miles north of Winamac in Pulaski County. The strutting, crane-like bird comes from Africa; how it reached America is not known. The largest number ever seen together in Indiana is 16.

THE *record number of sandhill cranes* in Indiana is the estimated 10,000 observed during the fall migration at the Jasper-Pulaski State Wildlife Refuge. The refuge is a regular feeding stop for the cranes, which also stop there in lesser numbers in the spring. The sandhill does not spend time in Indiana except during migration.

THE *first successful goldfish farm* in the nation was founded in 1899 by Eugene Curtis Shireman at Martinsville with 200 fish. Eventually the 1,500 acres, with 600 ponds and 350 acres under water, was producing 40 million goldfish annually. It became Grassyforks, Inc., in 1924, and still ranks among the biggest goldfish producers in the world.

DR. GARY BUTCHER of the Purdue University Animal Disease Diagnostic Laboratory is believed to be the only veterinarian in Indiana doing a *surgical procedure to determine the sex of young birds*. "Most people I talk to don't realize that you can't tell the sex of a bird by looking at it, and are really surprised when you tell them you have to do it surgically in many cases," said the doctor. The operation involves a 2-millimeter incision and insertion of an otoscope to examine the sex organs visually. It takes about 5 minutes and appears to be painless.

[SEE ALSO *Accidents and disasters; Research; Speed; Sports, Fishing*.]

ARCHAEOLOGY

THE *first official archaeologist* for the state was Gary D. Ellis, appointed in July 1977 to a post established as a section of the Indiana State Museum.

THE *first archaeological excavation* in Indiana for which the records and notes survived was done in 1898 in Posey County at the mouth of the Wabash River by Clifford Anderson, directed by Warren K. Moorehead. However, the *first dig using scientific methods* (plotting the area, cataloguing finds, etc.) was in 1926–27 on the farm of William Albee in Sullivan County. The archaeologist was J. Arthur MacLean, director of the John Herron Art Institute in Indianapolis. The site of the dig became known as the Albee Mound.

THE *first complete mastodon skeleton* found in the nation is possessed by the Earlham College Science Museum. It was unearthed in 1895 in nearby Preble County, Ohio.

THE *oldest mummy* in Indiana whose age has been calculated is that owned by the Wayne County Historical Museum at Richmond, said to date to 1580 B.C. It was purchased in Egypt in 1929 by Julia Meek Gaar, founder of the museum, and is the body of a female about six feet tall.

[SEE ALSO *Fossils; Indians.*]

ARMAMENTS

THE Liberty Pressed Metal Company at Kokomo manufactured the *first aerial bomb* with fins in 1918.

THE *first American howitzer shell* used in warfare was made by the Superior Machine Tool Company at Kokomo in 1918.

THE nation's *first 90-millimeter antiaircraft gun* was produced by Allis-Chalmers plant at LaPorte, coming off the assembly line September 17, 1941, and unveiled before a large crowd the next day. The gun weighed nine tons.

[SEE ALSO *Inventions.*]

ART AND ARTISTS

HENRY HAMILTON did the *earliest art* on record in Indiana in 1777 when, while leading 500 soldiers toward Vincennes from Detroit, he stopped along the Wabash River near what is now Logansport and sketched a rock formation called "the ship" because of its shape. Hamilton's sketch was done with gray washes.

THE *earliest known portrait* in Indiana is that of Gen. Hyacinth Lasselle, painted by Lewis Pickham at Vincennes in 1815. Lasselle, born at the Miami village of Kekionga, (present site of Fort Wayne) in 1777, lived at Vincennes and Logansport, where he died in 1843. The artist, born in Rhode Island, lived and worked at Vincennes, where he died in 1823.

THE *first professional artist* in Indiana appears to have been George Winter, who reached Logansport in 1837, became intrigued by the Potawatomi and Miami Indians, and moved freely among them, painting their everyday life until 1839. He also kept a journal.

THE *first exhibit of art works solely by female artists* was organized in 1912 at the John Herron Museum of Art in Indianapolis, a show of 31 oils, water colors, and pastels.

THE *first woman commissioned to do an official portrait* of an Indiana governor was Marie Goth, a native of Indianapolis, and later a member of the artist community at Nashville, who completed the portrait of Gov. Henry F. Schricker in April 1943 during his first term. Miss Goth died in 1975 when she was 88.

THE *biggest painting* ever done by a Hoosier was *Banvard Panorama of the Mississippi River*, by John Banvard of New Harmony. It was unbroken canvas 3 miles long and 8 feet high, 126,720 square feet, portraying 1,200 miles of the lower Mississippi. Displayed in Boston in 1847, the painting was believed destroyed either in a theater fire or in the blaze which destroyed P. T. Barnum's museum in the 1880s. Banvard, who arrived in New Harmony in 1836 when he was 21, did the painting in a warehouse in Louisville, using reels 20 feet apart. It was first exhibited in Boston, then taken on tour. Little is known of Banvard.

THE town of Nappanee, Elkhart County, has produced *more nationally successful artists and cartoonists per capita* than any other town. Achieving success from the town of about 5,000 residents were Merrill Blosser, creator of "Freckles and His Friends" for comics; Francis (Mike) Parks, cartoonist for papers in Chicago, Cleveland, New York, Omaha, San Francisco and the Newspaper Enterprise Association; Henry Maust, commercial artist and cartoonist for the *Cleveland Plain Dealer*, the *Birmingham Ledger*, and Chicago advertising agencies; Fred Neher, creator of "Some Punkins" and "Life's like That;" Bill Holman, who drew "Smokey Stover," and Max Gwin, who did a cartoon strip for *Prairie Farmer* and produced cartoons for some 300 publications.

THE *largest handmade paper* in Indiana comes in sheets 34 by 48 inches, made by Twinrocker Handmade Paper Company at Brookston, owned by Kathryn Clark. Such sheets are believed to be among the largest made by hand in the Western world.

MCGUIRE HALL at Richmond High School is the *only art gallery in the nation which is associated with a public school*. Operated by the Richmond Art Association, the gallery began in 1904 and was made part of a structure adjoining the present school through a gift from Charles McGuire. Art and band classes are conducted in the art gallery wing.

ASTRONAUTS

THE *first Hoosier in space* was Virgin I. Grissom of Mitchell, a graduate of Purdue University, who made a suborbital flight July 21, 1961, aboard a Mercury-launched capsule called the Liberty Bell 7. The ride, which took 15 minutes, soared 118.2 miles into space and 302.8 miles down range and was only the third effort in the entire U.S. space program. While Grissom was waiting to be picked up, the hatch blew off prematurely and the capsule sank, something which never happened before.

Grissom had *several other firsts* in the space program: the first Hoosier to *make an extended flight in space* as pilot of the Unsinkable Molly Brown, March 23, 1965, a three-orbit flight. On that flight he became the first Hoosier to *dine in space* when he took a bite of a corned-beef and rye sandwich smuggled on board by astronaut John Young. Finally, he was *first in losing his life*, January 27, 1967, during a rehearsal for an Apollo I flight. Fire swept the oxygen-pure atmosphere of the cabin in which he was locked with Ed White, who had been the first astronaut to walk in space, and Roger B. Chaffee, himself a graduate of Purdue

University, like Grissom. Faulty wiring was blamed for the blaze.

THE *first Hoosier to remain in space* an extended period of time was Frank Borman of Gary who, with James A. Lovell, Jr., remained in orbit 14 days in the Gemini 7 after being launched December 4, 1965. He accumulated a total of 477 hours, 36 minutes in space during his astronautical career, a record for a Hoosier.

Borman also became the *first Hoosier to rendezvous in space* with another vehicle. He and Lovell guided the space capsule to within a foot of another containing Walter M. Schirra, Jr., and Thomas P. Stafford on December 15, 1965.

On December 4, 1965, Borman became the *first Hoosier to eat a meal* in space. Aboard Gemini 7, he and Lovell consumed peanut cubes, sausage patties, fruit salad, and pudding.

In another first, Borman took off his space suit and *flew in his underwear* December 10, 1965.

THE *first non-astronaut in space* was Charles D. Walker of Bedford, 1971 graduate of Purdue University, who rode the 12th shuttle flight August 30, 1984. His job was to continue experiments in space conducted by his employer, McDonnell Douglas Astronautics Corporation of St. Louis.

THE *first Hoosier aboard a commercial space flight* was Joseph Allen of Crawfordsville, a member of the crew aboard the space shuttle Columbia. It was launched November 11, 1982, carrying only equipment from private firms destined for experimentation or release in space. Allen also was in the *first man to rescue a sattelite from space*. November 13, 1984, Allen and Dale A. Gardner walked into space to get a 1,265-pound satellite which needed to be brought back to earth for repairs. Allen seized the satellite, called Palapa, and wrestled it into the cargo bay of the space shuttle Columbia. At the time Allen, a graduate of DePauw University, was the *smallest man* among the astronauts; he weighed 130 pounds.

THE school which has graduated the *most students who became astronauts* is Purdue University, whose graduates in the U.S. space program have included Neil A. Armstrong, Eugene A. Cernan, Roger B. Chaffee, Virgil I. Grissom, John E. Blaha, Roy D. Bridges, Jr., Richard O. Covey, Guy S. Gardner, Jerry L. Ross, Loren J. Shriver, and Donald E. Williams.

A U T H O R S : SEE *Books and periodicals*.

AUTOMOBILES AND TRUCKS

THE *first commercially-built automobile* was that constructed by Elwood Haynes and tested July 4, 1894, on Pumpkin Vine Pike east of Kokomo. Haynes made automobiles with Elmer Apperson, who was with Haynes on the famed trial run. It is credited with being the first clutch-driven automobile with electrical ignition, weighed 240 pounds, and reached a speed of 8 miles per hour in the 1894 test. The manufacturing began the next year. Although Haynes experimented in the rear of a gas office, his prototype automobile was assembled at the Riverside Machine Shop on Main Street in Kokomo south of Wildcat Creek. From the time he got the idea in 1892, he experimented with electricity and steam before settling on gasoline as a fuel. He used a single-cylinder upright engine of marine type in the car, which was given to the Smithsonian Institution in 1910.

M. O. REEVES of the Sexto-Octo Company at Columbus, produced the *first motor bus* through his creation in 1897 of many-wheeled vehicles for multiple passengers. His "buses" were built on the concept that more wheels gave a smoother ride; his slogan was "No shock, no jolt, no bounce, no rebound."

THE *first honeycomb radiator*, similar to those used on

cars today, was made in Evansville by the Simplicity Auto Company between 1906 and 1912.

JOHN W. ESTERLINE, a Purdue University graduate who had developed an electrical recording instrument firm at Lafayette, thought a *6-volt starting system* for automobiles could be developed to be compatible with the wiring coming into use in 1912. Charles F. Kettering had devised a 32-volt electrical system for the Cadillac, which required a series of switches to start and operate the car. Esterline's system, powered by a battery developed by Willard Storage Battery Company in Indianapolis, was a success and, after introduction at the 1912 automotive shows, he was flooded with contracts. His plant at Lafayette, opened in 1913, employing 300, was flooded. This put him so far behind on orders that contracts were cancelled and the firm failed. Because the system was merely improvements on already existing methods and patents, there was no protection for Esterline; his system was taken over by others and became the widely used electrical setup for automobiles. Among Esterline's major backers were Carl G. Fisher and James A. Allison, whose Presto-o-lite firm making gas lighting for cars was put out of business by the battery system. Esterline later was a partner in the Esterline Angus Company, an electrical instrument firm in Indianapolis.

THE *first pneumatic rubber tire* was invented at Kokomo in October 1894 by D. C. Spraker, president of the Kokomo Rubber Tire Company. It was made of strips of three-ply rubber, canvas, and other wrapping of vulcanized rubber wound around a slender pole.

THE *first license* for a motor vehicle was the city hall permit acquired in Indianapolis by Charles Black in 1891; it permitted him to drive his kerosene-flame-ignited automobile downtown. Black, who operated a carriage shop, ran his motor-equipped buggy only at night, to avoid horses. The vehicle was a carriage imported from Germany and fitted with a one-cylinder, flame-ignited gasoline engine. Black had his Indianapolis carriage firm in a shop at Pennsylvania and Maryland streets in what is now the downtown area. Although some like to think the car was the first gasoline-powered vehicle in America, that claim has been pretty well disproven. His family gave the car to the Indianapolis Children's Museum, where it is displayed.

CHARLES BLACK of Indianapolis is also credited with having the *first automobile crash* when his car ran into two store windows during an outing around 1891.

WHAT is surely the *first automobile publicity tour* out of Indiana, and probably the wildest, occurred when two Anderson men, A. T. Mosher and Harry Harter, left Anderson November 3, 1908, in a Buick to make a 6,000-mile trip through the South to prove that the high-tension magneto of Frank and Perry Remy was a superior product. They went across Kentucky, Tennessee, and Georgia into the Florida swamps in an era when roads were almost nonexistent. Although the battery gave out in the water, the magneto performed admirably, supplying electrical power to the car. The two drove through cotton fields in Georgia, along cowpaths up Lookout Mountain, and returned to Indiana via Daytona Beach, Tampa, New Orleans, Crescent City, and Vicksburg. All along the way the Buick carried signs and banner explaining the mission and proclaiming the magneto under the hood.

THE *first Indiana car believed to have traveled* 1,000 *miles* was a model made in 1899 by Elwood Haynes and Edgar Apperson in their plant at Kokomo. The car was driven from Indiana to Brooklyn to show to a potential customer.

THE *earliest cross-country group auto trip* was organized by Carl G. Fisher of Indianapolis. To promote his idea of a transcontinental auto route, to be called the Lincoln Memorial Highway, Fisher and 71 others, termed the Trail-Blazers, set out from Indianapolis on July 1, 1913. Among the drivers was Ray Harroun, first winner of the Indianapolis 500-Mile Race. The vehicles represented every automobile manufacturer in Indiana and included

Pathfinder "40" trucks, some of which carried extra equipment, such as an entire load of spare tires. The caravan reached San Francisco in 34 days and the Lincoln Highway later followed 500 miles of the route taken by the Hoosiers. The name Lincoln Highway was given to U.S. 30 in northern Indiana.

THE *first fire truck* put into official use in Indiana was one which Fire Station No. 9 in Terre Haute began operating June 6, 1910. The station now is an historical building displaying the original alarm system, horse stalls, and brass pole, and the fire truck, an Oldsmobile model.

THE *first female driver* in Indiana is said to have been Mrs. Mary Landon of Elkhart, although there appear to be few details of her driving record. She died in 1965 at the age of 89.

THE *first car used by a president* was a Cole made in Indianapolis in which William Howard Taft rode to state occasions. Taft was the first president to use a gasoline-powered automobile.

A trip from Indianapolis to New York City January 3–6, 1930, by Clessie Lyle Cummins of the Cummins Engine Company at Columbus, was the *first diesel engine automobile trip* in Indiana and the nation. The journey of 792 miles, using a stock model engine weighing 1,200 pounds, cost $1.38 for fuel. The engine was installed in a seven-passenger Packard sedan.

CLESSIE LYLE CUMMINS also set the *first official speed record for a diesel-powered vehicle* on March 20, 1930. He was driving a Packard roadster at Daytona Beach, Fla., to an average speed of 80.398 miles an hour. The vehicle had a 4-cylinder marine-type engine and had been stripped of fenders, windshield, and excess body trimmings.

CUMMINS ENGINE COMPANY, Columbus, assembled the *first diesel engine tractor* with an American-build engine in May 1930, using a Cummins model U 4-cylinder, 4 1/2-inch bore, 6-inch stroke engine. It weighed 1,400 pounds and was placed in an Allis-Chalmers track type tractor.

THE Studebaker engine, built at South Bend, was the power for the *first automobile-airplane combination* in the U.S., the Arrowbile, built by the Waterman Arrowplane Corporation at Santa Monica, Cal. After tests February 20, 1937, the first five Arrowbiles were delivered to Studebaker Corporation in Indiana August 15, 1937. The six-cylinder engine, which developed 100 horsepower, gave the craft a top air speed of 120 miles an hour and a cruising speed of 105 miles an hour.

STUDEBAKER was the *largest car maker* in Indiana, selling 22,555 models in the first year of full operation as car manufacture and sales, 1910, and 114,000 three years later. In pre-World-War-II days, Studebaker was the fifth largest producer in the nation.

ON the basis of the number of makers, Indianapolis holds the record as the *biggest automobile center* in Indiana. At one time or another 44 different cars were made in the Hoosier capital, still a small number compared to the 208 different autos which have been manufactured throughout the state.

THE *first miniature automobiles* in the U.S. were constructed at Richmond by Crosley, and first offered for sale April 28, 1939. The prices, FOB Richmond, were $325 for the two-passenger convertible coupe and $350 for the four-passenger convertible sedan. The maker was Powell Crosley, Jr. The cars had an 80-inch wheelbase, were 10 feet long, had two cylinders, three forward speeds and reverse, four-wheel mechanical brakes, and a four-gallon fuel tank.

THE *first trucks to carry freight to Alaska* via the Alcan Highway were two vehicles from Alcan Express in Warsaw, which left July 20, 1948, to make the 5,500-mile trip, slated to take about 20 days. They carried gas, tools, auto parts, and light motors.

THE *first traffic light* is said to have been that installed in 1923 at Carmel, which also became Indiana's first speed trap. Invented and built by Leslie Haines, it was 8 feet high, had only red and green signals, and was placed atop a concrete base at Range Line Road and Ind. 234. The curious attracted to it soon were being arrested because without a caution light they could not judge when the signal would change and were running the red light. Haines and others began manufacturing the light, but, without a patent, their efforts stopped in 1933. The original light was taken down in 1934.

THE Vance Corporation at Hammond has what is considered the world's *most powerful wrecker*. Called Monster No. 2, it is 30 feet long, weighs 28 tons and can lift more than 179 tons.

THE 275 acres of stacked automobiles at seven locations in central Indiana is said to constitute the *largest auto junkyard* under the ownership of one family, that of Marion Pierce of Lewisville and his five brothers.

[SEE ALSO *Accidents and disasters; Inventions; Manufacturing; Radio; Research; Speed.*]

AVIATION

THE *first Hoosier to try flying* by mechanical means appears to have been Horace Rockwell, a painter of Roanoke, Ind., who, about 1852, launched himself from the second floor of his home with machinery he designed to mimic bird wings. He suffered fractures in the accident; observers said he forgot to flap his wings.

THE *first person in the nation to make a glider with cambered (convex) wings* was Octave Chanute in 1895; he made some 2,000 flights at Miller's Station near the site of Gary in 1896 and 1897.

THE *most successful hang glider* made by a Hoosier is the Valkyrie, created during the winter of 1974 by Bill Wolf of Columbus, later of Seattle, Wash. Weighing 50 pounds, the machine's 31-foot wingspan required that it be disassembled to get it out of Wolf's basement. The glider was placed in the Smithsonian Institution in 1978, the same year Wolf moved to Seattle. He died March 30, 1983.

HEAVIER-THAN-AIR machines, usually in the form of gliders, were flown in Indiana well before the Wright brothers put the nation's first motor-driven craft aloft. The *first heavier-than-air flights* in the state were taken by Octave Chanute near where Gary now stands; he flew gliders in the sand dunes seven years before the Wright brothers' flight in 1903. Chanute, a Frenchman, made 2,000 flights in 1896 and 1897 and studied glider designs. Some of his findings were used by the Wrights in construction of their craft.

THE world's *first wind tube*, a device for testing model aircraft, was built in 1901 at the University at Notre Dame by Albert Francis Zahm, who had been a student of Notre Dame and was a faculty member after graduation in 1883. Zahm was involved in the development of many flight theories, constructed models of aircraft, and helped organize the first International Aeronautic Congress in 1893 at the Chicago World's Fair.

THE *first monoplane* was built at Terre Haute by the Johnson brothers, Harry L., Louis and Julius, whose first model was airborne in 1910. The plane used a 50-horsepower motor built by the brothers in a barn. It developed 1,250 revolutions per minute and could send the monoplane to a height of 2,000 feet at a speed of 60 miles an hour. Water for cooling the engine was contained in the metal frame of the plane. They built a better model in July 1911 and took it on tours of fairs. That model was given to the Smithsonian Institution. A tornado which destroyed their plant ended plans to go into production with the monoplane engines. Instead, the brothers turned to making an outboard boat motor and became the famed Johnson Motors; they moved to Waukegan, Ill., in 1927.

THE Indianapolis Motor Speedway was the site of the *first licensed aviation meet in the nation* in 1910, a six-day event. The first man to circle the track, which had been built in 1909, was Orville Wright, flying as high as 125 feet. Competitors circled the track in the air, guided by pylons on the ground. Walter S. Brookins, 21, set a new altitude record of 4,384 feet.

BLANCHE STUART SCOTT became the *first woman* in the nation *to make a public solo flight* on October 23, 1910, in an exhibition at Driving Park, Fort Wayne. A student of Glenn Hammond Curtiss, the aviation pioneer, she took an Ely machine to a height of 12 feet and flew across the field, saying that she could have gone farther. "I believe I could have turned and circled the track, but Mr. Curtiss has absolutely forbidden me attempting the turns until I have mastered the straightaway flights," she was quoted as saying in the *Fort Wayne Journal-Gazette*.

ART SMITH of Fort Wayne was dubbed "the *most daring aviator in America*" by magazines in 1916. He was the *first to fly at night*, the *first to do skywriting*, the *first to set off fireworks from an airplane*. In 1911, at 17, he built his own plane, but it crashed. As a barnstormer, his loop-the-loop and death dives were highlights of the Pacific Exposition in San Francisco in 1915. He gave foreign exhibitions and was a flight instructor and test pilot for the Army in World War I, winning 58 medals. After the war he barnstormed and flew the mail. In 1925 he made the *first elopement by air*, crashing in Hillsdale, Mich. He and his wife, both hurt, were wed in the hospital. In 1926, carrying mail from New York to Chicago, he crashed against a tree near Montpelier, O., and was killed.

LEE O. EIKENBERRY of Flora was the *first man to fly a plane with retractable landing gear*. Born in Kokomo, Eikenberry learned to fly in the Army in 1917. The plane with the retractable landing gear was designed by Al Moody of Colorado, called the Eagle Rock Bullet, and was the forerunner of the first Boeing airliner.

EIKENBERRY also was the *greatest barnstorming pilot* on record. He made 17,000 flights carrying 32,000 paid passengers during the 1930s. Eikenberry, born near Kokomo in 1893, also set a record in a Waco 3-place biplane by *flying it 928 hours without an overhaul* in an era when overhauls usually were required after 100 hours in the air.

THE endurance *record for keeping a Piper Cub aloft* by a Hoosier was set in Muncie circa 1925 by Lee O. Eikenberry of Flora and Muncie, Kelvin Baxter of Richmond, and Robert McDaniels of Muncie, who kept the plane in flight for three weeks. Refueling was done by hoisting 5-gallon cans into the plane from a moving pickup truck.

CAPT. GEORGE W. STEELE, JR., of Marion and Lt. Commander Sydney M. Kraus of Peru were the first recorded Hoosiers *to cross the Atlantic in dirigibles* as observers on the ZR 3 from Germany, which reached Lakehurst, N.J., in August 1927. Steele was the ranking American observer among 17 men on board. The 5,006-mile, non-stop crossing in 81 hours was a record at the time.

THE sole Hoosier flier to win the *Thompson racing trophy* three times was Col. Roscoe Turner, who flew his last competition in that event in 1939 at the age of 43. Turner also held records as the *first to run an airplane engine at more than 2,000 horsepower*, the *first to fly an air-cooled engine with a streamlined cowling*, the *first to lower a plane via parachute* and the *first to fly 400 miles an hour*. Turner settled in Indianapolis at the behest of city officials who thought he could help lead a drive to develop a major airport. During three days beginning September 2, 1934, Turner made headlines by setting a *trans-continental speed record* from Los Angeles to New York of 10 hours and 2 minutes, stopping at Cleveland to refuel and take off at air races in weather which had grounded all the other planes, then returning to Cleveland to win the Thompson trophy. He was known for his flashy uniforms, which he designed himself, and for his pet lion, Gilmore, who went with him everywhere on a leash. Once in the Waldorf-Astoria Hotel in New York, Turner, a notorious sleepwalker, awakened in the lobby, nude, walking Gilmore. Of him, aviation giant Eddie Rickenbacker once said, "Roscoe Turner has done more for aviation than any man in the United States." When Turner died in June 1970, his wife abolished a museum he had established in Indianapolis; some of his planes were sent to the Smithsonian Institution.

LAYING claim to being Indiana's *first flying judge* was Grant Rogers of the Johnson-Brown Circuit Court, who commuted from Franklin to Bedford in his own Fairchild cabin plane on October 1, 1945, to serve as a special judge in the trial of Earl Fry, who was charged with killing his wife, Dora, with a shotgun. Judge Rogers took to the air because it cut his one-way travel time from 2 hours to about 30 minutes.

HERBERT O. FISHER of Indianapolis was the *first pilot to reverse all propellers* at the same time on a four-engine transport plane in flight, about 1952. He was experimenting for the Curtiss-Wright Corporation at Caldwell, N. J., on methods for making emergency descents, and showed that the engines could be reversed and the plane could still maintain a low forward speed.

THE record for *circumnavigating the earth* by Hoosiers in a twin-engine, turboprop plane is 76 hours, set March 25, 1983, when two Hoosier pilots and a pilot from Arkansas landed at Elkhart. The pilots were David Webster, president of Durakool Corp. of Elkhart; Joe Harnish, also of Durakool; and Forrest Ogden, Mena, Ark. They flew a Gulfstream Commander 1000 on the trip.

THE *nation's first airport on a college campus* was Purdue Airport, which opened at the West Lafayette campus of Purdue University in 1930, serving both the university and the surrounding community.

PURDUE became the *first university in Indiana to inau-*

gurate regular airline service from the campus to a major city in 1950 when Lake Central Airlines began service between West Lafayette and Chicago.

THE *first woman to obtain a commercial pilot's license* in Indiana was Lenora Harper McElroy about 1930; she took training at Indianapolis Municipal Airport.

THE *first radar for civilian flying* in the U.S. was installed at Weir Cook Airport (now Indianapolis International Airport), May 24, 1946; it was an experimental unit which covered an area 30 miles in all directions from the airport.

THE *first marked air route for private planes* was the Wrightway, established between Indianapolis and Dayton, O., in 1948 as part of the trail 40 miles wide marked from Washington to Los Angeles. The Indianapolis-Dayton route of 100 miles was designated Skyway 1.

THE first *independent air passenger line* in Indiana was that approved February 6, 1948, for Roscoe Turner Aeronautical Corporation, which planned to fly passengers from Grand Rapids to Cincinnati via South Bend, Logansport, Indianapolis, and Connersville and from Chicago to Louisville via Lafayette, Indianapolis, Bloomington, and Bedford.

INDIANA'S *first overseas charter airline* was American Trans-Air, with headquarters at Indianapolis International Airport; it became a carrier in 1981 after nearly eight years as a leasing and aircraft management firm. With a fleet of 13 aircraft, including a Boeing 707, a 727, and a DC-10, the firm carried 618,000 passengers in 1983 and flew 1.043 million passenger-miles. Dan Bradford, general manager of the firm, says the aircraft can be chartered for transportation to any place in the world.

THE record holder of *parachute jumps from a balloon* is Ray Porter, credited with 3,000 leaps in a career which began at 14 with a jump in Westside Park at Muncie. Porter jumped in an era when crowds gathered to see a jumper hauled aloft by a balloon with its basket attached to an open parachute. Porter's *world record career total* was recognized by the Civil Aviation Authority, and the CAA cited him as the *oldest certified hot-air balloon jumper* in the U.S. in 1954, when Porter was 55. He also recorded the *highest jump*, 10,500 feet, at Dixon, Ill., during a July 4 exhibition about 1923.

WHEN Roger Reynolds of Indianapolis, a parachutist with the U.S. Army's Golden Knights, stepped from an airplane April 24, 1974, over Charlottesville, Va., and his chute failed to open, he made the *longest drop by a Hoosier who survived*, 2,000 feet. Reynolds landed on his left side in soft soil in a doctor's backyard, suffered multiple fractures and injuries, and returned to parachuting after 12 months in the hospital. The fact that a doctor was there to administer emergency treatment was believed to have been an important factor in his survival.

THE Hoosier with the *most accuracy in parachuting* is believed to have been Charles F. Collingwood of Fountaintown, a member of the U.S. Army parachute team, "The Golden Knights." During one year, 1976, Collingwood hit the bull's-eye on the ground 37 times at night and 33 times in the daytime.

JACK SWOPE of Cloverdale claims the *freefall altitude record* in the Midwest and is the oldest Hoosier to free fall more than five miles. Swope dropped 28,400 feet in 1973 at the age of 46 near the intersection of I-70 and Ind. 234 as part of a promotion for a nearby event. A skydiver 23 years, Swope still was active as of 1984, when he dropped into the White River Park State Games on July 20, carrying an American flag.

[SEE ALSO *Accidents and disasters; Automobiles and trucks; Colleges and universities; Crime and criminals; Mail; Military; Police; Wars, world.*]

THE AUTOMOBILE OF CHARLES BLACK (left) of Indianapolis was
involved in the first car crash in the state when it struck two
windows in 1891. It is part of the collection of the Indianapolis
Children's Museum. (Photo courtesy of Indianapolis Children's
Museum.)

THIS DRAGLINE, *the B-E 3270-W, is the largest in Indiana and second largest in the world. The bucket can hold four automobiles. (Photo courtesy of Amax Coal Co.)*

HARRIETTE B. CONN, *Indianapolis, was the first black named a public defender in Indiana. (File photo.)*

A Wooton Desk, *part of a record display assembled at the Indiana State Museum in Indianapolis in 1983. This desk is part of the museum's own collection. (Photo courtesy of Indiana State Museum.)*

THIS FERRIS WHEEL, *the first in the world, was erected by a Hoosier, and a segment of it was turned into the most unusual bridge in Indiana. (Photo courtesy of Smithsonian Institution.)*

THE MADISON HEADQUARTERS *of the oldest volunteer fire company in Indiana. It is not, however, the first building used by the company. (Photo by author.)*

THE PURDUE UNIVERSITY BAND *displays the largest state flag in Indiana during a performance at half-time of a football game. (Photo courtesy of Purdue Audio-Visual Dept.)*

The familiar Coca-Cola bottle *was designed in Indiana by a team at the Root Glass Company at Terre Haute. Alexander Samuelson, plant superintendent, carried out the idea of making it resemble the cacao bean pod. The bottle shown is one of the early versions. (Photo courtesy of Root Glass Co.)*

THE MUSEUM AT VEVAY *houses the oldest surviving piano in the state, a Clementi, rescued in disrepair from a dilapidated building. (Photo by author.)*

HARRY VON TILZER, *credited with giving the name Tin Pan Alley to the songwriting section of New York, has probably written more songs than any other Hoosier. (File photo.)*

THE RECONSTRUCTED OFFICE OF ELIHU STOUT, *the first newspaperman in Indiana. He was with the* Indiana Gazette *at Vincennes in 1804, later the* Western Sun. *(Photo by author.)*

MARY E. BERCIK, CHOSEN MAYOR OF WHITING, *was the first woman chief executive of an Indiana city elected to the post in modern times. (Photo by author.)*

RED SKELTON *(right) in his radio heyday. Skelton had the longest-running show of any Hoosier comedian. (File photo.)*

THE LONGEST VIADUCT IN INDIANA *extends 2,295 feet across a valley near Solsberry. It is 157 feet high and was dedicated in 1906. (Photo by author.)*

B

BALLOONS

THE *altitude record* for a hot-air balloon is held by William K. Kepner who, with two others, ascended to 61,000 feet July 28, 1934, in South Dakota on a flight sponsored by the National Geographic Society. Kepner, born near Miami in Howard County, was a major in the Army Air Corps and undertook the ascension with Capt. O. A. Anderson and Capt. A. W. Stevens. At 61,000 feet, the balloon disintegrated, sending the steel gondola plummeting earthward. Capt. Anderson bailed out; Maj. Kepner climbed atop the gondola and helped Capt. Stevens disentangle from the rigging. Kepner parachuted when only an estimated 300 feet from the ground, probably qualifying him for the record speed of descent from 61,000 feet, although there seem to be no documents for such a record. The damanged gondola was placed in the Air Force Museum at Dayton, O.

THE *first major balloon race* in Indiana was at the site of the Indianapolis Motor Speedway June 5, 1909, where a crowd of 40,000 saw six balloons take off in the main race. The Indiana entry, carrying Carl Fisher, developer of the Speedway, traveled 280 miles but was disqualified because it was tied up briefly during the race. The winner of the event was Goethe Link; the silver loving cup he won later was placed in the Smithsonian Institution.

[SEE ALSO *Aviation; Mail.*]

BICYCLES

The *first pneumatic* tires for a bicycle in Indiana are said to have been those brought in about 1890 by Harry R.

Hearsey, who organized a trip from Indianapolis to Rushville by bicycle to introduce the "safety tire."

THE *largest single Indiana bicycling event* is the Hilly Hundred, held annually at Bloomington and involving road courses of 50 miles on each of two days. In 1984 the event had about 3,500 participants.

THE *largest modern-day bicycle rally* in Indiana was held July 3 to July 8, 1984, in Indianapolis. An estimated 1,000 members of the League of American Wheelmen attended from around the country and were joined by about 1,000 members of the Central Indiana Bicycling Association, the host organization. Competitive events, seminars, and demonstrations were part of the program.

THE *record speed* for a bicycle set by a Hoosier and a world mark at the time is 138.7 miles an hour, accomplished in 1972 behind a pace car at the Utah Salt Flats by Al Abbott, a graduate of Indiana University and a physician. The son of Mr. and Mrs. Horace E. Abbott of Marion County, he was guided by his brother, Dwight Abbott, a Purdue University aeronautical engineer, who rode in the rear of the pace vehicle, and Barry DeVries, and Air Force aircraft mechanic, who drove the pace car. At one point during the measured mile Abbott reached a speed of 140.2 miles an hour. The pace vehicle was a special car fitted with a plastic shield in the rear. Dwight Abbott, seated facing backward so he could watch Al, had control of the accelerator. The vehicle towed Abbott until he reached speeds of 60 to 70 miles an hour, because it was impossible for him to turn the large sprocket on the special bicycle until it was moving that fast. It was the first time a bicycle had tried for a speed record on the salt flats and on his first run Abbott set a new American record at 118 miles an hour. This surpassed the mark of 108.92 miles an hour set in America in 1941 by Alfred LeTourner, but was short of the 127.2 miles an hour done by Frenchman Jose Meiffret on the German autobahn. High winds held off a second attempt for a day and when Abbott did try it, he slipped on the salt and hit the rear of the car without damage or injury. On the last attempt before the official timer was scheduled to depart, Abbott reached his record speed. The purpose of the car in such events is not only to tow the vehicle up to pedalling speed, but also to break the wind resistance for the rider.

THE world's first *collegiate course* in competitive cycling was offered during the first semester of 1985 at Marian College in Indianapolis. Roger Young was instructor in the course, which began January 15 and included basics in competition and conditioning.

[SEE ALSO *Sports, bicycling.*]

B I R D S : SEE *Animals*

B O A T S

THE *first steamboat* on the Ohio River along Indiana was the *New Orleans*, owned by Nicholas J. Roosevelt, which reached Louisville from Ohio October 1, 1811. On board were Roosevelt, his wife, an engineer, a pilot, six hands, two female servants, a waiter, a cook, and a New-foundland dog named Tiger. The boat halted there for several days waiting for water to rise so it could pass over the falls and continue its trip to New Orleans. The day before arrival at Louisville, Mrs. Roosevelt gave birth to a daughter. After taking many for rides, the boat finally passed the falls and tied up December 15 at Yellow Bank in what is now Spencer county, and was set rocking by the great earthquake of 1811 which altered much of the shore landscape. While trying to cut fuel on the Indiana shore, crewmen could barely raise axes without injury because of continuing tremors. The boat finally made its way to New Orleans, a trip which was related by J. R. Latrobe,

Roosevelt's grandson, in a book titled *First Steamboat on Western Waters*.

THE *first time a steamboat sailed into the interior of Indiana* was during May 1823 when Capt. Donne of the *Florence* left Louisville and reached Terre Haute via the Wabash River.

THE *first iron-hulled boat built* in Indiana was the W. W. *Fry* built at Jeffersonville in 1840, using material sent from England. The boat served on the Western waters until 1870.

THE *largest military shipyard* in Indiana was at Evansville where 160 LSTs (landing-ship–tanks) were built during World War II. The first was launched October 31, 1942, under a contract obtained by seven companies who formed the Missouri Valley Bridge & Iron Company– Shipbuilding Division. An estimated 18,000 persons were employed in the shipbuilding. Ten Evansville-built vessels were lost in battle.

THE *largest inland shipyard* in the nation is Jeffboat, Inc., at Jeffersonville. In 1980 it employed about 1,800, although those numbers were reduced because of the economic recession of the early 1980s. In 1984 the firm had contracts to build an ocean liner and a 300-foot paddlewheel showboat.

THE *record time by boat from Cincinnati to Louisville*, 267 miles, is 267 minutes, 49 seconds, set October 9, 1924, by the *Hoosier Boy*, a 400-horsepower, 24-foot hydroplane piloted by J. W. Whitlock of Rising Sun. Duplication of the record is unlikely because of dams and locks installed since then, which make a straight run over that route impossible.

THE Indiana *speed record for an unlimited hydroplane* is 140.818 miles an hour, set in June 1984 on the Ohio River at Evansville by Chip Hanauer, driving the Atlas Van Lines boat.

THE first and probably only large *boat to occupy the*

lawn at the Indiana Statehouse was the replica of the *Kearsage*, constructed in 1893 for the convention of the Grand Army of the Republic. The *Kearsage* had been a Union gunboat in the Civil War.

THE *smallest battleship* in Indiana is a model of the USS Indiana in 1-64 scale, completed in 1964 after about 4 1/2 years work by an estimated 20 inmates of the Indiana State Prison at Michigan City. The model, 11 feet long and believed to be the only accurate model of the ship, is displayed in the prison administration building lobby. The work was guided by Jay Darling, an inmate, and Charles Moore, then a director of classification at the prison.

[SEE ALSO *Accidents and disasters.*]

BOOKS AND PERIODICALS

THE *first book published* in what is now Indiana was printed by Elihu Stout in 1804 at Vincennes. Authorized by the Indiana Territory, it was titled *Laws for the Government of the District of Louisiana, passed by the Governor and Judges of the Indiana Territory at their first session begun and held at Vincennes on Monday the first day of October,* 1804.

THE *first work of fiction* in Indiana was *Miahnomah; a Legend of the 'Dark and Bloody Ground,'* by B. V. Thorn, printed 1839 by Elihu Stout and Son, Vincennes. Thorn came to Aurora in 1811 from Kentucky, where he published an earlier volume; he was later coroner of Knox County. The slender book tells the story of an Indian girl of 17 who falls in love with a white hunter.

THE *first novelist* to reside in Indiana probably was Jesse Lynch Holman, who wrote *The Prisoners of Niagara, or Errors of Education, a New Novel, Founded on Fact* in 1810 in Kentucky; he moved to Indiana the next year and remained most of his life. He died in 1842 and did not produce another novel while on Hoosier soil.

THE *first non-government book* published in Indiana was *The Life of Bonaparte, Late Emperor of the French*, covering his life from August 15, 1769, until his deportation to St. Helena. The book, written by an anonymous author, was printed in 1818.

THE *first poet* in Indiana was Rebecca Lard of Vermont, who moved to Indiana in 1820. Although facts of her life are sketchy, she is believed to have written the state's first book of poetry, *The Banks of the Ohio*, published in 1823.

THE *first "true" confession* was *The Life and Adventures of John Dahmen* by Reuben Kidder, native of Germany and a lawyer at Paoli, who wrote about a classic murder trial, conviction, and hanging at New Albany. The book was published at Jeffersonville in 1821 by George Smith and Nathaniel Bolton.

THE *first guide designed to attract people to Indiana* was written by John Scott, a Pennsylvanian who came to Brookville in 1816 and published *The Indiana Gazetteer* at Centerville in 1826 with William M. Doughty, later coroner of Wayne County. The volume was a fairly accurate description of the state, considering the difficulty of gathering data and the constant changes in roads, towns, etc.

THE *first books circulated by a library* in Indiana were those of W. Bunten in Vincennes, August 23, 1806; he provided them for the Vincennes Library Company, formed July 20, 1806, at a meeting in the William Hays home, at which time stock was offered. The first librarian of this rental library was Peter Jones, also auditor of the Indiana Territory.

THE *first library for public use* was at the Cathedral at Vincennes, established in 1807.

THE *first bookmobile* in Indiana was that of the

Plainfield Library which, in 1916, sent out a custom wagon on a Ford chassis to serve rural patrons in a neighboring township. The bookmobile was the idea of Mrs. Mayme Snipes, librarian in Plainfield from 1909 to 1919.

THE *largest library system* in the state is that of Indiana University; its more than 4 million volumes rank it 15th in the world in size of collections.

THE *largest public library* in Indiana is the Allen County Public Library at Fort Wayne with 1,661,185 volumes. The *smallest public library* is Markle Public Library with 3,197 volumes.

THE *largest collection of American and English dictionaries* in Indiana and perhaps in the nation is the Cordell Collection of some 5,000 volumes at Indiana State University. They date to 1475 and were given to the university by Warren N. Cordell, an alumnus, in 1933.

JEREMIAH FARRELL possesses what is probably the *largest private collection of dictionaries* in Indiana, an estimated 635 volumes. Farrell, director of Holcomb Observatory at Butler University, has a dictionary publishd in Germany in 1525, his oldest, and a 1910–11 century edition, his thickest at 1.5 feet thick.

The *best personal collection of old hymnals* is that of Dr. William R. Eberly of North Manchester, with 100 rare books dating to 1724. The collection is among the finest in the Midwest.

THE *largest source of material on Abraham Lincoln* is the Lewis A. Warren Lincoln Library at Fort Wayne, which has 10,000 books on Lincoln, 7,500 magazine articles on Lincoln, 6,000 books and pamphlets in some way related to Lincoln, and some 400 books of the type that Lincoln read. Exhibits and memorabilia also are contained in the library, which serves mainly as a source for telephone and mail inquiries about Lincoln facts.

THE *largest collection of reference volumes on the Men-*

nonites in Indiana, and one of the largest collections in the world, is that in Mennonite Historical Library, part of the Harold and Wilma Good Library at Goshen College.

THE *oldest collection of books* is probably that in the Old Cathedral Library at Vincennes. Completed in 1843, the library contains parish records for 1749 and books and periodicals printed before 1700.

THE *largest private optics library* in the world, of volumes pertaining to the human eye, the microscope, the telescope, and other optics, is owned by Dr. James Leeds of Carmel. The collection of more than 3,000 volumes includes some dating from the eighteenth century and volumes in nearly 100 languages. "I know of only one person in the United States who collects what I do," says Dr. Leeds.

THE *most unusual inducement* was one offered by W. B. Harris, a publisher at Ellettsville, who once offered Shetland ponies as a premium for people subscribing to one of his magazines, *Our Boys and Girls*. Others copied the idea, including the *Saturday Evening Post*; ponies were rather inexpensive in those days before 1900.

THE *largest circulation of a fraternal magazine* based in Indiana is that of *American Legion* with more than 2,500,000 copies a month.

THE Bulletin of the Indiana State Board of Health was first issued as a quarterly in 1897 by Dr. John N. Hurty, making it the *oldest continuing medical publication* in the state. It became a monthly late in 1899.

THE first person to be designated *state poet laureate* by the Indiana General Assembly was E. A. (Big Rich) Richardson of Evansville, who addressed the legislature on the occasion of Lincoln's birthday, 1929, and read a poem about the Great Emancipator. The legislature then voted him state poet laureate and reaffirmed the honor in 1965. Richardson died September 17, 1965. Born Emory Aaron Richardson April 30, 1886, on a Pike County farm, Richardson published eight books of poems, the most popular being *Indiana and Other Poems, Hoosier Holly-Hocks,* and *Turkey Run and Selected Poems.*

THE *creator of Dick and Jane,* the child characters in reading primers used all over the U.S., was Zerna Sharp, a native of Frankfort and a reading consultant to Scott-Foresman Publishers in Chicago in the mid-1920s. Noting reduced reading ability of school pupils in a five-state area she traveled, she urged a new format for primers. While at the beach, she struck on the idea of introducing a word at a time to new readers in primers adhering to a strict formula. She chose the names Dick and Jane for the characters in the stories because they were easy to sound out. The primers sold from 1927 to 1973. Miss Sharp did not write any of the primers herself, but her formula was strictly carried out by those assigned to write the volumes. She died in 1981 at the age of 91.

THE *only basketball player* ever to appear on the cover of *Time* Magazine was Oscar Robertson of Indianapolis, player with Crispus Attucks High School, the University of Cincinnati, and several National Basketball Association teams. The date was February 17, 1961.

THE *first high school athlete* to appear on the cover of *Sports Illustrated* magazine was Rick Mount, star at Lebanon High School and Mr. Basketball in 1966. He was on the cover February 14, 1966.

THE only Hoosier writer to do a *novel and the play and the screenplay* from the novel without collaborators was Joseph Hayes of Indianapolis, author of *The Desperate Hours,* who created a play and screenplay for the work in 1955.

THE *longest known book* by a Hoosier issued by an established publishing firm was *Miss MacIntosh, My Darling,* which ran 1,198 pages and included sentences running over several pages. The author, Marguerite Young of Indianapolis, worked on the book 17 years before it came out in 1965. It was not a big hit.

THE record for *number of books on the best-seller list simultaneously* by a Hoosier is seven, established in 1982–83 by Jim Davis, cartoonist creator of Garfield, the cat. His first three books on the list at the same time established a record. They were *Garfield at Large, Garfield Gains Weight,* and *Garfield Bigger Than Life.* They were joined on the list by *Garfield Weighs In, Garfield Takes the Cake, Garfield Eats His Heart Out,* and *Garfield Treasury.*

JACK TRACY of Bloomington is the acknowledged Indiana *expert on the British fictional character, Sherlock Holmes,* by virtue of his writing on the subject in four books, including *Encyclopedia Sherlockiana* (Doubleday, 1977). Tracy also has edited books about Holmes. A member of the Baker Street Irregulars, Tracy issues Holmes-related publications through Gaslight Publications and is one of only two full-time Sherlockians in the nation. His encyclopedia was nominated for an Edgar Allen Poe Award by the Mystery Writers of America.

[SEE ALSO *Art and artists.*]

BRIDGES

THE *first covered bridge* completed in Indiana was the National Road span across Symons Creek, about three miles east of Straughn in Henry County; it was finished in 1834 and demolished in 1921. A *contract to build a covered bridge* over White River in Indianapolis for the National Road was the first let in Indiana. It was part of a package for four bridges on the road, now U.S. 40, and was awarded in 1831 to Lewis Wernwag, a builder from the east. Wernwag sublet the job to his sons, but because of financial problems the work reverted to him and delays pushed the completion up to 1835.

THE Edna Collins Bridge, built by Charles Hendrix in Putnam County near Clinton Falls in 1922, was the *last covered bridge* constructed in Indiana. There had been an estimated 400 built in some 91 years. The Edna Collins was an 80-foot span using Burr trusses, patented by Thomas Burr in 1806.

THE *longest covered bridge* in Indiana still open to traffic is southwest of Williams in Lawrence County; it is 376 feet long and was opened in 1884.

THE *greatest builder of covered bridges* in Indiana was Joseph J. Daniels of Rockville, who is credited with 60. His first bridge was on the first section of the Rising Sun–Versailles turnpike. Born in Rockville in 1826, Daniels was only 25 when he built a bridge over a White River fork for the Evansville and Crawfordsville Railroad. At 29 he became superintendent of that railroad. In 1861 he built the single span Jackson Bridge at Rockport in Parke County. His last span was the Neet Bridge in Parke County in 1904 when he was 78. *Other bridge builders* were Joseph A. Britton, credited with 40, and three generations of the Kennedy family, credited with a total of 60.

THE *only covered bridge in Indiana using the Post truss* design, a combination of wood and iron, is Bell's Ford Bridge, two miles west of Seymour on Ind. 258 over the east fork of White River. Built in 1869 at a cost of $2,500, the 325-foot-long bridge, still standing, was closed in September 1967 and bypassed by a new bridge in 1970.

PARKE COUNTY has *more covered bridges* than any other Indiana county with 35. There are 104 such bridges in the state in 34 counties. Among the Parke County bridges is one on the Rockville golf course, making it the *only fairway* in the known golf world *with a covered bridge* over a waterway.

THE *most unusual material* put into a bridge in Indiana was part of the original Ferris Wheel. The wheel, developed for the World's Columbian Exposition in Chicago in 1893, was 250 feet in diameter and made to haul 2,160 passengers at a time. After use at the St. Louis

World's Fair in 1904, the wheel was sold for scrap. A section was purchased by Isaac Dunn, who made a bridge connecting land he had on both sides of the Kankakee River, near Tefft in Jasper County. See (*Fairs and festivals.*)

THE *longest suspension bridge only for pedestrian traffic* completely in Indiana spans a portion of Lake Shafer from the parking lot to an island amusement center, a total of 400 feet. The two-span bridge was built in 1970 and is unusual because it has a top cable anchoring the three towers. The bridge walkway is 14 feet wide.

THE *only true suspension bridge for vehicular traffic* in Indiana is one on Ind. 154 across from Hutsonville, Ill. It crosses the Wabash River with three spans, two of 150 feet each and a center span of 350 feet. There are seven spans of 50 feet each in the Indiana approach to the bridge. Built in 1939, it has a roadway of 14 feet, 6 inches. In 1984, however, the state of Illinois was making plans to replace the bridge with a more modern structure.

BUSINESS

THE *oldest funeral home* in Indiana is Dexter Gardner & Sons, Inc., at Vincennes, started in 1816, but no longer at its original location. It also is said to be the *oldest funeral-directing business in a single family in the nation,* and the *second oldest funeral home in the U.S.*

THE *oldest continuous business* at the same site in Indiana is the Acme-Evans flour milling firm, originating in 1821 when Isaac Wilson built a grist mill along the banks of the White River in what is now Indianapolis. In 1840 the mill started shipping flour outside the Indianapolis area.

THE *oldest business* in Indiana *operating in the original building* is believed to be the Log Inn at Haubstadt, begun in 1825 and once a trading post and stage coach stop. A meal was served to Lincoln there, it is said, and the inn is thought to have been part of the pre-Civil War underground railroad for slaves.

THE *oldest drugstore* in Indiana is Wells-Yeager-Best in Lafayette, established in 1829 by Canada Fink. The store moved in 1841 and has remained in that location through a succession of owners. The present name was established in 1983 when A. A. Wells, owner, went into partnership with two of his associates, Frank M. Best and Emory L. Yeager.

THE *oldest bank building* is at Vincennes and was constructed in 1838. It now is called the Old State Bank and Art Gallery and houses the Northwest Territory Art Guild.

THE *oldest glass distributor* in the nation is Stewart-Carey Inc., founded in 1840 at Greensburg and moved to Indianapolis in 1963. Daniel Steward began the business selling glass in a drugstore.

BOHLEN, MEYERS & GIBSON of Indianapolis is the *oldest continuous architectural firm* in the nation. Founded by Diederich A. Bohlen in 1853, one of its early buildings was the convent and chapel of St. Mary-of-the-Woods at Terre Haute, done in 1858.

THE first *shoe store exclusively for ladies* in Indiana was opened in 1861 in Indianapolis by David Chase of Nineveh, who curtained off a section for women and carpeted it. The store was the largest in the city at that time.

THE *tavern in business the longest at the same site* is the Slippery Noodle Inn in Indianapolis, which can prove its existence back to 1865. It is operated by Harold Raymond Yeagy.

THE *oldest manufacturer of desks and office furniture* in the U.S. is Jasper Desk Company at Jasper, founded by four men in 1876 and now producing 300 to 400 units a week.

THE *oldest and largest mutual life insurance company* in Indiana is American United Life in Indianapolis. It was founded in 1877.

THE *oldest active farm equipment dealer* is thought to be Cordes Hardward Company, Inc., in Seymour, founded in 1880.

THE first *interior decorating salon* in Indiana was Coppock Brothers in Indianapolis, established in 1888 by McClellan and William Coppock.

FRANK B. SHIELDS of Seymour moved to Indianapolis in 1913 and in 1918 launched Barbasol brushless shaving cream, the *first successful commercial shaving cream*. Radio commercials featuring Singing Sam, the Barbasol Man, made the product a leader in sales in the mid-1930s.

THE *first employment service in Indiana* was the Brown Efficiency Bureau of Indianapolis, established December 13, 1913; it was one of the earliest in the U.S.

THE *first commercial brewery* of record in Indiana was one opened at Richmond in 1827 by two men from London, although it soon was discontinued.

ALTHOUGH Odus G. Faulkinbury of Lebanon is said to have been the *first person* in Indiana *to demonstrate and sell an electric permanent wave machine*, the date of this event does not appear to have been recorded. He died in 1962.

THE *first bank to become employee-owned* was the Bank of Indiana in Lake County. About 230 employees of the Money Management Corporation of Merrillville, a holding company which owned the bank, sought permission to purchase the holding company and the bank in August 1984 for $6 million. The bank, headquartered in Gary, has 14 branches and is the second largest in Lake County.

BARNES AND THORNBURG of Indianapolis, formed in 1982 through the merger of three firms, is the *largest law firm* in Indiana with 160 lawyers, 70 partners, and 75 associates. It ranks 118th in the nation, according to a *National Law Journal* survey of 1983.

The nation's *largest inland shipyard* is Jeffboat, Inc., at Jeffersonville. Founded in 1938, the firm has launched 6,200 vessels in 46 years. (See also *Boats.*)

THE *largest black-owned business* in Indiana is the L. H. Smith Oil Corporation of Indianapolis, founded in 1962 by Lannie H. Smith, Jr.; it is among the top 15 black businesses in the nation, with sales exceeding $27 million annually.

THE world's *largest maker of underwater photographic equipment* is Ikelite of Indianapolis, owned by Ike Brigham; it is the source for more than 100 types of lights, camera housings, and similar items for underwater photography.

THE *largest weekly horse auction* in North America occurs each Thursday at the Rushville Horse Sale Barn at Rushville, with the sale of up to 600 animals.

INDIANA'S *largest flea market* convenes each Tuesday and Wednesday at Shipshewanna where booths occupy 53 acres and draw crowds estimated at 40,000 on a busy weekend. The flea market, also the site of auctions, is owned by Robert Lambright and his sons Kevin and Keith.

THE *largest automated laundry* in Indiana and one of the largest in the U.S. is United Hospital Services of Indianapolis, which serves 10 hospitals and does 20 million pounds of laundry a year; it has 17 dryers each capable of holding 400 pounds of laundry.

THE *first company to move a water tower*, still containing the water, *and to elevate a bridge without disrupting traffic* was the LaPlante-Adair Company of Indianapolis. The water tower, containing 160,000 gallons, was moved in 1957 at the Ford plant in Atlanta, Ga. The 1,500-foot bridge at Lincolnton, Ga., was raised 17 feet in 1951 to allow for a higher dam downstream. The bridge weighed 4,000 tons. In 1964 the same Indianapolis-based firm *moved a German submarine* from Lake Michigan across the Outer Drive to the Museum of Science and Industry in Chicago in nine hours while crowds of up to 15,000 persons watched. The firm later moved from Indianapolis to Florida.

STEAM *carpet cleaning originated* in Indiana February 4, 1876, when the first such firm in the nation, the Howard Steam Cleaning Company, opened in Indianapolis. It used steam cleaning equipment similar to that used today, but less refined. The firm was honored in 1976 at the Steam Carpet Cleaners National Association convention in Indianapolis.

HOWARD E. CADLE of Fredericksburg is credited with originating the *while-you-wait shoe shops*. Cadle, who started adult life as a traveling salesman, became an evangelist whose name was memorialized in Cadle Tabernacle, a long-time landmark in Indianapolis.

The *first Indiana Craft Market* was held in March 1985 in the Indianapolis Hilton. It was financed by the Indiana Arts Commission and the Indiana State Museum Society. Craftsmen displayed material for both wholesalers and the public.

[SEE ALSO *Automobiles and trucks; Desks; Food and drink; Legislation; Manufacturing; Plants.*]

C

CATAPULTS

THE Indiana *catapult champion*, based on six national catapult contests from 1972 to 1977 when the contests were discontinued, is Wayne High School of Fort Wayne, which won four of the six competitions on the basis of most points accumulated. The four victories were in 1973, 1974, 1975, and 1977.

THE *greatest distance a catapult has thrown a rock* in Indiana is 798 feet, done by *Zephyrus*, a catapult built at North Central High School in Indianapolis, at a 1977 meet in Indianapolis. The same catapult holds the record for distance with a 100-pound rock: 579 feet in 1977 in Indianapolis.

The *farthest a* 1-pound spear has been thrown is 701 feet by *Remus II*, a catapult built at Eastwood Junior High School, Indianapolis, in a 1977 meet in Indianapolis.

THERE are three classes of catapult: those using counterweights for power, those using a twisted rope, and those using bent wood.

Counterweight Records

10 **pound rock:** 779.5 feet, by *Zephyrus*, North Central High School in Indianapolis; 1977, at Indianapolis

20 **pound rock:** 737 feet, by *Zephyrus*, North Central High School in Indianapolis; 1977, at Indianapolis

30 **pound rock:** 763 feet, by *Zephyrus*, North Central High School in Indianapolis; 1977, at Indianapolis

40 **pound rock:** 798 feet, by *Zephyrus*, North Central High School in Indianapolis; 1977, at Indianapolis

50 **pound rock:** 750 feet, by *Zephyrus*, North Central High School in Indianapolis; 1977, at Indianapolis

75 **pound rock:** 623 feet, by *Zephyrus*, North Central High School in Indianapolis; 1976, at Indianapolis

1 **pound rock:** 191.5 feet, by *Machina Belli*, St. Mary's of Rushville; 1977, at Indianapolis

1 **pound spear:** 196 feet, by *Hastatus II*, Wayne High School in Fort Wayne; 1976, at Fort Wayne

Twisted Rope Records

10 **pound rock:**	554 feet, 11 inches, by *Imperator*, Wayne High School in Fort Wayne; 1977, at Fort Wayne
20 **pound rock:**	369 feet, by *Imperator*, Wayne High School in Fort Wayne; 1975, at Fort Wayne
30 **pound rock:**	280 feet, 11 inches, by *Imperator*, Wayne High School in Fort Wayne; 1974, at Fort Wayne
40 **pound rock:**	145 feet, 5 inches, by *Imperator*, Wayne High School in Fort Wayne; 1975, at Fort Wayne
50 **pound rock:**	131 feet, by *Imperator*, Wayne High School in Fort Wayne; 1976, at Fort Wayne
75 **pound rock:**	103 feet, 1 inch, by *Imperator*, Wayne High School in Fort Wayne; 1974, at Fort Wayne
1 **pound rock:**	239 feet, by *Dux Parvus II*, Wayne High School in Fort Wayne; 1976, at Fort Wayne
1 **pound spear:**	701 feet, by *Remus II*, Eastwood Junior High School in Indianapolis; 1977, in Indianapolis

Bent Wood Records

20 **pound rock:**	37 feet, 5 inches, by *Magnus Ignis*, Wayne High School in Fort Wayne; 1977, at Fort Wayne
30 **pound rock:**	24 feet, by *Magnus Ignis*, Wayne High School in Fort Wayne; 1977, at Fort Wayne
40 **pound rock:**	19 feet, by *Magnus Ignis*, Wayne High School in Fort Wayne; 1977, at Fort Wayne
50 **pound rock:**	13 feet, 5 inches, by *Magnus Ignis*, Wayne High School in Fort Wayne; 1977, at Fort Wayne
75 **pound rock:**	7 feet, by *Magnus Ignis*, Wayne High School in Fort Wayne; 1977, at Fort Wayne
1 **pound rock:**	186 feet, 3 inches by *Machina Gigantum* of Ben Davis High School in Indianapolis; 1977, at Indianapolis

C A T T L E : SEE *Animals*.

CAVES

THE *greatest cave explorer* in Indiana was the Rev. Horace Carter Hovey, born near Rob Roy, January 28, 1833, credited with exploring more than 300 caves, many of them in Indiana, and author of *Celebrated American Caverns*, the bible of spelunking in early times. Hovey was the first man in the nation to extensively examine caves and detail them in writing; at the same time he was serving as a Presbyterian minister with ministries at North Madison, Vevay, and New Albany. He left Indiana in 1869. He urged a national speleological society and a Mammoth Cave National Park, both of which came to pass.

THE world's *largest travertine dam formation*, which still is active, is in Squire Boone Caverns, south of Corydon. A travertine dam is one created by mineral deposits from water flowing over it and, if active, such a dam continues to increase in size. That in Squire Boone Caverns is 15 feet across and 3 feet deep, with water still spilling over it and adding to its dimensions. It is about 90 feet down in the caverns, which were discovered in 1790 by Daniel Boone's brother, Squire. Although the dam was known to exist for years, it was only made accessible to tourists 11 years ago.

THE *largest underground mountain* found in any cave in the nation is that in Big Wyandotte Cave in Crawford County; it rises 136 feet.

[SEE ALSO *Animals*.]

CEMETERIES SEE *Graves*.

CIRCUSES

THE *first recorded circus* to visit Indiana was in 1830 when McComber & Co. Menagerie played in Indianapolis on a lot near Henderson's Tavern.

NELLIE KEELER of Kokomo is the *smallest known Hoosier* to be exhibited. P. T. Barnum billed her as the "smallest lady in the world" in 1879 when, at 11, she was 28 inches tall and weighed 11 pounds. She was the second of four children, all normal in size, as were her parents, Maria and Ezra Keeler. There is no record of the size to which Nellie finally grew.

THE *best-known circus clown* in Indiana was Emmett Kelly of Lafayette, who joined the John Robinson Circus in 1922. He worked with the Sells-Floto Circus of Peru, the Hagenbeck-Wallace Shows, also of Peru, and the Cole Brothers Circus out of Rochester; he spent two years in England before joining the Ringling Brothers Circus in 1942, where he remained until it folded.

THE *greatest number of circuses headquartered in Indiana* was 14, during the heyday of the big tent shows (1900 to World War II). It was estimated that it would have required 412 railroad cars to haul the canvas, animals, and equipment, and 50 more cars to hold all the people. The American Circus Coporation near Peru was one of the big providers of winter quarters, with large red sheds for beasts and equipment and large land holdings to provide pasture for animals. The tradition of wintering in Indiana began when Ben Wallace bought a defunct traveling show in 1883. It consisted of a band wagon, a one-eyed lion, a camel, two monkeys, a few dogs, a spotted horse, and an elephant named Diamond. Wallace, joined by James Anderson, began exhibitions, training the elephant in a railroad roundhouse. They staged their first shows in Peru and their little outfit developed into the large Hagenbeck-Wallace Circus. Ben Wallace's home in Peru was at 6th Street and Broadway. Headquarters for the Cole Brothers-Clyde Beatty Circus was at Rochester where a $500,000 menagerie of wild animals was housed and trained during the winter at the north end of Erie Street. At Peru, a new circus tradition has begun in modern times, the staging of a circus by youths in the town each summer.

[SEE ALSO *Accidents and disasters*; *Collections*; *Marriage*.]

CITIES AND TOWNS

THE *first civil settlement* in the Northwest Territory in what became Indiana was Clarkesville, which became the first incorporated town in the state. Homesites were begun there in 1783 and the first town book was begun in 1784.

THE settlement at New Harmony in 1825 by Robert Owen and his associates was the nations *first communistic non-religious settlement*. New Harmony was purchased for about $150,000 from George Rapp and his Rappites, and existed until May 1827 with about 1,000 members.

THE sole city in Indiana and the *largest city in the nation founded in this century* is Gary, created in 1906 because of the erection of steel mills there; it was named for Judge Elbert H. Gary, chairman of the board of U.S. Steel.

AUGUST 1, 1950, Jasper became the *first city in the nation to discontinue garbage collection* and install waste disposing units in each household instead. The reduction in taxes was calculated to help pay for the disposers. Thirty-five years later the law still required disposal for garbage, although the city continued trash pickup.

THE community of Arba in Randolph County, 2 1/2 miles west of the Indiana-Ohio boundary, is the *highest town* in Indiana, 1,210 feet above sea level. The *highest spot* in the state is just east of Arba at 1,240 feet above sea level.

THE *smallest official city* in Indiana is Woodburn, 15 miles east of Fort Wayne, population 1,002. Under Indiana law, an incorporated community in Indiana becomes a city only after its population exceeds 2,500. However, Woodburn obtained its special status in 1936 through a special act of the Indiana General Assembly because in those days cities received more state funds than did towns and Woodburn needed the money. Because of its city status, it has a major, city council, taxes, and a budget, but no police force. The one-man police force was eliminated in 1976 when he was shot by his wife. In 1984 Woodburn had a budget of $45,000.

THE *smallest incorporated town* according to the 1980 census is Spring Hills, a community of 19 persons in Washington Township, Marion County. It lies entirely within the confines of Indianapolis.

[SEE ALSO *Gas; Holidays; Land; Politics, city.*]

COAL

THE *first coal was noted* in Indiana by Col. George Croghan, an Indian agent of many years in the Vincennes area, who spotted the fuel on the Wabash River in 1763.

THE *first official coal locations* in Indiana were noted in 1804 when deposits were listed in land surveys and put on maps.

THE *first survey of mineral resources* in Indiana was made in the 1830s by David Dale Owen, who reported deposits of coal and building stone.

THE *first recorded use of Indiana coal* for something other than domestic household burning was in 1811 when the steamboat *New Orleans*, the *first steam powered vessel* to reach Indiana, mined coal from the Indiana shore to use as fuel. The boat spent several weeks off the Indiana shore waiting for a rise in the water so it could cross the falls of the Ohio River and continue on its voyage to New Orleans.

THE *first coal was advertised* for sale in 1832, available at various sites in Indiana.

THE *first coal shipped from the mining location outside*

a county for sale was that transported from Otter Creek in Perry County by John Weaver and Capt. Ezra Olds in 1852.

THE *first basic coal mine safety act* was passed in Indiana in 1879.

THE *state's first coal shaft* was sunk in 1850 by John Hutchinson near Newburg.

INDIANA was the *first state to have a system of reforesting strip mines,* beginning in the fall of 1920 in Clay County. At one place, 1,490 peach, 1,951 apple, and 990 pear trees were planted. Sherwood Coal Company and Central Indiana Coal Company experimented with trees and 2,500 cottonwoods were planted by Enos Coal Company at Oakland City.

THE *first coal company incorporated* in Indiana was the American Cannel Coal Company of Cannelton, chartered by the General Assembly in 1837.

THE *first mechanical pick,* a device much like an air hammer, was used in underground coal mining in Indiana in 1884.

THE *first strip mine* in Indiana is believed to have been operated from 1908 to 1936 near Patricksburg by George G. Rowland, a former civil engineer and the first president of the Indiana Strip Mine Operators' Association. Rowland died December 19, 1951, at 77.

THE *first all-mechanical mine,* in which coal was mechanically cut and mechanically loaded, was the Ayrshire Coal Company mine at Arthur, beginning in 1922. The operation was directed by David Ingle, Jr.

INDIANA in 1926 was the *first state to use liquid oxygen* for blasting in surface coal mines; it was a cheaper and safer explosive than the powder and dynamite used before that.

Horizontal drilling, which reduced costs and made it easier to get at deeper coal in strip mining, began for the first time in the nation in 1930 in Indiana. Overburden, the material covering the coal veins, was loosened by blasting and removed. As deeper coal was sought, deeper and deeper holes were required until the system of drilling horizontally into the exposed overburden was started.

THE *first all-welded cleaning equipment*, called a preparation plant, was installed in Indiana in 1932 at the Chieftain 20 mine in Vigo County. It replaced the riveted equipment which was more difficult and more expensive to build.

INDIANA was the first state in the U.S. to *increase the shovels used in strip mining to 35 cubic yards* in 1935. The replacement of much smaller shovels increased production in coal strip mining.

THE nation's *first knee-action coal mine stripping shovel* was installed at the Tecumseh Coal Corporation at Boonville in 1935. Use of a boom which bent like a knee allowed stronger and bigger shovels to be made.

THE *first 25-cubic-yard walking dragline* in the U.S. was installed in Indiana in 1945. The walking dragline, which did not require rails, made the removal of soil covering coal deposits easier and cheaper because of its mobility and flexibility.

AKREMITE, the *first ammonium nitrate and fuel oil explosive*, was used for the first time in the U.S. in 1955 at Maumee Collieries Company in Indiana. The mixture of fertilizer and 6 percent fuel oil was a cheaper and safer explosive than the material which had been used in coal mining.

THE production of 6.4 million tons makes 1900 the year for the *least amount of coal mined* in Indiana since records were kept, beginning with that year.

THE best *record for deep mine production* in Indiana probably is that of American No. !, which four times held the world record for coal tonnage in an 8-hour day before the advent of more mechanized equipment. The last record for the mine was June 5, 1926, with 7,157 tons in one day.

THE *record year for coal production* was 1980, when 30.8 million tons were mined in Indiana.

IN the early 1900s, when coal use was at its peak, *more than* 200 *deep mines and surface* mines were operating in Indiana, the largest number known to have been used at one time.

IN 1982 *only three deep mines* were in operation in Indiana, the *lowest number* since the beginning of statistical records in 1900. The total of 25 deep and surface mines in 1964 is the lowest total for all mines operating.

THE *largest single hunk of coal* excavated in Indiana is believed to have been the piece weighing 7,400 pounds sent to the World's Fair in 1893. It was taken from Otter Creek west of Foleyville on the James Foley place. A steam shovel was used, possible for the first time in Indiana.

THE *largest walking dragline* (a machine like a steam shovel used for moving earth or coal) in Indiana is the Bucyrus-Erie 3270-W, which operates at Amax Coal's Ayrshire Mine near Chandler, Ind., 12 miles northeast of Evansville in Warrick County. It is the second largest walking dragline in the world. The dragline is "walked" by two giant shoes, each 71 feet long and 16 feet wide, which take 6-foot strides at a speed of .10 miles an hour. The B-E 3270-W is 455 feet long, almost as long as 10 Greyhound buses parked bumper to bumper. It is 121 feet wide. Using its long boom, it can swing a circle equal to the span of the St. Louis Gateway Arch, a working area 622 feet in diameter, equal to the 300,000-square-foot Houston Astrodome. The bucket of the dragline is large enough for four automobiles; it can hold 176 cubic yards of material. The dragline weighs 17.5 million pounds. In one day the B-E 3270-W could uncover 6,000 tons of bituminous coal, or 2 million tons a year. The Ayrshire mine went into operation in October 1973.

COLLECTIONS

THE *king of baseball collectors* in Indiana is Paul C. Frisz of Terre Haute, said to have the largest private collection of baseball items in the nation. Frisz, who began collecting in 1922, was inducted into the Baseball Hall of Fame in honor of his collecting in 1971 and was an officer in the Society of American Baseball Researchers. Born in Terre Haute, he went to Dayton, O., to attend school because of deaths in the family. He played baseball and football, but not well. After college he worked as a salesman until returning to Terre Haute in 1940 to become an insurance agent. In 1948 he opened the Central Hotel in Terre Haute, which became headquarters for baseball fans and player alike. Frisz's sole involvement in baseball was taking over the Terre Haute farm team of the Detroit Tigers in 1956 when it was in danger of folding. It did fold, but Frisz paid off all debts and lost only $600. He retired in 1968. Frisz received about 700 letters a year about his collection and was noted as an expert on statistics. He once found 40 errors in a baseball record book, which he brought to the attention of the publisher. Among his material are photographs of every pennant-winning baseball squad in the major leagues since 1871, a copy of the first action photograph taken of a baseball game, and a cane which once belonged to Three-Finger Brown, a noted Hoosier major league pitcher. Said Frisz once, "If I could make such a trade, I would trade all this to have been a great player."

THE largest collection of *autographs of major and minor league baseball players* is believed to be that of Henry West of Greenfield, who collected at least 10,000 signatures from active players, beginning in 1940.

IT is doubtful that anyone in Indiana has a larger collection of *teddy bears* than Jack McCutchan of Lebanon, who has 400 to 500 of the critters, two or three of them worth $700 or more.

THE most complete collection of *circus artifacts* in Indiana is that possessed by the Circus City Festival Museum at Peru, which has an extensive group of lithographs, costumes, rigging, miniature circuses, and other items from bygone tent circus days.

THE largest collection of *coincidences* is that of Frank F. Deller-Penna of Indianapolis, who has gathered data on more than 2,500 since he started at age 14. Most of the coincidences in his collection occurred in Indiana. An example: On September 22, 1963, the Jackie Browns and the Donald Browns both had girls at Community Hospital in Indianapolis; the Kenneth Toneys and the James Toneys both had daughters at St. Vincent Hospital in Indianapolis; the LeVonne Whitfields and the Joe Whitfields had sons at Wishard Hospital in Indianapolis; and the Walter Davises had a son and the James Davises had a daugher at Methodist Hospital, Indianapolis. The families were unrelated and didn't know each other before going to the hospitals.

THE largest collection of memorabilia of Hoosier bank robber *John Dillinger* is that possessed by the John Dillinger Historical Museum at Nashville, which claims to have 90 percent of all the artifacts known to exist in connection with the Mooresville badman.

PROBABLY the finest collection of fancy *paperweights* made by a Hoosier are the 23 produced by Benjamin F. Leach of Fowlerton and now owned by the Chicago Art Institute Museum. Discovered in 1929 by art dealer F. Sumner Ettinger, the paperweights were the finest unearthed because they were authentic, all from the same factory, and all done by the same man, Leach, who founded a glass plant at Fowlerton in 1896. The paperweights found their way to Mrs. Potter Palmer, Jr., of Chicago, who gave them to the museum in 1931.

THE first *plate collector's convention* in the nation was held in 1975 at South Bend when 1,000 exhibitors and 18 companies gathered at the invitation of Winnie Watson Sweet.

CAMERON PARKS of DeKalb County assembled the largest collection of *ceremonial and ornamental slate Indian relics*, earning him the title of the slate king.

RAYMOND E. WILSON of Indianapolis has assembled more than 1,300 *antique tools*, all in working condition and dating from the period 1790–1900; it is probably the state's largest collection.

THE largest collection of *model trains* in Indiana is that assembled by Robert R. Vickers of Anderson, numbering well over 500 trains. His first collection was donated to the Indianapolis Children's Museum. His second collection is kept by his widow at Anderson, and yet a third collection is possessed by his son, Robert V. Vickers, at Cleveland, O.

[SEE ALSO *Books*; *Music*; *Phonographs*; *Screen*; *War*; *Civil*.]

COLLEGES AND UNIVERSITIES

THE *oldest comprehensive junior college* in the nation is Vincennes Univeristy, founded in 1801 as Jefferson College at the urging of William Henry Harrison.

VINCENNES UNIVERSITY became the *first state college in Indiana* by provision of the Indiana Territorial Act of 1806. It was formed from the nucleus of a private school operated by Presbyterian minister Samuel Scott, who was largely responsible for full activation of the university in 1810. Vincennes University was the second university to open in the Northwest Territory.

THE *oldest private college* in Indiana is Hanover College, founded in 1827 by the Presbyterians as a manual labor academy and the first church-affiliated institution of higher learning in the state.

THE first person in Indiana to carry the *title of professor of mathematics* was John Hopkins Harvey, who taught at Indiana University, Bloomington, 1827 to 1832.

THE *oldest nonsectarian liberal arts college for men* in Indiana, or anywhere west of the Alleghenies, is Wabash College, founded by Presbyterian ministers and laymen in 1832 on 50 acres which now are located in the midst of Crawfordsville. The school has one of the highest endowment-per-student ratios in the nation and its student body of about 850 is destined to remain that size under a 1973 policy decision to remain small. The school has a faculty-student ration of about 1 to 10.

THE *oldest women's college* in Indiana is St. Mary-of-the-Woods College on U.S. 150, five miles south of Terre Haute. It was founded in 1840. In October of that year the Sisters of Providence, a religious congregation from Ruille-sur-Loire, France, reached the wilderness there, led by Mother Theodore Guerin. By July 4, 1841, they had opened Saint Mary's Female Institute. In 1846 a *charter* from the Indiana General Assembly was the *first granted in the state for the higher education of women*.

THE *first private Indiana college to switch to coeducational* was Franklin College in 1842. The college was founded in 1834 as Indiana Baptist Manual Labor Institute.

THE University of Notre Dame at South Bend was the *first Catholic college* in the state; it was started in 1842 by eight French priests of the Congregation of the Holy Cross.

THE *first college* constructed in Indiana *specifically as an anti-racial institution* was Eleutherian College at Lancester, Ind., founded by Thomas Cravens in 1849 and dedicated to abolition and equal rights for blacks and whites. By 1866 the school was nearly inactive. It was re-established in 1878 as a normal school and in 1890 was taken over as a township grade school, abandoned in 1938.

BUTLER UNIVERSITY, when it opened in 1855 as Northwestern Christian University, was the *first Indiana school created co-educational*, vowing to enroll students without regard to sex, race, or color.

THE *first university* in Indiana to let *students select their own subjects* was Butler University, which started the elective program with parental consent in the late 1850s when it was known as Northwestern Christian University.

INDIANA UNIVERSITY at Bloomington was the first state university in the nation to grant equal privileges to women and produce a *female graduate*. Sarah Parke Morrison was graduated in 1869 as the first woman to enter the school and receive a degree. The school began in 1824 and was designated a university in 1838.

THE first *law school in a Catholic institution* in the U.S. was that of the University of Notre Dame at South Bend, which began in 1869.

THE nation's *first sorority* was Kappa Alpha Theta, which began at Asbury University, now DePauw University, at Greencastle on January 27, 1870.

CREATION of the Department of Civil Engineering in 1873 at the University of Notre Dame, and the start of the Department of Mechanical Engineering in 1886 at Notre Dame, marked the *first engineering departments in America in a Catholic college or university*.

THE *first person to acquire an engineering degree* in Indiana was William K. Eldridge, who was graduated from Purdue University in 1878.

GERTRUDE MAHORNEY, who received a degree from Butler University in 1887, was the state's *first black college graduate*.

THE *first coed* in the nation to pass a Civil Aeronautics Administration test and *acquire a pilot's license* was Joann Greer of Lowell, who got her license at Purdue University in March 1940. A year earlier she and Panette Morris of West Lafayette had been the first coeds to start flight training. *Purdue* was the *first school* in the U.S. to qualify students for *private pilot certification.*

THE first school in the nation to offer a bachelor's degree with a *major in professional aircraft piloting* was Purdue University whose Department of Aviation Technology started the program in 1965.

THE *first female Hoosier to become a Rhodes scholar* was Barbara Toman of Crown Point, a student in journalism and English at Indiana University when chosen in 1983. She planned to study politics and economics at Oxford. Before 1976 no females were chosen Rhodes scholars, an omission corrected only by an act of parliament.

A *longevity record for college presidents* was set in 1984 by the Rev. Theodore Hesburgh, president of the University of Notre Dame at South Bend, who had been in office 33 years, more than any other college president in the nation.

THE Rev. Theodore Hesburgh also has *more honorary degrees* than anyone in the U.S. His honorary degree in May 1984 brought his total to 100, far ahead of the only other person to come close, President Herbert Hoover, who received 89.

PURDUE UNIVERSITY leads the nation in *doctorate degrees in pharmacology*, in *bachelor degrees in engineering*, in *engineering degrees for women*, and in *chemistry students.*

THE first school in the nation to offer a *course on cable television* was Indiana Central University in Indianapolis, which started a 45-minute lecture course in management for the first semester of 1985. Those wishing to take the course for credit had to attend an orientation session on campus and return there for mid-term and final exams.

[SEE ALSO *Astronauts; Aviation; Bicycles; Flags; Medicine; Newspapers; Organizations; Photography; Radio; Television.*]

COUNTIES

THE *most prolific designer of courthouses* is believed to have been George W. Bunting, credited with at least seven in Indiana. Son of a sea captain, he came to Indiana from Pennsylvania. In 1881 courthouses of his design were being erected simultaneously in Clinton County and Madison County, only 70 miles apart.

THE *first county agent* in Indiana was Leonard B. Clore, who got the job in 1912 in LaPorte County. Born in 1866 in Johnson County, he had been the first international corn grower at the Paris Exposition in 1900 and was declared Corn King of the World in 1909. He rejected an offer to serve as agricultural advisor to the czar of Russia in 1909.

THE *county which has had the most county seats* (although courthouses were not erected at all of them) was Martin County, with nine county seat cities in 50 years: Hindostan, Mt. Pleasant, Memphis, Harrison, Hillsborough (later Dover Hill), Harrison again, West Shoals and, finally, Shoals.

[SEE ALSO *Land*.]

COURTHOUSES: SEE *Counties; Structures*.

COURTS

THE woman credited with obtaining the *right for women to practice law* in Indiana was Antoinette Dakin Leach, who was denied admittance to the bar in Sullivan in 1891 and appealed the decision to the Indiana Supreme Court which granted her admittance to the bar in 1893. There is dispute, however, as to whether Antoinette was actually the first woman to practice law in Indiana. Mrs.

Stelle Colby Meeker claimed that she began practicing law at Crown Point in 1892, and other sources cite Mary Harry Peacock and even Mrs. Willkie, mother of Wendell Willkie, as the first women to practice law. However, Antoinette Leach's struggle is the best documented.

THE *first woman admitted to practice before the Indiana Supreme Court* was Miss Mary Harry Peacock in 1896. A native of Lawrenceburg, she was deputy clerk of the court 16 years until 1894. She died in January 1942.

THE *first juvenile court judge* and the organizer of the system was George W. Stubbs of Indianapolis. Concerned with the youths who appeared before him when he was elected police court judge in 1901, Stubbs pushed through a bill setting up a juvenile court in 1903 and was appointed its judge. He won election to the post the next year.

INDIANA'S *first all-woman jury* sat at Vernon to hear a case of breach of the peace against B. B. Cox, brought by George Russell, who claimed Cox had threatened him. The jury, which found Cox innocent on the afternoon of June 6, 1921, included Mrs. N. J. Benson, Miss Maggie Abbott, Mrs. E. P. Trapp, Mrs. Jessie Richardson, Mrs. Kate Wenzel, Mrs. Anna Hengstler, Mrs. Zelpha Webber, Mrs. Nellie Long, Mrs. Isabelle Waltermire, Mrs. Myra Culp, Mrs. Louisa W. Barth, and Mrs. Mary Stemm. The bailiff was Mrs. Maggie Hartwell.

THE *first black judge* in Indiana was Mercer M. Mance, elected in 1958 to the post in Superior Court, Room 2, in Indianapolis.

INDIANAPOLIS attorney Harriette B. Conn, named a *public defender* in May 1970, was the *first Indiana black* to hold that post.

THE *first court in the nation devoted exclusively to environmental matters* was the Indianapolis Environmental Court, started in 1978 to hear cases involving health, housing, and land use codes. The *first judge* was David A. Jester.

THE *first woman county court judge* in Indiana was Linda Chezem, appointed in January 1976 as judge in Lawrence County, after passage of a bill creating county courts to replace justice-of-the-peace courts in some counties. Mrs. Chezem later won election on the Republican ticket to keep the court post another term.

THE *first woman federal judge* in Indiana was Sarah Evans Barker, confirmed to the U.S. District Court for Southern Indiana March 13, 1984, and sworn in March 31, 1984. Mrs. Barker, 40, was a U.S. attorney for the same federal district where she was appointed a judge to fill the vacancy caused by the death of Judge Cale Holder. She is a native of Mishawaka, a graduate of Indiana University, and earned her law degree from American University in Washington.

[SEE ALSO *Crime and Criminals*.]

COVERED BRIDGES : SEE *Bridges*.

CRIME AND CRIMINALS

THE *first robbery of a moving train* was the work of the Reno Gang, which boarded an Ohio and Mississippi line train at Seymour the night of October 6, 1866, and took $15,000 from an Adams Express man. Two years later they captured a one-car train at Marshfield in Scott County and got $96,000 in gold and government bonds. Members of the gang were Frank Sparks, John Reno, and Simeon Reno. Although caught for their first train robbery, they were never tried and were later convicted of other crimes.

THE *first state prison* was at Clark Street and Clark Boulevard in Clarksville, established in 1821. Built by the state, it was leased to private individuals who were paid to care for inmates. The first lessee was Capt. Seymour Westover, who was killed at the Alamo in 1836.

THE *female with the most murders to her credit* is Belle Gunness of LaPorte, whose slaying of at least 14 men was discovered during an investigation after her farm house burned April 28, 1908. Belle, 5 feet, 8 inches tall, weighing 280 pounds, is believed to have lured the men into marriage and disposed of them for various insurance policies, said to have brought her a total of $30,000. Although discovery of a tooth in the fire ashes suggested Belle died in the blaze, one theory is that she pulled her own tooth as a false clue and fled.

THE *largest number of bank robberies in one year* in Indiana occurred in 1933, when 35 bank jobs were reported.

THE first Hoosier *murder on an aircraft in flight* was committed by Earnest P. Pletch of Frankfort, who shot Carl Bivens, a Missouri flying instructor, to death somewhere over Missouri with a .32 caliber pistol in October 1939, then flew back to Indiana, landing the single-engine plane in a pasture 4 miles south of Bloomington on the Meredith Dillman farm. Pletch was seized by police called by an alert telephone operator who saw the plane, the object of a widespread hunt, land in the pasture. The bizarre case, according to Pletch's confession, started when he took his sister's car and headed for Hannibal, Mo., seeking his estranged wife. When unable to find her because she had left with a road show, Pletch said he decided to take some advanced flying lessons because it was something he always had wanted to do. He found a teacher at Brookfield, Mo., Carl Bivens, who was using somebody else's plane to give lessons. Pletch had one lesson, spent the night in the car, and went up again the next day. It was then, during conversation, that Bivens learned that Pletch had enjoyed some notoriety because he had recently stolen an airplane, taken it to Missouri, and been caught. Bivens advised that there were ways to fly stolen planes to Mexico and obtain fraudulent ownership documents; the two of them hatched a plan to steal the plane Bivens was using and head south. First, however, Pletch wanted to visit his folks at Frankfort. On the way Bivens seemed to have second thoughts and objected to the gun he thought Pletch was carrying, the revolver that was to be the murder weapon. Their falling out as criminal partners led to a struggle and Pletch, who was riding in the back of the plane, was pulled against the controls, sending the craft into a dive. He pulled out the revolver and shot Bivens twice in the back of the head, regained control of the plane and, about 15 minutes later, landed in a field and got rid of Bivens's body. After another landing to refuel, Pletch said he stopped at a farm in eastern Missouri to spend the night. Next day he returned to Indiana, circled Frankfort near his home and then headed south, perhaps for Mexico. Next stop was Bloomington, however, and apprehension.

SAM BASS, born on a Lawrence County farm in 1851, went west in 1870 and became the *best known Hoosier outlaw* of that era. After being a ranch hand and deputy sheriff, Bass developed a love for fast horses, gambling, and easy money and organized a gang which raided a Cherokee reservation to steal horses. Living in Denton, Tex., Bass and his gang then committed numerous crimes in the area. When they took $60,000 from a Union Pacific train in Nebraska, two gang members were killed; a third decided to betray Bass by tipping off authorities to the next job. When Bass tried to rob the Round Rock bank in 1878, he was killed, ending a five-year reign as an outlaw. He was buried on his 27th birthday.

THE *most unusual defendant* tried in Indiana probably was a chimpanzee named Jocko Dooley, who was charged in 1905 with violating a then-new law against smoking. The arrest probably was a semi-humorous test of the new law. The chimp, 15 at the time, had a habit of about 200 cigarettes a day; he was part of the Carl Hagenbeck Circus. Records are unclear as to the outcome of the trial, although there is little doubt Jocko was found guilty. The anti-smoking law in Indiana was amended in 1909, changed to apply only to persons under 18 in 1973, and the ban was completely lifted in 1977. However, Indiana has had a law prohibiting the sale of cigarettes to anyone younger than 13 and this age limit was raised to 16 on September 1, 1983. Sale to anyone younger than that can bring a fine of $500.

THE *oldest Hoosier sentenced for a felony* is John Stolarz, three months short of 88 when he was given a 6-year term in 1983 in Lake County for shooting his wife, Helen. Stolarz was imprisoned at the Westville Correctional Center.

THE *first man officially executed* in Indiana was Harry Jones, hanged May 7, 1897. Department of Corrections records contain no further information about the man or his offense.

JOHN RINKARD at 63 was the *oldest man to be hanged* in Indiana, executed January 17, 1902, for killing his wife.

THE *youngest to be hanged* in Indiana were 26 years old: Ora Copenhaver, executed June 12, 1903, for killing his wife, and Edward Hoover, hanged November 13, 1903, offense unrecorded.

THE *first man to die in the electric chair* in Indiana was John Chirka, an Austrian executed February 20, 1914. Chirka, 40, a flour miller, was convicted in Lake County on September 22, 1913, of killing his wife.

INDIANA was the first state to use *iron rods* instead of leather straps to hold condemned men in the electric chair to prevent the victim jerking loose from the effects of electricity. The chair was created from the hanging scaffold at the Indiana State Prison and was first used in 1914.

THE *youngest felons electrocuted* in Indiana were William Ray, who died August 5, 1920, for killing during a robbery, and James Swan, executed June 23, 1939, for the same kind of offense. Both were 18.

THE *first execution in the nation of a white convicted of killing an Indian* occurred at Pendleton December 1, 1824, when James Hudson was hanged from an oak for his part in the slaying of two Indians, three squaws, and four children in their camp on Fall Creek. Hudson was one of five whites convicted of the March 22, 1824, murders. Sentence was passed by Judge W. W. Wick. One of the condemned was John Bridge, only 19. As he stood ready to be hanged, Gov. James Brown Ray, one of the state's most flamboyant chief executives, rode up on a horse, announced that only he, the governor, had the power to save the boy. He then dramatically granted Bridge a reprieve. The strain of it all caused Bridge to collapse, however, and he was hopelessly deranged the rest of his life.

THE *oldest man executed in the electric chair* in Indiana was Cleveland Greathouse, 63, sentenced for killing his wife; he was put to death November 26, 1945.

More persons have been sentenced to death in Lake County than in any other Indiana county—11 of the 73 in Indiana up to 1984.

THE *crime most frequently committed* by the 73 persons executed in Indiana up to 1984 is that of killing in the perpetration of a robbery or burglary, which brought death to 31 felons.

THE nation's *first horse thief detective association* was organized in June 1845 near Wingate, and incorporated three years later as the Council Grove Minute Men. This evolved into the National Horse Thief Detective Association, which was granted extraordinary policing powers by the state. The Council Grove Minute Men was the last such group to dissolve, in 1957, years after horse thievery had ceased to be a major problem.

THE Indiana Reformatory Institution, later the Indiana Women's Prison, was the *first in the nation built for women and managed exclusively by women*. It received its first prisoners in Indianapolis October 8, 1873, when 17 went behind walls under supervision of Sarah J. Smith, the first superintendent, who held the job from June 10, 1873, to December 1, 1883.

VALJEAN DICKINSON became the *first black to head an Indiana penal institution* in January 1969 when he was elevated from acting superintendent of the Indiana Women's

Prison in Indianapolis to superintendent. Dickinson later became program manager of the Division of Continuing Studies at Indiana University–Purdue University, Indianapolis, and in 1981 was appointed executive director of the Fall Creek Parkway Branch of the YMCA in Indianapolis.

INDIANA was the first state to establish *flogging as the penalty for convicted wife beaters*, a measure passed by the Indiana General Assembly in 1891.

THE *first use of a lie detector* device in Indiana was in the case of William J. Newell and Josephine and Edward McCloud, involved in a disturbance in the Newell home in Indianapolis in 1924. Attorney Edward New gave tests with the device, called a sphygmomanometer, and reported to Indianapolis city judge pro tempore Lloyd Claycombe that the defendants had been lying. Edward McCloud was fined $1 and costs on a charge of drunkenness. Charges of assault and battery against Newell and Josephine McCloud were continued.

THE *first black Federal probation officer* in Indiana was Webster L. Brewer, who served from April 1964 to November 1968 for the Southern District of the Federal Court.

THE *first black criminal court judge* in Indiana was Webster Brewer, who became judge in superior court, criminal division, in Indianapolis in 1978. Brewer earlier had been a judge in the civil division.

THE *first black appointed to the Indiana Parole Board* was Milo Murry, who was appointed July 1, 1961, and retired May 31, 1975.

THE *first Hoosier to charge a corporation with homicide* was Michael Cosentino, prosecuting attorney at Elkhart, who brought criminal charges against the Ford Motor Company because of a fatal rear-end crash involving a Pinto automobile. In a trial in 1980 Ford was found not guilty.

A warehouse in Brazil, Ind., seized in mid-August, 1982, contained the *biggest bundle of counterfeit money* ever confiscated in the state. The phony $100 bills totalled $2,942,000; six men were indicted after the raid.

THE *first black to be agent in charge of an FBI office* in Indiana was Wayne Davis, who took charge of the Indianapolis office in 1977. He left March 16, 1981, to become special agent in charge in Detroit.

[SEE ALSO *Courts; Police; Organizations, Radio.*]

C R O P S : SEE *Inventions; Plants.*

D

DENTISTRY

THE earliest person to practice *dentistry as a sole profession* in Indiana was J. P. Ulery of Rising Sun, well before 1850. Others had been dentists as a sideline.

THE *first female dental school faculty member* in Indiana was Dr. Edith Davis, part-time instructor in periodontia at the Indiana University Dental School clinic in Indianapolis. She was appointed in late 1945.

DESKS

THE *largest number of Wooton desks* assembled in modern times was a collection of 15 of the masterpieces displayed in the Indiana State Museum from April 9 to August 8, 1983. The desks were the work of William Wooton, a Quaker, who worked on his patented furniture in Indianapolis from 1874 to 1884. Some of the desks for the exhibit were acquired from the collection of Richard C. Dubrow of New York, founder of the Wooton Desk Society.

THE *most expensive Indiana desk* was one created by Wooton for Queen Victoria, which in 1979 was valued at $125,000. The desk was a superior Wooton with a British lion on the pediments. The Wooton desk patents passed to the Richmond firm of Haynes, Spencer & Co., which stopped making the desks in 1898.

DOLLS

THE most popular Indiana dolls are Raggedy Ann and Raggedy Andy, still selling in 1984; they were created in Indianapolis by John Gruelle, artist, children's author, and political cartoonist. It happened like this. In December 1914, Marcella Gruelle found a battered doll in the trash, rescued it, and took it to the office of her father, John Gruelle, cartoonist for *The Indianapolis Star*. He recognized it as one of his mother's old dolls, now grubby and faceless. The artist applied a new face to the doll and two buttons from his desk drawer as eyes. Her name was chosen from the poems of James Whitcomb Riley, a friend of Gruelle. Marcella adored the doll and her father began to make up stories about Raggedy Ann, mainly to get his daughter to go to sleep. When Marcella died of tuberculosis March 21, 1916, her despondent father continued writing the stories during his spare time and illustrating them with drawings of the doll. A Chicago company published the books and a bookstore operator, so the story goes, made a doll as a window display to spur sales of the book. It spurred sales of the doll, too. When an old friend of John Gruelle's mother showed up with a similar doll, it turned out to be

Raggedy Andy. The two girls had played together with their dolls in Indianapolis. Eventually there were nearly 40 Raggedy Ann books for children, all written and illustrated by Gruelle before his death in 1938. Years later another artist did an update on the illustrations for the Bobbs-Merrill Company of Indianapolis, then publishers of the books. The dolls were manufactured by the Knickerbocker Company, which went out of business in 1983, turning rights over to Hasbro, Inc. Two of the early dolls are in the collection of the Indianapolis Children's Museum.

DRUGS

WHEN the Indiana registry law went into effect in 1899, Bruno Knoefel of New Albany became the *first registered pharmacist* in the state.

THE *first law in the U.S.* designed to *curb adulteration of food, drugs, and cosmetics* was the Food and Drug act instituted in 1899 by Indiana, and later used as a model for a similar Federal law.

THE *first state-wide Alcoholics Anonymous conference* in Indiana was convened May 8–9, 1954, in the Hotel Lincoln in Indianapolis, attended by more than 100 groups from Indiana and elsewhere.

THE *first black appointed to the Indiana Pharmacy Board*, Spurling Clark, was named to the post August 26, 1968, and served until his death in February 1971.

THE antiseptic *Merthiolate* was introduced in 1930 by Eli Lilly and Company of Indianapolis, but was not successful with customers until the company added dyes to make it stain the skin and alcohol to make it sting.

Alka-Seltzer was developed by Miles Medical Company (later Miles Laboratories) at Elkhart in 1931 after Andrew Beardsley, son of one of the men who founded the company along with Dr. Franklin Miles, discovered the "secret" medicine used in the city room of the Elkhart newspaper to ward off the flu which swept the country after World War I. It was a mixture of aspirin and bicarbonate of soda. Miles came up with its own version, plus fizz.

INDIANA became the first state to permit the manufacture, sale, and use of *laetrile* May 1, 1977, when the legislature overrode a veto by Governor Otis R. Bowen. The drug, used by some in cancer treatment, had been banned from interstate commerce by the Federal Drug Administration.

[SEE ALSO *Inventions; Medicine.*]

DRUGSTORES: SEE *Business.*

DUELS

THE *first duel* known to have occurred in Indiana was January 19, 1809, when Henry Clay, then a member of the Kentucky legislature, and Humphrey Marshall, also a Kentucky legislator, journeyed across the Ohio River a little downstream from Silver Creek in Floyd County to settle an argument over a bill to boycott articles made by the British. Clay sponsored the bill; Marshall was against it and called Clay a poltroon, a term encompassing everything bad which could be said about a man in that era. Clay was hit in the thigh and suffered a flesh wound in the right hip in the duel. Marshall was unharmed.

THE *most humorous duel* involving Indiana pitted William G. Terrell and William S. Lingle, both of Lafayette, in a face-off over a dog. Terrell was editor of the *Lafayette Journal* in 1858, Lingle editor of the *Courier* in the same city. When Lingle's dog ran into the *Journal* shop, it was kicked out; the second time, cans were tied to it; and the third time it wandered into the shop, it was doused with turpentine. The dog, according to reports, was so burned by the chemical that it leaped through a window glass, ran to the Wabash River to cool off, and drowned. Lingle's editorial on the incident was so stinging that Terrell challenged him to a duel. They headed with their parties for Covington, Ky., to do the fighting, but en route the banter overcame the anger, they shook hands, and made a night of partying, the duel forgotten.

E

ECONOMICS

INDIANA went *bankrupt for the first time* in 1837–38 because of a drain on capital caused by the construction of a canal system and a panic in 1837, among other factors.

THE *nation's first comptroller of the currency* was Hugh McCulloch, a Fort Wayne banker, who served from May 9, 1863, to March 8, 1865, resigning to become Secretary of the Treasury under Presidents Abraham Lincoln, Andrew Johnson, and, later, Chester A. Arthur. McCulloch was comptroller under the National Bank Act of 1863, which gave the comptroller authority to grant bank charters pretty much at his own whim. Before that, McCulloch was involved in the establishment of Bank of the State of Indiana, chartered in 1855. With the charter of the Second State Bank of Indiana due to expire in 1859, it began recalling capital and a group of promoters sought to have the charter renewed. Lobbyists offered to do the job for $200,000, but J. M. Ray, the cashier, refused to do so, saying it smacked of corruption. Instead, promoters pushed for a new bank charter, which they got; McCulloch became president of the new bank and J. M. Ray became its cashier. With the passage of the National Bank Act, McCulloch's bank went out of business because of competition and its branches for the most part became national banks.

WHEN John P. Frenzel became president of Merchant's National Bank in Indianapolis in 1882 at the age of 28, he became the *youngest president of a national bank* in the nation, a mark believed unsurpassed in Indiana. Frenzel started at the bank at 12 as a messenger.

THE Chamber of Commerce of Franklin issued the world's *first self-liquidating script* money March 8, 1933, during the Depression. The method used to liquidate the money was to place a two-cent stamp on each dollar every time it was circulated. Had the banks not reopened, the full amount would have been paid. The amount issued was $2,400.

INDIANA'S *first black-owned bank* (although there also were white investors) was Midwest National Bank, which opened in October 1972 in Indianapolis.

THE *biggest loss on paper* in the nation in a single day was $24,768,630, lost December 26, 1972, by Arthur Decio, chairman of Skyline Corporation at Elkhart, due to a drop in the stock market.

THE Madison Bank and Trust Company, Madison, is the *oldest bank* in Indiana with continuous service. It began in 1833.

THE *largest bank* in Indiana is the American Fletcher National Bank in Indianapolis, with 1982 assets of $2,864,000,000; it provides an estimated 2,500 jobs and has an annual payroll of $30 million. It was started in 1939 by Stoughton A. Fletcher.

THE *smallest* of the 404 banks in Indiana is Western State Bank at South Bend, with assets of $4,227,841 as of the end of 1982.

THE *largest savings and loan institution* in Indiana is

the Federal Savings and Loan Association in Indianapolis with 1982 assets of $586,167,738.

THE *smallest savings and loan* in Indiana is United Savings and Loan Association at Gary, with assets of $19,818 as of the end of 1982.

THE *largest credit union* in Indiana is the Teachers Credit Union in South Bend which, as of the fall of 1983, had assets of $147 million.

[SEE ALSO *Business*].

EDUCATION

THE *first teacher* in Indiana was the Rev. John Francois Rivet, sent to Vincennes in 1791 by George Washington to teach the Indians at a salary of $200 a year. Rivet organized the Jefferson Academy in 1801 and at his death in 1804 became known as the "father of teaching" in the state.

THE *earliest teacher of agriculture* in Indiana was Philip Dennis, sent to the state in 1804 by the Quakers to pass on farming techniques to the Indians. Little Turtle had obtained a program with federal funds to teach farming and when the Quakers were asked to assist, they sent Dennis from Maryland with some helpers. He returned to Maryland in the fall after harvest. The Quakers continued the project two more years, but it failed after Little Turtle died and Indians became violent against the whites. The site of the agricultural school was on the Wabash River two miles below Andrews in Huntington County.

Instruction in printing, lithography, and engraving was given in the social community school at New Harmony in 1826, said to be the first time for such a curriculum in the nation. The school was founded by Robert Owen.

THE *first known diploma mill* in Indiana was that of John Bennett of New Albany. He issued certificates as early as 1830 to anyone wishing to become a doctor who could pass the exam Bennett gave while travelling around the country. It is not known how many got medical diplomas that way because at that time there was no prescribed course of training for doctors anyway.

MONROE COUNTY SEMINARY, opened in 1833, was the first such institution in Indiana for women.

THE *first free schools* in Indiana probably were the academies for boys and girls opened by Bishop Simon William Gabriel Brute de Remur, first bishop of Vincennes, some time before his death on June 26, 1839. The bishop was called the founder of free education in Indiana.

INDIANA was the *first state to permit use of the school facilities by the community* when classes were not in session, although this 1859 act was confined mainly to playgrounds attached to schools.

THE Valparaiso Technical Institute, established in 1874, is the *oldest school* in Indiana and the nation *teaching electronics*.

MARY RANN became the *first black graduate of an Indiana high school* in 1876 by her completion of work at Indianapolis High School, later renamed Shortridge.

THE *first junior high school* in Indiana was established at Richmond when 7th and 8th grade pupils were moved to a separate building in 1896. They also were given special courses, and departmental teaching was put into effect, using a mathematics department, an art department, etc. That was also the first time pupils were passed or failed by subject rather than by a grade in school.

THE state did not *require that youths attend high school* until 1897; staying in school until the age of 16 was mandatory in 1901.

THE *first platoon school* in the nation was Central School at Bluffton. William Wirt directed the school, begun in September 1899, and organized with specific times devoted to study, work, and play. All three elementary schools in Bluffton adopted the method in September 1902.

THE *first consolidated school* in the U.S. was at Raleigh in Rush County, where all the township schools were centralized in a single school about 1920. The school closed in the 1960s, but the building still stands.

THE *first all-electric school* in Indiana was one at Hartford City, which opened in 1954 with American Electric Power Service Corporation providing the electrical heat.

THE Edgelea Elementary School on the south side of Lafayette was the *first prefabricated school* in the nation, built of units produced on the factory assembly line of the National Homes Corporation in 21 days. The four units, each containing two classrooms, two washrooms, and a furnace room, were donated by the manufacturer in 1955.

THE *first black in Indiana to hire teachers in public schools* was Walter D. Bean; he took this position in Indianapolis in 1966. His teaching career began in 1936. Bean also was the *first black admitted to the Indiana Society of Public Accountants*.

THE first school district in the nation to establish a *rehabilitation program for students* violating laws while in school was Perry Township in Marion County which, in 1983, set up Alternatives, Inc. Those guilty of arson, assault, possession of stolen property or weapons, sexual misconduct, or inciting others to violence were tossed out of school but given the option of taking Alternatives, Inc., for 10 days at a cost of $250. The program was designed to teach those expelled how to behave, how to get back in school, and how to stay there without misbehaving.

THE *oldest high school* in Indiana is New Albany High School, founded October 3, 1853, but interrupted during the Civil War. The *oldest high school in continuous operation* is Central High School at Evansville, opened in 1868.

THE *oldest elementary school still in operation* is Myers Grade School at Cannelton, which began in 1868 as Free School and was renamed for a teacher and principal known as Daddy Myers.

THE *largest high school* in Indiana is North Central High School, Indianapolis, with a 1982–83 enrollment of 3,707, well ahead of the second-place school, Indianapolis Washington with 2,717.

THE *smallest high school* in Indiana is Worthington-Jefferson Junior and Senior High School at Worthington, with a 1982–83 enrollment of 157.

THE *largest elementary school* in Indiana is Charles N. Scott Elementary and Middle School in Hammond with an enrollment of 1,053.

THE *smallest elementary school* is Hayesville Elementary School in DuBois County, with an enrollment of 42.

[SEE ALSO *Aviation; Colleges and Universities; Electricity; Flags; Medicine; Music; Newspapers; Organizations; Radio; Religion; Research; Structures.*]

ELECTRICITY

THE first city in the nation to have *electric street lighting* was *Wabash* which switched on its system in 1880. The Brush Electric Light Company of Cleveland, O., installed lights on the dome of the courthouse. Owner of the firm, Charles F. Brush, had invented his arc light in 1879. Four lights were put in place March 31, 1880, powered by a generator in the courthouse basement, which was driven by an old steam engine on the courthouse lawn. April 8, 1880, a further payment of $1,800 for the system was approved. In 1881 the firm got a franchise to install the same lighting in Indianapolis, and put sample lights on Monument Circle.

INDIANA was the first state to have a *state-wide electrical co-operative organization* with establishment in 1935 of Statewide Rural Electric Cooperative, Inc., a service arm for Rural Electrical Membership Cooperatives.

THE *first loan sought* in Indiana under Rural Electrification Administration legislation signed May 11, 1935, was by the Boone County REMC at Lebanon. It joined in the application with two other rural electric cooperatives.

THE *first home to be electrified* under the Rural Electrification Administration was that of Clark Woody in Boone County, May 22, 1936.

THE *first electrical heat pumps* in Indiana were those offered for sale by the Indiana and Michigan Electric Company in 1950, according to Arnold Hogan, then vice-president of the firm at Marion. The firm served an area from Muncie north into southern Michigan.

THE five 635-megawatt generating units of Public Service Company of Indiana, Inc., near Princeton are the *largest generating units* for electricity in Indiana and among the largest in the nation. They burn 7 million tons of coal a year, require 680 people to run them, and use a 3,000-acre lake for cooling.

[SEE ALSO *Inventions; Presidents.*]

EXPLORING

THE *first white man* whose appearance in Indiana is documented was René Robert Cavalier Sieur de La Salle, who reached the St. Joseph River in December 1679 at a point now occupied by South Bend. Although he may have been preceded by Father Jacques Marquette or Father Claude Allouez, both Jesuits, there are no surviving records providing exact dates of their visits.

[SEE ALSO *Caves.*]

EXPLOSIONS:
SEE *Accidents and Disasters.*

F

FAIRS AND FESTIVALS

THE *first rural fair* was held in Knox County in 1809.

GOVERNOR JOSEPH A. WRIGHT was responsible for the *first Indiana State Fair*, October 19–23, 1852, in Military Park in Indianapolis. An estimated 15,000 visitors showed up for the first day to view 1,365 exhibits, and overflow crowds continued to assemble to see plowing matches, hear speeches, and watch fireworks. With admission at 20 cents each, the revenue was $4,600, enough to cover expenses and repay a $2,000 loan to launch the fair. It was planned to move the annual event to various cities about the state, Lafayette in 1853 and Madison in 1854, but the plan was abandoned and Indianapolis became the regular location.

THE *first street fair* in Indiana is believed to be one conducted at Peru in September 1894.

THE *oldest organized festival* in Indiana is the Rose Festival of Hillsdale Nursery in Indianapolis, first held in June 1937 for garden clubs and similar groups, and opened to the public in 1938. After a patriotic theme in 1942, the festival was discontinued during World War II, recommencing in 1947.

THE *first Ferris wheel* was erected by Hoosier Luther V. Rice at the 1893 Columbian Exposition in Chicago; the developer, George W. G. Ferris, could find no other person to attempt the job. The wheel was 265 feet tall and had 36 cars, each capable of holding 60 passengers. Rice was born near Ladoga. (See Bridges.)

THE *largest county fair* in Indiana is the Marion County fair with more than 5000 4-H members participating in 67 exhibition categories, and annual visitors of more than 200,000.

THE *largest display of pyrotechnics* in Indiana was the 2,000 rockets shot aloft in synchronization with music September 3, 1983, at the first Indiana Festival at White River Park in Indianapolis. The fireworks were launched by Jim Souza of Pyro Spectaculars, a firm at Rialto, Cal., which also claims to have produced the largest fireworks display in the world in 1981 at Hong Kong. The rocket show in Indianapolis, which lasted 20 minutes, was accompanied by appropriate music over radio station WENS, which sponsored the fireworks and played 21 songs and six jingles during the display. Souza estimated that the fireworks weighed about a ton; they were readied in two days by a crew of 10.

JAMES BUCHANAN III became the *first black member of the Indiana State Fair Board* when appointed to the post November 15, 1983, by Gov. Robert D. Orr. Buchanan, who had been a chauffeur for Indiana Gov. Ralph F. Gates during the 1940s, was a retired employee of the State Board of Health where he had worked 37 years. He had been head of the housekeeping section. Buchanan also was vice-president of the Indianapolis Real Estate Brokers Association, a director of the Indianapolis Urban League, and a former member of the Indianapolis Metropolitan Board of Zoning Appeals.

[SEE ALSO *Radio*.]

FIREMEN

THE *first paid female firefighter* in Indiana was Michaellyn Mauer, 27, approved by the LaPorte Board of Works and Safety in January 1978 as a member of the force after she had served a year's probation.

THE Fair Play Company No. 1, a fire station at Madison, is *the oldest volunteer fire company* in the state, dating from September 15, 1841. Madison has four companies more than 100 years old.

[SEE ALSO *Health and sickness; Structures*.]

FLAGS

THE *first school in the nation to regularly fly a flag* outside on a flagpole was School No. 32 in Indianapolis, at Illinois and 21st streets, which dedicated a flag and pole February 20, 1891, as part of a patriotism program initiated by Capt. Wallace Foster, known nationally as "the flag-man."

THE *largest flag made in Indiana*, and also the *largest in the world*, is a banner 210 feet by 411 feet presented to President Ronald Reagan by Great American Flag, Inc., in 1983. It was finished March 22, 1980, by Anchor Industries at Evansville; eight seamstresses worked six weeks to construct the flag. It was designed for the Verrazano-Narrows Bridge in New York City, but never installed.

A state flag made for the Purdue University band is the *largest state flag* in Indiana, measuring 45 by 75 feet. It made its first appearance during the Purdue-Stanford football game September 11, 1982.

THE *largest British flag* in Indiana is a 100-by-60-foot Union Jack used by the Wapahani High School band in its marching formations. The British banner is said to be one of the largest in existence.

THE *highest-flying flag* in Indiana is the 20-by-30-foot banner atop the American United Life Building in downtown Indianapolis. The building rises 533 feet and the flag is atop an 80-foot pole, making its top 613 feet above the ground.

FLOODS: SEE *Accidents and disasters*.

FLOWERS: SEE *Plants*.

FOOD AND DRINK

THE *first whiskey produced for widespread sale* was that of the Rappites of New Harmony, who brought a still from Pennsylvania. The operation turned out an estimated 3,000 gallons of rye whiskey annually, sold in a wide area in southern Indiana.

IN 1831 Dunlap & Dougal of Indianapolis installed a *soda fountain*, a full year before its invention was credited to John Matthews in New York. Who operated the soda fountain seems unknown. J. P. Pope and Company in Indianapolis was serving soda water flavored with mead, made of fermented honey, in 11 flavors by 1853.

THE *oldest operating soda fountains* in Indiana are those in Zaharako's ice cream parlor in Columbus; they were purchased at the 1905 St. Louis World Exposition and installed in the business, now operated by Manuel and Lewie Zaharako.

THE Rev. Benjamin Nyce, a school principal of Kingston, began tinkering with fruit preservation in 1856 and two years later patented a means of preserving it by *refrigeration*, believed to be the first use in Indiana. Nyce opened a business at Cleveland, O., which was successful and he refused offers to buy him out. When his health failed, his wife took over. Commercial preservation by refrigeration was not achieved until 20 years after Nyce's patent.

MRS. GILBERT VAN CAMP, wife of an Indianapolis grocer, tinned beans cooked with pork and a tomato sauce to prevent spoiling. People who purchased the tins liked the flavor; this good seller was the *first commercially canned pork and beans* in the state. More than 6 million cans a year were being prepared and sold by 1890, using Mrs. Van Camp's secret recipe—and her name on the product.

THE *first recipe for butterscotch pie* allegedly was created by Sarah Wheeler of Connersville, who published her version in 1904 for a Methodist church cookbook. Sarah, operator of Wheeler Creamerie Exchange at Connersville, found that her filling for a cream pie had burned and, as a result, tasted like butterscotch candy. She repeated the "mistake" for other pies and this helped build the Wheeler restaurant chain.

WITNESSES testify that an *ice cream cone* may have been *invented at Fairmount in 1904,* before the first recorded serving of the delicacy at the Louisiana Purchase Exposition in St. Louis that same year. Cyrus (Sykie) Pemberton and a relative devised a mold made on a lathe. Into this was placed dough which was baked, then filled with ice cream.

Tomato juice as a drink was invented in 1917 at the French Lick Springs Hotel by chef Louis Perrin and head waiter Dan Hughes, who discarded the pulp and seeds of squeezed tomatoes and thickened the resulting beverage. It was not a huge success, but gradually use of the drink rose to 4,000 gallons a year and by 1921 the developers were supplying tomato juice to a wide southern Indiana area. Tomato Products Company was formed in 1925 with factories at French Lick and Paoli; this is believed to be the first time tomato juice was produced under factory conditions.

Canned tomato juice was developed by Walter Kemp of Kemp Brothers Canning Company in Kokomo; he devised the canning method in 1928 in response to a request by a St. Louis physician seeking a baby food to use in his clinic.

IN 1937 C. J. Morris of South Bend devised a way to liquify honey so that it could be bottled or canned. Before that honey was shipped and stored in the comb and crystallization was a problem. Morrison had a processing plant in his home.

THE *first report on adulteration of food* was made by Harvey Wiley for the State Board of Health in 1879. The report came during the same era in which Wiley instituted the state's first investigation into the adulteration of honey, syrups, and molasses by the addition of glucose.

THE Coca-Cola bottle was designed by a team at Terre Haute headed by Chapman J. Root of the Root Glass Company. The soft drink company announced a sweep-stakes in 1913; the Root entry was chosen the best at a 1916 bottlers' convention in Atlanta, Ga. The bottle was pat-ented in 1915 by Alexander Samuelson, Root's plant super-intendent; he carried out an idea conceived by T. Clyde Edwards, Root auditor, to make the bottle resemble the shape of the cacao bean pod. In 1923 the patent passed to the Root Company, and Coca-Cola acquired the rights in 1937.

THE *first Burger Chef* in the nation opened in 1954 at Little America Amusement Park on North Keystone Ave-nue in Indianapolis; it was an experiment by the General Equipment Manufacturing Company which produced res-taurant equipment. Eight more of the restaurants, using a special brazing method for hamburgers, opened in Indiana, Illinois, and Wisconsin in 1958.

THE *first Hoosier to win the Pillsbury Bake-off*, which started in 1949, was Mrs. Edwin J. Smogor of South Bend, whose All-American Apple Pie containing apples, caramel, and cheese took the honors in 1962. The next *Hoosier win-ner* was Mrs. Barbara Gibson of Fort Wayne who won in 1974 in the refrigerated division (the contest had two sec-tions by that time). Her entry was Easy Crescent Danish Rolls, large rolls filled with cream cheese and preserves.

THE *first champagne for commercial sale* produced in Indiana was probably that made by Carl Banholzer of Hesston, using grapes from LaPorte and the French system to bottle 150 cases in 1978. The wine was priced at $12 a bottle.

THE *biggest order of fast food* prepared in Indiana was 12,900 White Castle hamburgers shipped to Arizona and

New Mexico in November 1980. The sandwiches were part of a total order of 227,000 placed by the Fountain Hills, Ariz., Chamber of Commerce and the Queen of Heaven School at Albuquerque, N.M., for festivals in their communities. The Indianapolis truckload was driven by Pete Rasmussen and the order was prepared under the supervision of Paul Ferguson, White Castle area manager in Indianapolis.

JOHN BRUCE, 21, of Tell City, journeyed with another student from London to New York in March 1983 to pick up $400 worth of pizza and return with it to Harlaxton College, an affiliate in England of the University of Evansville. It was the *longest route to pick up a pizza* by anyone, Hoosier or otherwise. The two were selected by other students to make the trip.

INDIANA in the nation's No. 1 *supplier of duck feet*. The state exports its supply to the Far East, where it is a delicacy.

TITLE of the *world's largest popcorn producer* is claimed by Weaver Popcorn Company in Van Buren, Grant County; it distributes corn for popping throughout the U.S. and to 29 foreign countries on five continents. The firm, which buys popcorn from about 400 farms in eight states and processes it in plants at Van Buren and Ulysses, Kan., puts out 100,000,000 pounds of popcorn a year. The corn is grown on an estimated 36,000 acres of land. The Rev. I. E. Weaver, a Church of the Brethren minister, founded the company in 1927 with the planting and harvesting of 10 acres near Eton. The headquarters was moved to Van Buren in the 1940s. Welcome I. Weaver followed in his father's footsteps to become president of the firm about that same time. The company's statisticians estimated that Americans consume about 2 pounds of popcorn per person per year, which makes about 32 quarts of popped corn per capita.

THE *largest pork producer* in the U.S. is Wilson Foods Corporation at Logansport, opened in December 1968. It handles 12 to 15 percent of all the federally inspected pork slaughtered in the nation, and has annual sales of $2.2 billion.

[SEE ALSO *Business; Crops; Inventions; Railroads.*]

FOSSILS

THE *most complete fossilized beaver* in the world is at Earlham College's Science Museum. Discovered in 1889 in Randolph County, it is believed to be at least 10,000 years old.

THE *most unusual collection of fossils* in the nation is found at Richmond where their abundance is evident in outcroppings of limestone in the Whitewater River gorge, now part of the city park in Richmond.

[SEE ALSO *Archaeology.*]

G

GAMES

THE first Indiana *billiards* champion was Parker Byers, who won the title in 1869 and did not lose it until 1875, when beaten by Jake "the Kid" Schaefer, whom Byers had taught to play.

THE best *checkers* player in Indiana probably was Walter F. Hellman of Gary, who was world champion from 1948 to 1972 except for two years. A Swede who came to Gary when he was 11, Hellman won the checker grand slam in 1972—the Florida Open, the Southern Open, the Northern Open, and the national championship.

THE fastest *jigsaw puzzle* solver of record in Indiana is Martha May of Lafayette, who finished second in the 1982 national jigsaw puzzle championships at Athens, O., completing a puzzle in the singles competition in 3 hours, 36.05 minutes. The puzzle was "Shades of Childhood," with 500 pieces.

THE first *world horseshoe tournament* in 1909 at Bronson, Kas., was won by Frank Jackson of Kellerton, Ind.

BY all odds the best *horseshoe pitcher* in Indiana has been H. Curtis Day of Frankfort, who was four times national champion and three times world champion. His world championships came in 1969, 1971, and 1974 and national titles in 1966, 1969, 1971, and 1974. He was Clinton County champion 17 times, Indiana champion 21 times, Midwest champion 15 times, and Indiana-Ohio champion 15 times. In his 1974 world championship play he had 83 per cent ringers. Day also set the *best tournament record for ringers*. He won the national title at Murray, Utah, in August 1966 with a mark of 86.6 per cent ringers in 17 games, the best since the tournament started in 1915.

THE first world champion of *putt-putt golf* was Eric Smith of Indianapolis, who took $15,000 prize money in the tournament at Fayetteville, N.C., in August 1969. He also set a world record of 13 consecutive holes-in-one and tied the previous best score of 21 on a 36-par round. Eighteen when he won the championship, Smith, son of Mr. and Mrs. Walter K. Smith, had turned pro at 15 and won $1,000 in his first season.

THE top Hoosier player of *roque* (rhymes with croak) is George Atkinson of Indianapolis: he won the national title in 1937, was runnerup three times, was third twice, and served as vice-president of the American Roque League. He is the only Hoosier to win the national crown. The game, devised in 1901 in Connecticut, is a combination of croquet and billiards and involves four hard-rubber balls and 10 arches in a game played to 32 points.

It is doubtful if any Hoosier has won more in a single *slot machine* payoff than Celesta Graham of New Albany, who hit a jackpot of $250,000 in July 1983 at the Flamingo Hilton Hotel in Las Vegas.

The most won at *Monopoly* by a Hoosier is $107,980, collected in June 1984 by Paul Day of Indianapolis by winning a two-hour tournament held by Pepsi Cola in the Tropicana Hotel and Casino at Atlantic City. Day got $100,000 first prize plus $7,980 for all the Monopoly money and property he held.

GAS

Ezechiel Clampitt of near Sheridan drilled the *first gas well* in Indiana, although he was drilling for water. When the gas came in it was ignited with a flame that could be seen for miles, and Clampitt dug another well for water in 1832.

The *champion driller* in Indiana is believed to have been Almeron H. Crannel, who came from New York to Hartford City and is credited with 1,400 oil and gas wells drilled in Blackford County, the first being sunk in 1876. It was Indiana gas well No. 1; at 922 feet it reached a deposit which produced a flame 10 feet long, visible from as far away as 20 miles. It could be said to have introduced the gas boom in north-central Indiana. Crannel, who lived in Hartford City 24 years, died October 28, 1950, in the Marion Soldiers Home Hospital.

The *first Indiana city to use gas for street lighting* was Madison, which installed the lights in 1851.

Northern Indiana Gas and Electric Company at Michigan City put in use the *first waterless gas storage tank* in the nation February 10, 1925. A piston inside the tank rose and fell as the amount of gas varied. Made of steel plates 20 feet long and 32 feet wide, the tank was 105 feet in diameter and 160 feet high, and held a million cubic feet of gas.

GEMS

THE *biggest recorded diamond* in Indiana was 4 7/8 carats, found by Calvin Stanley at the base of a high cliff of blue shale three miles west of Brooklyn and three miles northwest of Centerton. It was later purchased by G. E. Nordyke of Indianapolis.

GLASS: SEE *Collections; Manufacturing*.

GLIDERS: SEE *Aviation; Recreation*.

GOVERNORS

THE *youngest person elected* governor in Indiana was James Brown Ray, who served from February 12, 1825, to December 7, 1831. He was born in 1794. Ray was an Indiana senator and became president pro tempore when Ratliff Boon quit as lieutenant governor to run for Congress. When William Hendricks resigned as governor, Ray became governor, then ran for election. There was controversy because some accused him of being younger than the age of 30 required by the constitution.

BROOKVILLE, which provided *three governors in a row*, holds a position unmatched by any other Hoosier city. The governors, serving from 1825 to 1840, where James Brown Ray, Noah Noble, and David Wallace. Wallace also served as lieutenant governor under Noble. In 1856 Brookville produced yet another governor: Abram H. Hammond, elected as lieutenant governor, became governor in 1860 when Ashbel P. Willard died.

THE first Indiana governor *to succeed himself after passage of the 1972 constitutional amendment* permitting it was Otis R. Bowen, governor from 1973 to 1980.

THE first Indiana governor *to die in office* was Ashbel Parsons Willard, governor from January 12, 1857, to October 4, 1860. A heavy drinker, Willard went to Minneapolis to try to regain his health and died there. A native of New York, he had been elected from New Albany and was called at one time the "best popular orator in the United States."

THE first Indiana governor *born in the state* was Oliver Perry Morton, a native of Salisbury (Wayne County) and chief executive from 1861 to 1867, after which he became a U.S. senator until his death in 1877.

THE *shortest term* for an Indiana governor is two days, served by Henry Smith Lane under a Republican agreement in 1861. Lane and Oliver P. Morton, his running mate, agreed that if they won the election and the Republicans won control of the legislature, Lane would become U.S. senator and Morton would assume the governorship. Lane was sworn in January 14 and left January 16. Morton served out the term and was re-elected, serving until 1867.

THE only Indiana governor *born in a log cabin* was James F. Hanly, born in 1863 in Illinois. He migrated to Warren County in 1879, was governor 1905–1909, and died in 1920.

THE only Indiana governor to *resign* was Warren T. McCray, who took office January 10, 1921, and left April 30, 1924, after being convicted of mail fraud in connection with personal financial problems. He served three years in federal prison and was late pardoned by President Herbert Hoover.

WHEN Paul Voreis McNutt became governor of Indiana, the Democratically-controlled legislature empowered him in February 1933 to reorganize the state government, making him the *first chief executive with dictatorial powers* in the state's history, and probably the first in the nation. McNutt was given the right to hire and fire all state employees and raise or lower salaries. Only legislative appropriations and possible court review provided limits to his power. He reorganzied 168 boards and commissions into the nine departments of executive, state, audit, treasury, law, education, public works, commerce, and industry.

THE first governor *elected to separate four-year terms* was Henry F. Schricker, elected in 1940 and again in 1948 during a period when governors were prohibited from succeeding themselves. Schricker was a native of North Judson.

THE *first governor to use music video* in an election campaign was Robert D. Orr, who broadcast one titled *Stay with Me* during the 1984 campaign. Orr, who was re-elected, appeared with a group of 18-to-24-year-olds while Henry Lee Summer sang the song. Orr was then the *oldest governor* in office in the nation at 66.

[SEE ALSO *Art and artists; Fairs and festivals; Politics, state.*]

GRAVES

THE *oldest marked grave* in Indiana is that of Janne Bonneau in the French Cemetery at Vincennes. She was the second wife of Toussaint DeBois, a French nobleman disinherited for leaving his country to accompany Lafayette to America. Janne Bonneau died November 15, 1800, at the age of 28.

THE *earliest U.S. military veteran* buried in Indiana was Sgt. John George, thought to be the personal drummer boy at George Washington's headquarter guard during the

Revolution. He came to Perry Township, Marion County, in 1838 at the age of 80, and was buried in Round Hill Cemetery on his death November 28, 1847. George left Kentucky for Indiana after the death of his wife to live with a daughter and her husband, Peter Stuck, near the present site of Indiana Central University.

CROWN HILL CEMETERY in Indianapolis, begun in 1863, is the *largest cemetery* in Indiana, 550 acres with more than 160,000 graves. Among notables buried there are President Benjamin Harrison, poet James Whitcomb Riley, novelist Booth Tarkington, bank robber John Dillinger, U.S. Senator Albert Beveridge, and three U.S. vice-presidents: Charles Fairbanks, Thomas Hendricks, and Thomas Marshall.

H

HEALTH AND SICKNESS

THE *first health officer* in Indiana was a constable at Vincennes, who took the job when the city passed a law to eliminate health nuisances in 1819. His name evidently is unrecorded.

THE *first state board of health in the nation* was established in 1881 in Indiana and went into operation in 1882 with Dr. Thaddeus M. Stevens as secretary, using a budget of $5,000.

THE *first epidemic* of major proportions in Indiana was an outbreak in 1826 at Hindostan, then a town of nearly 2,000, which was nearly wiped out. There is disagreement over whether the malady was typhoid, influenza, cholera, or all three.

A culture done on the throat of Earl Kendy of Richmond on April 1, 1897, is believed to be the first *test for diphtheria* in the state, done under a State Board of Health provision. Sent to the state laboratory by Dr. J. J. Johnson, the culture was reported positive. The second diphtheria culture was taken by Dr. R. W. Clay on the throat of Maude Rice of Newton seven days later.

THE brain of a dog and a heifer were first examined for *rabies* in Indiana in November 1905. The Nelis-Van Gehuchten method gave an inconclusive answer as to whether the disease, then a serious threat, was present in the animals.

DR. JOHN N. HURTY, state health commissioner, and Dr. Ada E. Schweitzer, director of infant and child hygiene for the Indiana State Board of Health, conceived the *first state baby contest*, held at the Indiana State Fair in 1920. The champion was chosen on the basis of a point system.

INDIANA first had a *Disease Prevention Day* October 1, 1914, proclaimed by Governor Samuel Ralston. Planned by John N. Hurty, secretary of the Indiana State Board of Health, the observance called for school programs, exhibitions, parades, and displays urging prevention of disease.

THE *first company to manufacture synthetic vitamin D*, the first vitamin to be made synthetically, was Mead, Johnson and Company at Evansville, which put it on the market in the spring of 1928. Ergosterol exposed to ultraviolet light was used in creating the vitamin.

SOUTH BEND claims to be the *first city in the U.S. to require food handlers to take a Wasserman Test*; although the date of this requirement is unknown, it predated the 1940s. Such tests detected VD.

KAY AND CHARLOTTE SINGLETON of Georgetown were victims of a *rare ailment*, Morvan's Syndrome, known to have struck only seven persons in the world. Discovered in the girls around 1947 when they were toddlers, the ailment, known as chronic peripheral osteomyelitis, led to the removal of fingernails and bones and deterioration of joints. It is not inherited and not contagious. A sister of the victims had no traces. Both Kay and Charlotte married and had children. They were seen by specialists all over the world and attended numerous medical conferences.

THE *record for performing cardio-pulmonary resuscitation* for a person not in a medical profession in Indiana is probably that of Craig Kenworthy of Indianapolis. Two weeks after receiving CPR training in the spring of 1979 at Lawrence North High School, Indianapolis, Kenworthy performed CPR on a car accident victim, and within less than two years had used the life-saving method on seven accident victims.

THE nation's *first fitness academy* was the National Fitness Academy in Indianapolis near the campus of Indiana University-Purdue University-Indianapolis (IUPUI), which began operation in September 1983. The academy, which trains fitness leaders, does fitness research, and studies equipment, moved to California in 1985.

More people died in Indiana of *influenza in* 1918 than in any other disease outbreak. The mortality list totalled 5,553, plus an additional 5,958 who died of pneumonia associated with the flu.

THE victim of the *world's longest coma* was Oscar E. Mills of Gary, an Indiana State Policeman. He suffered a skull fracture in a crash while chasing a suspect November 30, 1957 , and died without regaining consciousness April 12, 1966, after being unconscious 8 years, 4 months, and 12 days. Mills struck a turning car on Ind. 18 near Lafayette and careened against a grain crib on the farm of Charles Block.

[SEE ALSO *Fairs; Medicine.*]

HOLIDAYS

THE first official proclamation calling for *observance of Thanksgiving* in Indiana was issued by Gov. David Wallace November 4, 1839, calling for the holiday November 28th that year. Thanksgiving was not proclaimed a national holiday until 1864.

THE *first observance of Memorial Day* in Indiana was at Huntsville in Randolph County in 1865 after issuance of orders by Gen. John Logan, commander of the Grand Army of the Republic, that May 30 was to be observed in honor of the Civil War dead and that graves should be decorated.

TERRE HAUTE claims the *first observance of citizenship day* in Indiana, held October 8, 1939, and instigated by Ethel M. Ray, a teacher.

Creation of the Easter Lily as the symbol of the Easter Seal Society for Crippled Children and Adults was the work of Ruth McClellan of Petersburg, who got the idea while washing dishes. It was presented to the national headquarters of the organization in Chicago in October 1952 and chosen as the society's symbol at a convention in San Francisco which Mrs. McClellan attended as one of three delegates from Indiana.

THE *largest parade* in the state, both in units marching and in spectators, is the annual "500" Festival Parade, held in Indianapolis in connection with the Indianapolis 500-Mile Race.

THE *largest Independence Day celebration* in Indiana and the midwest is the Jaycee street fair in downtown Indianapolis begun July 4, 1976, and held annually since on the Saturday closest to July 4. The crowd is estimated at 300,000 each year.

THE *Santa Claus* who occupied the role *full-time* the longest was Raymond J. (Jim) Yellig, who began work as St. Nick in 1946 with the opening of Santa Claus Land in

Southern Indiana. Yellig had first played Santa in 1915, and around 1930 began answering letters for Jim Martin who ran the store-post office at Santa Claus. Yellig still was on the job as of Christmas 1983, although only on Sundays. He died July 23, 1984, at 90.

THE *largest Christmas tree* in Indiana is that formed annually when the Soldiers and Sailors Monument in downtown Indianapolis is strung with lights, creating a tree shape which rises 284 feet.

THE only city in the U.S. to have a *continuous annual observance for veterans* since World War II is Seymour, which has had a V-J Day Parade each August since 1945. The event includes a parade and a 21-gun salute; it attracts crowds of up to 50,000.

HOSPITALS: SEE *Medicine*.

HYDROPLANES: SEE *Boats*.

I

INDIANS

THE *largest of numerous mounds* left in Indiana by early tribes is the Sugar Loaf Mound at Vincennes, a cone 140 feet high with a level top measuring 16 by 25 feet.

THE *largest single earthwork* constructed by prehistoric people in Indiana is an earthen wall 9 feet high and forming a circle 1,200 feet in circumference at Mounds State Park at

Anderson. The wall is 50 to 60 feet wide at its base. It surrounded a mound 4 feet high and 30 feet in diameter.

Most agree that Meshekinnoquah "Little Turtle" was the *greatest Indian known* in the state. Born near Fort Wayne in 1752, he became chief of the Miamis and made first serious contact with whites in 1780, in a massacre in retaliation for the burning of an Indian village and trading post. This was known as Labalme's massacre. In 1790 he led his forces into Ohio to rout an American expedition led by Gen. Arthur St. Clair. When he saw that the forces of Gen. Anthony Wayne were too strong, he refused to join other tribes in battling Wayne; the Indians were defeated.

Little Turtle joined in the Fort Greenville, O., treaty, bringing peace to Indiana. In 1797 he visited Washington, spoke with John Adams and Thomas Jefferson, and posed for a portrait by Gilbert Stuart. He stopped the sale of liquor to Indians in Indiana and obtained a school for his people in 1804 near Andrews so Indians could learn white culture (although the school was ultimately unsuccessful). He died July 14, 1812, at Fort Wayne.

THE *last battle* with Indians on Indiana soil was December 17 and 18, 1812, when the Miami Indians were defeated on the banks of the Mississinewa River in Grant County.

THE *richest Indian* in the state, said to have been the richest Indian of all times, was Jean Baptist Richardson, chief of the Miamis from 1815 until his death in 1841, who amassed a fortune of more than $1 million, chiefly through land deals, and built an impressive home in 1833 on Ind. 9 near Huntington. It has been restored.

THE *oldest Indian* on record to die in Indiana was Chief White Eagle, 107 when he passed away February 15, 1983, in Wishard Hospital in Indianapolis. He had entered a nursing home in Indianapolis in 1976. Eagle, an Osage, had lectured around the nation. He was not a chief, but was named for his father and grandfather, who were.

[SEE ALSO *Art and artists; Collections; Education; Medicine.*]

INDUSTRY

THE *first aluminum casting* was made by William (Billy) Johnson at the Ford and Donnelly Foundry at Kokomo in 1895.

THE *first industrial union* in Indiana and the nation was the American Railway Union, formed in 1893 at Terre Haute by Eugene V. Debs.

[SEE ALSO *Coal; Gas; Jobs; Manufacturing.*]

INTERURBAN

CHARLES LEWIS HENRY organized the *first interurban street car line* in Indiana and the nation with establishment of the Union Traction Company in 1898. The first car ran June 1 between Anderson and Alexandria, with Hadley Clifford aboard as the *first conductor*.

THE Chicago, South Short & South Bend Railroad, traveling daily between South Bend and Chicago, is the state's *last surviving electric interurban* out of a total which once reached 250 lines.

[SEE ALSO *Railroads; Structures.*]

INVENTIONS

THE *cooking stove* was invented May 26, 1835, at Richmond by Solomon Dickinson, supplanting the fireplace or open blaze.

ALTHOUGH there are printed references to the invention of the *dishwasher* by Mrs. W. A. Cochran, a Shelbyville housewife, 1879–89, Shelby County historians have been unable to uncover any evidence of the feat and suspect that the inventor may have lived in Indiana at one time, but developed the dishwasher elsewhere.

ARCHIE FREDERICK COLLINS of South Bend, a nationally known physicist, invented the *wireless telephone* in 1899; he also discovered the effect of electric waves on brain cells in 1902.

THE *panic-exit device* on doors in public buildings was invented by Carl Prinzler of Indianapolis. They went on sale in 1908. Inspired by a fire in Chicago in which many died because they could not get out of locked doors, Prinzler devised the present system: The door can be locked, but pressure on a bar allows it to be opened from the inside. Prinzler's idea was engineered by a neighbor, Henry DuPont, of Von Duprin, Inc., then a division of Vonnegut Hardware Company.

THE first *ice shaving machine* for making snow cones was invented by Frank Thomas and installed about 1925 at Riverside Park in Indianapolis.

Dirilyte golden-hued tableware was invented by Carl Molin in Kokomo in 1926.

THE *frozen custard machine* using mechanical refrigeration was invented by Frank Thomas and installed in 1932 in the Teepee restaurant in Indianapolis. Before that, frozen custard machines got their refrigeration from salt and ice. The second Thomas machine was installed at the Northpole in Indianapolis for owner Pop Spencer in 1933.

THE *first plow with a chilled hard steel surface* which slipped soil better and remained hard longer was developed by James Oliver at South Bend. He became a multimillionaire with "the plow that broke the plains." The patent was granted to Oliver and Henry Little on June 30, 1857. The plow was credited with revolutionizing agriculture. Low in price, it made Oliver a major manufacturer by the mid-1870s.

THE *first plow on wheels* was invented by Asa M. Fitch of Lexington, Seymour, and Indianapolis, who got a patent November 17, 1885. He also invented *Fitch's chewing gum* in 1876. The confection was popular in Central Indiana. Fitch sold the business on Fort Wayne Avenue in Indianapolis during World War I. Fitch was born at Charlestown in 1850 and died October 20, 1923.

THE *first mechanical corn picker* was developed at Kokomo by John Powell in the early 1920s.

THE state's *first automatic mechanical walker for horses* was invented by Morton Walker, a Shelbyville welder, and first used in 1956 at Churchill Downs, Louisville. It was then made portable and taken to other places. Walker, a native of Wabash, used overhead arms attached to a central point, where they were powered by a 3/4-horsepower electric motor. His walker could handle four to 12 horses at a time, moving them in a circle.

THE *gasoline pump* was born in a barn at Fort Wayne, the brainchild of Sylvanus F. Bowser. The first one was delivered September 5, 1885, to Jake D. Bumper of Fort Wayne. Sylvanus and his brother, Augustus, got a patent for the device (No. 372,250) October 25, 1887, and later organized S. F. Bowser and Co., Inc.

FORT WAYNE was the site of the marketing of the world's first *computerizing pump*, which accurately measured the amount of liquid dispensed and provided the total price in dollars and cents. The pump went on sale November 1, 1932, marketed by the Wayne Company. Patent No. 1,888,533 was granted November 22, 1932 to Robert Joseph Jauch, Ivan Richard Farnham, and Ross Harper Arnold.

ELWOOD HANES of Kokomo successfully tested the *first gasoline powered, spark ignited car* in Indiana, driving it on Pumpkinville Pike July 4, 1894. Haynes, never highly successful at manufacturing automobiles, was an inventor of other things, of which the most potentially successful was a form of stainless steel which he invented in 1906 and called stellite; he was trying to develop tarnish-free dinnerware at the request of his wife. He never was able to take economic advantage of his inventiveness and gained little wealth from it. (See Automobiles and trucks.)

IN 1895 Frank L. and B. Perry Remy developed an *ignition system* for marine and stationary engines at Anderson, then turned to similar work on automobiles. In 1919 they were bought by General Motors Corporation; their names survive in Delco-Remy equipment.

GEORGE KINGSTON developed the *first carburetor* at Kokomo in 1902, using a piece of brass pipe 6 inches long with a cap fitted to one side in which a floater and wire gauge regulated the flow of fuel.

THE *first successful automobile heater* was invented in the early 1920s's by Richard Hood Arvin of Indianapolis, who traveled by car on his job as salesman for the Indianapolis Air Pump Company. The heater sold worldwide in 1927 under the name Noblitt-Sparks Industries, Inc., and beginning in 1950 under the name of Arvin Industries of Columbus, Ind. The firm was named in Arvin's honor.

THE *first diesel vehicle with an American-built engine* was put into manufacture in 1930 by Clessie Lyle Cummins at Columbus; his name has become internationally known for diesel equipment. Cummins also was involved in several history-making automobile trips. (See *Automobiles and Trucks*.)

A *headlight system which automatically dimmed* for an oncoming car and returned to bright after traffic had passed was developed by the Guide Lamp Division of General Motors Corporation at Anderson. It was offered to the public January 25, 1952, called "Autronic-Eye." There are few, if any, in existence today.

THE *first successful machine for testing the blood alcohol* content of humans was the Drunkometer, created in 1931 and patented in 1936 by Rolla N. Harger, an Indianapolis biochemist. Harger turned his patent over to the Indiana University Foundation, in part because he didn't think it would be a particularly big money maker; it was.

THE *most widely used portable device for determining blood alcohol* is the Breathalyzer, invented by Robert Borkenstein in 1955. Borkenstein, a chemist with the Indiana State Police, created the Breathalyzer as an improvement on the Drunkometer. The Breathalyzer was an improvement because it accurately measured breath from deep within the lungs, and because no expertise was required in analyzing the results.

THE *first successful machine to analyze blood* was invented by Jerry W. Denny of Carmel, Larry G. Durhos of Indianapolis, and Robert Cole of Zionsville in 1971. Called the Programmachen 1040, it performed 300 blood tests in about 30 minutes and was a great commercial success in hospitals and clinics.

THE operation begun in 1867 at Fort Wayne by the Hoffman brothers was the *earliest band sawmill* in the nation. It used a band saw 40 feet long with saw blades 4 to 5 inches wide. Jacob Rosecrans Hoffman applied for Patent No. 92,191 on July 6, 1869, for merely a "sawmill."

THE *first automatic engraving machine for making half-tones*, the method used to reproduce photographs in most newspapers, was invented by Noah Amstutz, a longtime resident of Valparaiso. His device was exhibited in the Royal Institution in London in 1899. Amstutz wrote a book on photoengraving and a series of articles on photoprinting.

THE *first "mechanical man"* invented by a Hoosier is believed to be that devised by R. J. Wensley of Indianapolis, a worker for Westinghouse Eectric Company at Pittsburgh; he exhibited a robot about 1927 which responded to commands given over the telephone.

INSPIRED by the sound of riverboat whistles, William Hoyt of Dupont in Jefferson County invented a *calliope* which made its debut in New York in 1856. The next year it was towed on a flatcar to Indianapolis, where Hoyt played "Old Dan Tucker" and "Oh! Susanna" for a crowd of his fellow Hoosiers. Hoyt took out no patent and the idea was used by others, so he realized no money on his invention. He also invented the *cogs which were used to pull Madison's first trains* up the steep grade north of the town.

A *soft rubber mouthpiece for a cornet* was invented by Capt. Charles Gerard Conn at Elkhart, cornetist in the town band. He devised it when he suffered a bruised lip; he began to receive orders for them and made them in a home workshop. In 1875 he organized the Conn & Dupont Company and began to manufacture brass cornets. This was the *first wind instrument factory* in the U.S. In 1888 Conn began the nation's *first manufacture of a saxophone* and on August 27, 1889, obtained a patent for the *first all-metal clarinet*, called the "Clarionet." Before this, clarinets had been made of wood. In 1921 the Conn company began manufacture of the nation's *first sarrusophone*, an instrument of the oboe class with a metal tube.

THE world's first effective *machine-gun* was invented by Dr. Richard Jordan Gatling of Indianapolis in an effort to provide a weapon so terrible it would halt wars. Gatling, who came to Indianapolis in 1854, obtained patent No. 36,836 on November 4, 1862, for what became known as the Gatling gun. It fired 250 shots a minute. The Navy used it on a few river boats, but there were reservations because of its awesomeness, and it was not adopted for official Army use until 1866. Gatling, a physician who never practiced medicine, manufactured the gun in an Indianapolis plant and opened a plant in Cincinnati, but it burned. After the Civil War he opened a factory in Connecticut. Born in 1818 in North Carolina, Dr. Gatling married an Indianapolis woman, the daughter of a doctor. Although he invented other things, they were not particularly successful, and he is little known for any of them except the Gatling gun.

THE *gas mask* used in the World War I and World War II was devised by James B. Garner of Lebanon in 1915 while he was working at the Mellon Institute at the University of Pittsburgh. Garner also was a professor at Wabash College.

THE *crow and duck call* was invented in 1930 by George Garrison of Delphi, then employed by Remington Arms Company. Garrison died in 1945.

THE nation's *most famous arch support* was invented in 1905 by William M. Scholl, a native of LaPorte, who was 22. By the time Scholl, a bachelor, died in Chicago in 1968, his name appeared on more than 1,000 foot aid products. A world traveler, Scholl was on the maiden flights of the Graf Zeppelin and the Hindenburg.

[SEE ALSO *Automobiles and trucks; Electricity; Food and drink.*]

J

JOBS

THE Hoosier with the *most jobs in a lifetime* was William F. Stevens, whose listing of 95 jobs once placed him second in the world. Stevens got his first job at 7 carrying water for a road crew near Bloomington for $1 a day. His record for jobs held simultaneously was 7, and his shortest job (selling vacuum cleaners in Greenwood) lasted five days.

*More people in Indiana are employed in the manufac-
turing of primary metals* (steel mills, foundries, etc.) than in
any other single category: a total of 82,400 (1984). The next
two highest categories are electrical machinery with 78,100
workers and transportation equipment, which occupies
68,300.

K

KING

THE *youngest monarch* ever crowned in Indiana was
Prince Ikot Alfred Ekanem of Ibibio, a nation in southeastern Nigeria, who was installed in 1966 in ceremonies televised world-wide from Indiana University at Bloomington,
from which he was graduated. The prince was 25. He came
to Indianapolis in 1961, was a graduate of Shortridge High
School, and became a permanent Indianapolis resident in
1973. His tribe maintains him as a prince as part of their
nation's heritage, although Ibibio now is divided into 19
states.

KNIGHT

THE *first Hoosier knighted* is believed to have been Sir
Henry W. Thornton of Logansport, who was honored with
the high British title for his work in organizing and expedit-
ing transportation for the allies in World War I.

L

LAND

INDIANA's oldest county is Knox, created in 1790 to include all of what is now Indiana and parts of Ohio, Michigan, Illinois, and Wisconsin. It was organized by Winthrop Sargent, secretary of the Northwest Territory, and named for Gen. Henry Knox, artillery officer of the revolution and secretary of war during the country's formation.

THE *"youngest" counties* in Indiana are Howard, Ohio, and Tipton, all formed in 1844. Howard County, organized as Richardsville in honor of a Miami chief, was renamed in 1846 for Tilghman Howard, a Hoosier lawyer and statesman. Ohio was named for the river it flanks, and Tipton was named for Gen. John Tipton, Hoosier soldier and a U.S. senator from 1832 to 1839. Indiana's *largest county* is Marion, with a 1980 census population of 765,233. Ohio County, with 5,114 residents (1980 census) is the *smallest county* in the state; nearly half the county's residents (2,478) live in Rising Sun, the largest community.

THE *first city to encompass an entire county* was Indianapolis, which extended its limits to the boundaries of Marion County by virtue of the Unigov law, which went into effect January 1, 1970.

INDIANA's *first state park* came into existence when residents of Owen County, with government backing, bought the estate of Dr. Frederick Denkewatter in May 1916 and gave it to Indiana. It became McCormick's Creek State Park. Negotiations for acquisition of land for Turkey Run State Park were underway when the Owen County group made their purchase.

THE *busiest Indiana state park* based on size is Bass Lake Park, which was only 14 acres of campground and 60 permanent camp sites, but had a 1982 average rate of 57 per cent occupancy, higher than all other state parks.

THE *largest Indiana state park* is Brown County State Park with 15,543 acres.

DEAM OAK STATE MEMORIAL on Ind. 116 northeast of Bluffton is the *smallest state-owned park* in Indiana. L. A. Williamson discovered an unusual tree there in 1904, which was identified by Charles Deam, Bluffton druggist and botanist, as a cross between white and chinquapin oaks. In 1915 when the tree was marked for cutting, Deam bought half an acre of land including the rare tree and deeded it to the state.

THE sole *park* in Indiana to *mix animal predators and prey* is Wolf Park near Battleground where wolves and bison roam together. It has been pointed out that wolves normally only attack sick and weak bison, so there is little danger of them threatening a healthy herd.

THE *largest state forest* in Indiana is Morgan-Monroe State Forest with 24,000 acres.

THE *largest remnant of untouched prairie* in Indiana is Hoosier Prairie State Nature Preserve, 304 acres at the edge of Griffith in Lake County. The tract contains more than 300 native plants, many of them rarely seen elsewhere in the state.

THE *first extensive wildlife refuge* in Indiana was 2,000 acres of swampy land purchased by the state in 1924 where the Kankakee and Yellow rivers came together. The land was bought by Thesburg Land Company on behalf of the state, which paid $1 and allowed the company to collect $13,000 for reclamation work it had done. The sanctuary was in LaPorte and Starke counties.

THE *largest city park* in Indiana is Eagle Creek Park in Indianapolis which has 1,500 acres of water and 3,500 acres of land. It is the largest developed municipal park in the U.S.

THE *first public playground* in Indiana was opened in 1817 in Vernon where about an acre of land was given to the city provided that it be used for nothing else but a playground. Called the Commons, it still is in use, equipped with swings, a concrete game-playing area, and barbecue equipment.

INDIANA'S *oldest farm* of record is that of Martha Ann McKinney Newhouse, 38 acres in Dearborn County, which has been in the same family since 1801.

THE *largest "farm"* in Indiana is 14,733 acres owned and operated by Purdue University. The land is used for instruction, experimentation, and research about crops and animals.

THE *largest private farm* ever operated in Indiana by one person was probably that of Moses Fowler of Benton County who had 20,000 acres in that county and 25,000 acres in White and Warren counties. His sales of grain and stock were said to have totalled $150,000 a year, circa 1820.

THE *greatest known single block purchase* of land in Indiana by an industry was the 9,000 acres acquired in 1906 by U.S. Steel Corporation in Lake County. It was to build U.S. Steel, then the world's largest steel-making facility; the result was the creation of the city of Gary.

THE *first county in the U.S. to be completely photographed from the air* was Jennings County, done in 1930, and followed by most of the other counties in the state. The photographs were used by experts at Purdue University in crop and land use study and evaluation.

INDIANA was the *first state completely covered by an aeromagnetic survey*, which provided a reading of the deep subrock of the land in hopes of detecting mineral deposits. The survey was made by the U.S. Geological Survey, beginning in February 1947, the covering about 1,500 square miles.

ALTHOUGH not officially pinpointed, the state's *lowest spot* is probably the confluence of the Ohio and Wabash rivers, where the river is at 324 feet above sea level, making Indiana soil about 325 feet above sea level, according to the U.S. Geological Survey.

THE *highest point* in the state is just east of Arba in Randolph County, 1,240 feet above sea level.

LEGISLATION

WHAT must rank as *the most unusual bill* in an Indiana General Assembly was the measure introduced January 18, 1897, to change the mathematical value of pi to 3.2 instead of the 3.1415926535 long recognized by mathematicians and school children. The bill was sponsored by Representative Taylor I. Record of New Harmony, who believed the story of Edwin J. Goodwin, a doctor at Solitude, south of New Harmony, that he had found a new value for the figure used in calculating the dimensions of a circle. The bill passed the House, 67–0, and was ready for action in the Senate when postponement was asked by Senator Orrin Z. Hubbell of Elkhart. Once delayed, action never recommenced on the measure and it died. Had the bill passed, it would have made impossible in Indiana calculations exact enough, for instance, to have launched and recovered a space vehicle. Although there were those who spoke in favor of changing the value of pi, an Indianapolis newspaper reported: "All of the senators who spoke on the bill admitted that they were ignorant of the merits of the proposition."

INDIANA had the *first law which permitted the state to sterilize males* to prevent "procreation of criminals, idiots, imbeciles, and rapists." It was promoted by Dr. Harry C. Sharp, a doctor for the Indiana Reformatory at Jeffersonville, who performed vasectomies on inmates to "relieve their frustrations." He operated on some 200 inmates by making sterilization a condition of parole. Sharp, Dr. John

N. Hurty, secretary of the Indiana State Board of Health, and Dr. Amos Butler tried to get the law passed in 1905, but failed. It did pass March 9, 1907, with the help of the National Christian League for the Promotion of Purity. A total of 120 sterilizations were performed before Warren Wallace Smith, a prisoner at the Indiana Reformatory, sued in Clark County Court before Judge James W. Fortune, pleading that his sterilization was done without due process. The Indiana Supreme Court upheld his contention May 11, 1921, and the legislation was declared unconstitutional.

One other state legislature had passed a sterilization law before Indiana, but the Pennsylvania measure of March 21, 1905, was vetoed by the governor and thus never became effective.

THE *first tax on chain stores in the nation* was enacted in Indiana March 16, 1929, and went into effect over Governor Harry Leslie's signature July 1, 1929. Setting up an annual license fee of $3 to operate a store in Indiana, the law required that additional stores opened by the same owner or management would pay a progressively higher licensing fee. An amendment in 1933 required chains with more than 20 stores in the state to pay $150 to license each additional store.

[SEE ALSO *Coal, Crime and criminals, Drugs, Electricity*.]

LIARS

INDIANA'S biggest liar, officially, is Charles Porter of Odon, the only Hoosier to earn the title of World Champion Liar in the annual competition by the Burlington Liars' Club in Wisconsin, an honor attained in 1977. Designation of a champion liar began in 1929. Porter earned his T-shirt, license plate and official letter of recognition for penning: "It was so hot last summer that you could take a frozen hamburger patty out of the freezer, toss it into the air, and when it came down you had one that was cooked well done. But you had to be careful and not toss it up too high. If you did, it came down burned."

Porter, 58 when he won the title, still was writing lies seven years afterward, with such observances as:

"It was so cold here one night that my thermometer knocked on the door and wanted to come in. I tell you, it was so cold here that my red barn turned blue.

"Why, it was so dry one summer, I seen a tree following a dog around."

Porter also tells, by way of a battered old typewriter on which he types his "tales," of the time the lightning bugs and mosquitos got crossed together so it was unsafe to go out after dark "because the mosquitos had a light to search you out." Once, he claims, he had a steak "so rare it kicked my front teeth out." His house, he says, is so old "the only thing that keeps it from falling in on itself is that the termites are holding hands."

A few years after gaining his title, Porter retired from his job as a government clerk.

LIBRARIES: SEE *Books and periodicals*.

LIMESTONE

THE *first recorded use of Indiana limestone* was in the foundation and sills of the Monroe County Courthouse in Bloomington in 1819. It was hauled from eight miles away.

THE first commercial limestone quarry of record in Indiana was that opened in 1827 by Richard Gilbert near Stinesville, which is at the north end of the limestone belt running from Owen County through Monroe, Lawrence, and Washington counties.

[SEE ALSO *Fossils; Structures*.]

LOOT

LOWELL ELLIOTT turned in the biggest cache of money in the state when he found $500,000 on his 119-acre farm near Peru in June 1972 and returned it to authorities. Elliott, 61, rejected an offer of $10,000 from American Airlines and a chance to fly anywhere for five years, saying he should have gotten 5 per cent of the recovery, or $25,000. The money had been dropped from an airliner by a hijacker and landed on Elliott's property.

[SEE ALSO *Crime and Criminals.*]

M

MAIL

WHEN John Rice Jones contracted in 1799 to carry mail once a month from Louisville, Ky., to Kaskaskia, Ill., by way of Vincennes, he became the *first official postman* in what is now Indiana.

IN 1800 a post office was opened at Vincennes, the *first post office* is what is now Indiana; payments for the first year were $85.49, while expenses were $600. Those receiving the mail paid for the postage, which was 8 cents for a single-sheet letter carried up to 40 miles. An increasing rate reached 25 cents for mail carried more than 500 miles.

THE *earliest mail service* into Indiana was in 1800 when a route was established from Louisville to Vincennes. Mail routes were established to Jeffersonville in 1803 and to Corydon in 1809.

INDIANA'S *first regular postman* was Lewis Jones, who carried six letters from Centerville to Indianapolis April 2, 1822, on horseback and continued deliveries for two years.

WHEN John Wise took off in the Jupiter balloon from Lafayette August 17, 1859, he was making the *first attempted airmail delivery* from Indiana to New York City. Winds took him instead to Crawfordsville, about 27 miles away, with his pouch of 123 letters and 23 circulars. Nevertheless, it was the first balloon flight, or air flight, of mail in history. The mail completed it journey by rail.

MILTON TRUSLER *proposed the concept of free rural delivery of mail* in 1880 at a meeting at the Bentley Grange near Fairfield. He traveled to other granges promoting the idea; Congress put in experimental service in 1896.

THE *first rural free deliveryman* was Raleigh Norman who took a letter by horse and cart to E. A. Jones in Nawcreek Township near Hope on October 15, 1896. Norman, son of postmaster Ephriam Norman, took over Route 14, delivering to 125 families over 25 miles. The route, now known as Hope No. 2, is believed to be the *oldest route* in use in the state.

THE *first rural mail buggy* in Indiana was designed by Albert Hitchcock of Hope and built by Neleig Brothers at Columbus. It was constructed soon after rural mail delivery began in 1896.

THE *first woman rural mail carrier* in Indiana is said to have been Della H. Collins, whose husband, Milton L. Collins, was *Muncie's first mail carrier* but details are skimpy.

THE *first Hoosier to officially fly the mail* for the U.S. government was Robert F. Shanks of Indianapolis, one of the four original mail pilots; he took his first delivery flight from New York City to Washington on August 12, 1918.

Air mail first arrived in Indiana December 17, 1927, when Lt. Homer Radar touched down his monoplane at

Mars Hill Airport southwest of Indianapolis. His historic first words are reported to have been: "Isn't anyone here from the post office to receive this mail?" The answer was no, because there had been a mixup in reporting his time of arrival.

THE nation's *first automated, do-it-yourself post office* was opened as an experiment in a grocery store at English Lake in 1960. It featured a box system and a stamp machine which made change.

THE *smallest post office* in Indiana operated by U.S. postal personnel is that at Millhousen in Decatur County, where postmaster Vera L. Walters serves 30 boxholders from an area just large enough for a door, the postal boxes, and one postmaster. It is in the corner of a grocery.

THE *oldest postmaster* in Indiana as of 1985 was Thelma Stouder, 83, operator of the post office at Goldsmith. She did not become postmaster until she was 70. The Goldsmith post office does not make deliveries; patrons pick up their mail from postal boxes.

[SEE ALSO *Aviation; Museums.*]

MANUFACTURING

THE *only cotton mill* to operate in Indiana was one at Cannelton which began operations January 7, 1851, making muslin with equipment shipped via New Orleans. Its 108 spindles were driven by oxen. The use of cotton in manufacturing by Bemis Brothers Bag Company, which had taken over the firm, stopped in 1954 because of the growing popularity of paper sacks.

THE *first glass manufacturing company* in Indiana was begun in New Albany in 1869 by John Baptiste Ford, who later was the *first man in the state to make plate glass*.

THE *first optical glass in the nation* was perfected at

Elwood by the George A. MacBeth Company in 1890. Until then all optical glass came from Europe. MacBeth brought in Edmond Fiel from the east to produce lenses for a Japanese telescope. After that the Elwood firm produced optics for the Dudley Observatory, Albany, N.Y., the Princeton Observatory, the University of Chicago, the U.S. Army Signal Corps, and Eastman Kodak Company. In 1935 the firm, by then MacBeth-Evans, was purchased by Corning Glass Works.

INDIANA had its *largest number of firms* making glass items around 1900, a total of 110 factories.

THE *first producer of lawnmowers* in Indiana was Dille and McGuire of Richmond, which in 1875 obtained a patent for a lawnmower after repairing one of only a few lawnmowers then known to exist and making improvements on its design. The firm had been established in 1870 and was known as Quaker City Machine Works before beginning lawnmower production.

WHAT is believed to be the *shortest contract* ever written and followed in Indiana was that of the Studebaker brothers, drawn up in 1863 for their wagon-making firm at South Bend. It read:

"I, Henry Studebaker, agree to sell all the wagons my brother Clem can make."

[Signed] Henry Studebaker

"I agree to make all he can sell."

[Signed] Clem Studebaker

THE *first truly successful automobile manufacturers* in Indiana were the Studebaker brothers, Clement and Henry, who had arrived in South Bend in 1852 from Ashland, O., to open a wagon and blacksmith shop. In 1899 they began to make bodies for electric cars; the Studebaker firm developed into the biggest in Indiana and at one time the fifth largest in the nation.

THE *first shipment of iron ore* to reach Indiana was discharged at Gary July 23, 1908.

THE *first heat of steel* in Indiana was tapped from an open-hearth shop February 3, 1909, in U.S. Steel Corporation's plant at Gary.

THE Crystal Chemical Works at Alexandria, which opened June 1, 1897, became the *nation's first rock wool factory*. Charles Corydon Hall ran the operation, which melted limestone rock in a special device, then blew it under steam pressure into fine, wool-like threads used for insulation. The works was purchased in 1929 by Johns Manville Corporation.

A *gas refrigerator* for household use was first introduced to the nation by the Electrolux Refrigerator Sales Company of Evansville in 1926. The Electrolux used a tiny gas flame and a tiny flow of water to take the place of all moving parts.

THE *largest producer of automotive piston rings* in Indiana is the Engine Products Division of the Dana Corporation, formerly Perfect Circle Corporation, with piston ring manufacturing facilities at Richmond and Hagerstown. The number of piston rings produced there annually is estimated in the millions.

Indiana leads the nation in the production of wood kitchen cabinets, vanities and other cabinet work, cut limestone, asbestos friction materials, raw steel, copper and steel rods, bars and shapes, magnet wire, nonferrous wire drawing and insulating, roller bearings, measuring and dispensing pumps, fractional horsepower electric motors, vehicle lighting equipment, radio and television receiving sets, engine electrical equipment, appliance wire and cord sets, travel trailers and campers, musical instruments, and burial caskets.

THE *largest manufacturer of baseball bats* in the nation is Hillerich and Bradsby Co. at Jeffersonville, maker of the Louisville Slugger bats. The firm was established in 1859 and moved to Indiana from Kentucky in 1974.

[SEE ALSO *Automobiles and trucks; Music; Organizations; Radio.*]

MARRIAGE

THE *world's most married man* is a Hoosier, Glynn (Scotty) Wolfe, who in May, 1984, announced plans to divorce his 26th wife and also admitted he might marry again. Wolfe, 75, is a native of Knox County and first married in 1927. His wives included four he married twice.

THE *first Sikh wedding* in Indiana was in Indianapolis in June, 1978, between Amarjett Luphra of New Delhi and Toronto and Susan Wilson of Salem. They met at the *Jewish Post* in Indianapolis where he was sales manager and she was editor. They also were wed in St. Mark Catholic Church in Indianapolis.

THE *most unusual married couple* from Indiana undoubtedly was Bernice Smith of Bluffton and Fort Wayne and Al Tomaini, birthplace unknown. Bernice, born without legs, was 30 inches tall and worked in the circus. Tomaini, the circus tall man, was 8 feet, 4 inches in height. The Tomainis were wed 26 years until Al's death in 1962. Bernice, known in the circus as "Jeanie, the living half-girl," moved to Gibsonton, Fla., where she operated a motel, restaurant, and fishing camp.

[SEE ALSO *Crime and criminals.*]

MEDICINE

THE *first Caesarean operation* in Indiana is believed to be that performed in 1827 by Dr. John Lambert Richmond of Indianapolis, whose action with crude instruments by candlelight saved the life of the mother, although the infant died.

THE *first American doctor believed to have used a hypodermic syringe regularly* in his practice was Dr. Gonsolvo C. Smyth of Greencastle, who practiced medicine from 1836 to 1897.

DR. JOHN STOUGH BOBBS performed the *first gallstone operation in the world* June 15, 1867, in Indianapolis. The patient was Mary E. Wiggins (Mrs. Burnsworth) of McCordsville. The procedure was reported to the Indiana Medical Society in May 1868 in a paper titled "Lithotomy of the Gall Bladder." Bobbs was known as "the father of cholecystotomy."

As well as historians can determine, the first physician in Indiana to *use the X-ray* was Dr. Frank E. Weidemann of Terre Haute who, in 1892, used a Ruhmkorff coil and Crookes tube to show that the equipment could reveal the image of a key hidden in a book.

THE first Hoosier to *operate on a prostate* was William Niles Wishard between 1890 and 1895. He developed a new method of catheter drainage, and was the first to use a cautery on the prostate with the operative area under visual observation.

THE first *use of chloroform* in Indiana is believed to have occurred when Dr. William H. Wishard of Indianapolis employed it to reduce pain for a Greenwood farmer being treated for a dislocated arm. The date is uncertain.

THE champion surgeon in Indiana history for *thyroid operations* was Dr. Goethe Link, who performed more than 20,000 such surgeries in his career.

THE first doctor to perform a *caudal drainage of the pancreas*, in which a tube was affixed and remained in place throughout the patient's life, was Dr. Goethe Link of Indianapolis, who described the 1910 operation in the *Annals of Surgery* the next year. Drainage continued, relieving the pancreatitis for over 30 years, until the patient, a woman, died in December 1942.

THE *first kidney transplant* in Indiana was performed in 1963 at the Indiana University Medical Center in Indianapolis. David Strombaugh, an employee at the South Bend Studebaker plant, received the kidney from his twin brother, Darwin, an engineering student at Purdue University. They were 22. The surgery was the first such operation for Dr. Robert Rhamy and Dr. Harold King, who headed the 25-member transplant team.

THE *first person in the world to survive a kidney transplant* was John M. Riteris. He had been living in Indianapolis 12 years when he died on August 20, 1979; he had been the longest living kidney-transplant patient. Riteris underwent the transplant at Boston in January 1959. He headed the philosophy department at Indiana University-Purdue University-Indianapolis.

THE *first person to undergo kidney dialysis* in the state was Claude M. Spilman, Jr., at the Indiana University Medical Center in Indianapolis in 1966. Two Floridians, in Indiana to set up a state-wide program, devised a kidney machine from spare parts, since no machine existed in Indiana, and used it to cleanse Spilman's blood over a six-hour period three times a week. The initial dialysis was marked by a broken hose which caused some of Spilman's blood to be distributed onto the ceiling. Spilman died in May 1983 at the age of 62.

THE *earliest heart-transplant patient* from Indiana was Louis B. Russell, Jr., an Indianapolis teacher, who underwent the nation's 34th heart-transplant operation August 24, 1968, at Richmond, Va., when he was 44 years old. He returned home that Thanksgiving. Russell died November 27, 1974; he had at the time been the world's longest-living heart-transplant recipient.

ANNA GARDNER, 38, of Crawfordsville, became the *first person to undergo a heart transplant in Indiana* when she had surgery October 30, 1982, in Methodist Hospital, Indianapolis. She left the hospital in good health January 7, 1983.

METHODIST HOSPITAL in Indianapolis became the first in the nation late in 1982 to begin clinical evaluation of a device which uses *sonic waves to pulverize kidney stones* in humans. The machine, the Dornier Kidney Lithotripter, eliminates the need for surgery if it is successful in disintegrating the stones. It is manufactured in Germany.

THE first *implantation of a drug-releasing infusion pump* in a human was made in May 1983 at St. Joseph Medical Center in South Bend by Dr. Vincent Scuzzo and Dr. Juan Garcia on a 79-year-old unnamed cancer patient. The device, 4 inches by 1 inch in size and weighing 13 ounces, is designed to send precisely-controlled doses of drugs to a specific organ without side effects on other organs. It was made by Infusaid Corporation of Norwood, Mass.

THE *first internal pacemakers* to stop abnormal heart rhythm through electrical shock were implanted at Indiana University Hospital, Indianapolis, on August 31, 1983, in Marion A. Labig of Dunkirk and Robert M. Cope of Hatboro, Pa. The devices, called transvenous cardioverters, were invented by Dr. Douglas P. Zipes, professor at the I.U. School of Medicine, cost about $8,000, and were placed under the skin near the collarbone. They correct ventricular fibrillation by a shock administered through a catheter at the command of a small desk-top computer.

THE first Hoosier to undergo a *cochlea implant* was Trixy Taylor of Mishawaka, in surgery May 31, 1983, in Riley Hospital for Children in Indianapolis. Used to treat her deafness due to meningitis, the implant is an induction coil and two electrodes which stimulate the ear's nerves when sound reaches a microphone in a unit outside the body. The device does not restore hearing, but permits the wearer to distinguish certain sounds.

THE first Hoosier to receive an *artificial heart* was William J. Schroeder, who underwent surgery for the implant November 25, 1984, in Humana Hospital Audubon at Louisville, Ky. Schroeder, a resident of Jasper, was the second man in the world to live with an artificial heart. Normally kept beating by a large computerized unit, the heart was kept beating for 22 minutes on November 30, 1984, by a battery-powered portable pack, making Schroeder the first man in the world to use such a portable unit. Three weeks after the implant Schroeder suffered a stroke which affected his coordination and speech. March 17, 1985, he set the record for surviving with an artificial heart: 112 days.

THE *first person from Indiana to be vaccinated* was said to have been Little Turtle, chief of the Miamis, who was vaccinated while visiting Washington, D.C., a few years before his 1812 death. He carried the news of the procedure back to his people in Indiana.

THE first Hoosier to be given *antitoxin for diphtheria* was Mary Bosse, an inmate of the Indiana School for Feeble-Minded Youth, in 1895. She had been ill five days when she got 5 cubic centimeters of the Behring Product, No. 2; she died three days later. The next patient to get antitoxin was Willie Moore, who got the serum on the 6th day of his illness; he also died. The next 30 who got the antitoxin lived.

THE *use of malaria to treat syphilis* was introduced to Indiana by Dr. Walter L. Breutsch on patients insane due to the venereal disease. An Austrian had shown in 1927 that malaria killed the spirochete which caused syphilis. Dr. Breutsch, who had come to Indiana in 1924, tested this hypothesis on patients at Central State Hospital in Indianapolis. There seems to be little recorded on how long this treatment was used or its effectiveness.

THE *first psychology laboratory* in Indiana and the second in the nation was one at Indiana University at Bloomington which, in 1894, began the first detailed study of learning ever made by psychologists, the Bryan Study of the telepathic language.

THE *first uses* in Indiana of *insulin shock* (1937), *metrazol* (1938), and *electro-shock* (1940) in the treatment of mental illness were at Norways Sanatorium in Indianapolis, founded in 1898 by Dr. Albert E. Sterne and later operated by Dr. LaRue D. Carter.

A Hoosier, Dr. Ezra Reed of Terre Haute, served as *surgeon-in-chief of the Texas Navy* from 1811 to 1877. As far as is known, he also was the only person ever to do so.

THE Rev. Samuel H. Weed, an 1864 graduate of Indiana University and a Civil War veteran, is credited with *naming chiropractic medicine*. The treatment of ailments by reducing "subluxations" in the spine was devised by Dr. Daniel D. Palmer of Iowa, who asked Weed for a good name. Weed suggested the Greek for "done by hand," which is chiropractic.

THE first major *exhibit of pathological specimens* was organized by Dr. Frank B. Wynn of the Indiana Medical College and Indiana University School of Medicine, and taken to the 1899 meeting of the American Medical Association at Columbus, O. Aided by Dr. William N. Wishard, Dr. Wynn placed the exhibit in an empty room; it developed into the scientific exhibit of the AMA annual meetings.

THE *king of the body snatchers* in Indiana reportedly was Rufus Cantrell. Around the turn of the century, when using bodies for dissection was illegal, Rufus operated in Indiana and Ohio, and occasionally in other states, providing corpses for medical schools and doctors. By 1903 he had been jailed. He was paroled in 1909 after serving part of a 2-to-14-year sentence.

WHEN Elkanah Williams of Bedford specialized in ophthalmology and aural surgery, he was *one of the first eye and ear specialists in the U.S.*, and he also was the *first professor in those fields in the nation*. Dates of his achievements are uncertain.

THE first man to *transmit an electro-cardiogram by radio* was Dr. Jim C. Hirschman, a graduate of Indiana University, who sent the data from the ship *Hope* 4,300 miles to Miami. The exact date of this event seems lost in history.

SAMUEL E. ELMORE was the *first black doctor* in Indiana by virtue of a degree obtained, although it was first denied, from the Indiana Medical College. Elmore, who was born in Maryland in 1832 and didn't learn to read and write until he was 22, was in the first class at the college when it opened in 1869. He had previously studied two years at Oberlin College.

THE *first professionally trained nurse* in Indiana is believed to have been Margaret E. Iddings, who served Indianapolis City Hospital beginning in 1885.

THE *only doctors in the nation to have mountains named after them* are Hoosiers: Dr. John Evans, Dr. David Starr Jordan, and Dr. Frank Wynn. Evans, of Attica, *founder of the Indiana state hospital system* and the *first state hospital for the insane*, later was governor of Colorado and founder of Northwestern University. Mt. Evans, 62 miles south of Denver, was named in his honor in 1895. Mt. Jordan in the King's River Canyon in California was named for Dr. Jordan, naturalist, educator, philosopher, and president of Indiana University 1885–91. Mt. Wynn in Glacier National Park in Montana was named for Dr. Wynn, who unified schools into the I.U. School of Medicine and died in a mountain-climbing accident in 1922.

DR. JAMES O. RITCHEY was the first Hoosier elected a *master of the American College of Physicians*, gaining this highest membership category in the international medical specialty society in 1971.

THE *first black to head a national professional association* and call Indiana home was Dr. Theodore H. Clarke of Kokomo, installed in 1978 as president of the American Podiatry Association during its meeting in Portland, Ore. Dr. Clarke was associated with the Westview Osteopathic Medical Hospital in Indianapolis.

DR. SUZANNE KNOEBEL of the Indiana University School of Medicine became the *first female president of the American College of Cardiology* in April 1982. She is a native of Fort Wayne.

THE *first general hospital in Indianapolis* was Indianapolis City Hospital, opened in 1866.

THE first building erected in Indiana as a separate *obstetric and gynecological hospital* was William H. Coleman Hospital for Women at the University Medical Center in Indianapolis. It opened October 10, 1927.

INDIANAPOLIS METHODIST HOSPITAL is the *largest hospital* in Indiana, covering 35 acres and offering beds for 1,105 patients. The hospital, chartered in 1899, opened in 1908 with rooms for 100 patients.

THE most unusual hospital is the state in Kendrick Hospital at Mooresville, the *only hospital in the nation that does nothing but rectal work*; it is the world headquarters of the International Academy of Proctology, which moved there from New York in 1983.

INDIANA'S *first nursing school* opened in 1883 at City Hospital in Indianapolis (now Wishard Memorial Hospital) with a class of 9, graduating 5 in 1885. The Flower Mission Training School for Nurses was promoted by Dr. William Noles Wishard, after whom the hospital is now named, and was only the second such school west of the Alleghenies.

THE *largest medical school in the nation* is the Indiana University School of Medicine at Indianapolis which, in 1984, had an undergraduate student enrollment of 1,182 and a graduating class of more than 300.

THE *longest continuing medical postgraduate course* in the nation is the head, neck, anatomy, and histopathology clinic conducted for two weeks every July at the Indiana University Medical School in Indianapolis. It began in 1915 and long was known as the Barnhill course for its founder, Dr. John F. Barnhill.

THE Indiana University Medical Center in Indianapolis is the site of the state's only *kidney dialysis equipment for children*, the only *pediatric burn unit*, and the only *nuclear magnetic resonator*. The resonator is a new technique for

obtaining not only cross-section pictures of the body structure but also indications of body chemistry, by using bursts
of radio waves and a powerful magnet. The method provides better information than X-rays or scans and does not
require the use of tracer dyes or dangerous ionized radia-
tion.

THE world's *first DNA bank* was opened in April 1984
at the Indiana University School of Medicine in Indianapolis. It provides a place to store samples of the
human genetic material DNA (or deoxyribonucleic acid)
for study and analysis.

THE first *sperm bank* in Indiana was Follas Research
Laboratories, with offices in Indianapolis and Lebanon.
The firm went into operation in June, 1984.

THE *first body tissue bank* in Indiana went into operation in July 1984 at the Central Indiana Regional Blood
Center. The bank keeps skin, bone, sperm, and other tis-
sues frozen or freeze-dried until needed.

THE *first bone marrow transplant program* began in
January 1985 at James Whitcomb Riley Hospital, the 12th
setup in the nation to use marrow from donars to treat
leukemia.

[SEE ALSO *Drugs; Education; Health and sickness; Inventions; Legislation; Research.*]

MILITARY

THE *first fort* in what is now Indiana was *Vincennes*,
put under the command of François Morgane de Vincennes in 1732 by the French and brought under the American flag in 1779 when it was captured by troops led by George
Rogers Clark. It was then called Fort Sackville.

THE *first American fort* built in Indiana was Fort
Wayne, constructed in 1794 at the current location of Clay

and Berry streets in Fort Wayne by Gen. Anthony Wayne. The construction at the site of Indian Miami Town came after Wayne had defeated Little Turtle.

IT is doubtful if anyone from Indiana lived farther north longer than Sgt. Julius R. Frederick, a member of the Greely Expedition, which for three years occupied a hut on Cape Cabine, Pym Island, Ellesmere Land on Smith Sound, at about 78 degrees north latitude. The site was within 350 miles of the North pole and Sgt. Frederick was one of only six survivors rescued June 22, 1884; 17 other members had died. The expedition, led by Lt. Adolphus W. Greely, took weather observations as part of the International Meteorological Congress of 1879. Frederick, a volunteer, died in 1904. He was 51.

JULIUS R. FREDERICK of Indianapolis was the *first man commissioned from the ranks* by the U.S. Army and then retired for heroism. By Congressional act of December 24, 1895, Frederick was promoted from sergeant to second lieutenant for his efforts in the Greely expedition, whose members lived for three years within 350 miles of the North Pole. The new officer then was retired as a hero.

THE *first reunion* for the 8055 M*A*S*H *unit*, the military hospital which was the basis for the highly successful novel, movie, and long-running TV series, was in December 1972 at Evansville, then home of Dr. Dale (Ugly John) Drake, one of the characters of M*A*S*H, who moved to Indiana after the Korean War. It was the first time many members of the unit had seen one another in 20 years. A tent reminiscent of those used in Korea was headquarters for 22 ex-M*A*S*H members, including Dr. Richard Hornberger, known as Hawkeye, who wrote the book under the name of Richard Hooker. Also present were Dr. Agrippa (the Duke) Kellum, Dr. Jerry (the commanding officer) Holleman, Dr. Alphonse (the Painless Pole) Italie, and others.

THE *first female* from Indiana in the *Air Force Academy* was Terri Lynn Carmer of Bargersville, a graduate of Center Grove High School and one of the first 150 women admitted after coeds were approved in the fall of 1975.

THE *first female twins* to be graduated from the United States Military Academy at West Point were Melinda and Melissa Miles, daughters of Mr. and Mrs. William C. Miles of Bloomfield, who were in the class of 1981.

THE *youngest recognized Army recruiter* in Indiana was Adeia Dickinson who was 7 1/2 when she was responsible for two men joining the Army in 1983. Adeia wore a T-shirt saying "Army Brat" and told her schoolmates that her father, Sgt. 1st Class Dennis Dickinson, recruiter at Crown Point, could get people jobs during what was a recessionary period. As a result, two men joined the Army and Adeia got an Army T-shirt and a certificate for "exceptional assistance in the field of recruiting."

THE *longest line of family graduates* from the United States Naval Academy at Annapolis, Md., is that in which the most recent graduate was Christopher Kiergan of Indianapolis in 1983. Also graduates of the academy were Kiergan's grandfather, Capt. N. B. Kiergan, class of 1933; his great-grandfather, Commodore John K. Richardson, class of 1916; and his great-great-grandfather, Adm. Charles Dyson, class of 1883. No other family in academy history had graduated family members *exactly* 100 *years and* 50 *years apart.*

THE *largest payroll* issued in Indiana is the $1.7 billion a month sent around the world from the U.S. Army Finance and Accounting Center at Fort Benjamin Harrison, Indianapolis, to 2,056,000 members of the military and civilian military employees.

[SEE ALSO *Wars.*]

MINES: SEE *Accidents and disasters; Coal.*

MONUMENTS

THE *largest female figure* in Indiana is that of Miss Indiana atop Circle Monument in downtown Indianapolis; she is 30 feet tall and weighs 13,900 pounds.

THE *first monument to peace erected in the U.S.* was that at Decatur, erected in 1913, and cited as a "first" by Robert Ripley in his *Believe It or Not*.

MOTION PICTURES: SEE *Screen*

MUSEUMS

SINCE no other museum *exclusively organized for children* exists in Indiana, the Indianapolis Children's Museum is the largest, but it also is the *largest children's museum in the world* and *one of the largest museums of any kind* with 228,000 square feet of space. It opened at its present location October 2, 1976, and expanded in 1983. Attendance exceeds 1 million a year.

THE Children's Museum also has the largest collection of *model trains* in the state on public display. The collection includes 6,000 cars and engines.

THE *sole museum in the country dedicated to memorabilia on rural mail delivery* is the RFD Museum at Hope, site of the start of rural free delivery October 15, 1896. The museum contains mail buggies and related artifacts.

THE largest collection of *miniature buildings* in Indiana and one of the largest in the world is in the Birds Eye Museum at Wakarusa, exhibited by DeVon Rose, who, with his sons Garry Lynn and Terry Joe, created more than 80 buildings on a scale of 1 inch to 5 feet. All of the buildings are models of Wakarusa structures except a model of the Bonneyville Grist Mill of near Elkhart. Rose shows his collection by appointment.

THE *first natural history museum* in Indiana was the Jack D. Diehm Museum of Natural History at Fort Wayne, built in 1965 and rebuilt in 1981 after a fire. It contains 67 cases of more than 2,000 different stuffed and mounted animals.

THE *largest and rarest shells* in Indiana are in the Glory of the Sea Museum at Hartford City. They are a clam which weighs about 250 pounds, and a Kufus shell 42 inches long. The Kufus, which resembles a worm or sewer pipe, comes from the Philippine Islands and most are only about two feet long. The giant clam came from Australia. The museum, opened in 1962, is operated by Fred Glancy and is in an 18-room house.

[SEE ALSO *Archaeology; Collections; Phonographs; Railroads*.]

MUSIC

THE *first adult singing class* of record is one conducted in 1792 at Vincennes by Father Benedict Floget.

THE *first piano* brought to Indiana was a Clementi, which reached Vevay by flatboat about 1817 when Mary Wright and her parents arrived. It later was discovered by Effa Danner in an abandoned building and found its way to the Switzerland County Historical Society Museum, where it is displayed.

THE *first pipe organ* installed in a church in Indiana is believed to be that put in the Moravian Chapel at Hope, dedicated in 1837. The fate of the organ is unknown; only a pipe from it survives.

THE *greatest builder of calliopes* was George Kratz of Evansville, who was world renowned for his construction. His eight-ton calliopes used coal-burning boilers, each powering 32 whistles under pressure of 120 pounds per square inch. Kratz built the calliopes from about 1900 to 1914 in Evansville.

THE *first black* from Indiana to become a *successful entertainer of high society* was Noble Sissle of Indianapolis. He teamed with pianist Eubie Blake in a popular act at a time when most black entertainment was done in blackface, or by white performers in blackface. Sissle had organized a dance band while he was a student at Butler University in Indianapolis.

THE *first sousaphone* was manufactured by the C. G. Conn Company of Elkhart from designs suggested by John Philip Sousa. The first model was the "bell up" type. The first "bell front" type, such as those in use today, was made in 1908.

THE *first sarrusophone* was manufactured in 1921 at Elkhart by the C. G. Conn Company. It is an instrument of the oboe class with a metal tube.

THE *first high school to have an orchestra* is believed to have been the old Walnut Grove school in White River Township, in Hamilton County near Noblesville, directed by Prof. M. C. Burton sometime before the turn of the century. The school building was razed in 1939. The same school was the *first to introduce manual training*.

THE *first high school orchestra of note* in Indiana, and perhaps the nation, was formed at Richmond in 1898 by Dr. Will Earhart, music supervisor there until 1912. The Richmond orchestra was termed one of symphonic quality by critics, setting it apart from earlier groups. Earhart was a pioneer in the development of instrumental music in the public schools and developed a program which ran from the first through the 12th grades. Harmony and musical history were established by him as part of the high school curriculum in 1900. Among his achievements was the purchase of two dozen musical instruments for the school at a time when public funds were not used for such purposes. A native of Ohio, Earhart left Richmond to become supervisor of public schools at Pittsburgh.

Recording of jazz was begun at Richmond about 1918–19 when King Oliver and his troupe cut a disc of "Dippermouth Blues" in the Gennett Records Division of the Starr Piano Company, a dingy room in one part of the piano firm. Although the firm had begun recording music in 1916, this was the first genuine jazz recording in Indiana and one of the first in the U.S. The Oliver group included Louis Armstrong. Others who cut records there were Hoagy Carmichael, who recorded "Stardust," Duke Ellington, Fletcher Henderson, Jelly Roll Morton, and Guy Lombardo. Henry Gennett, the owner, was sued by Victor, which claimed that the record-cutting stylus he used was solely theirs. Gennett won, which put the stylus in the public domain.

THE *first jazz record*, cut in New York City about January 13, 1917, and released May 31 that year, was of the song "Indiana." The flip side had "The Dark Town Strutter's Ball." The music was the Original Dixieland Jazz Band conducted by Dominick (Nick) James La Rocca.

PRODUCTION of the *first compact audio disc in the U.S.* began at Terre Haute September 21, 1984, at Digital Audio Disc Corporation. The almost indestructible audio disc, expected to revolutionize the stereo industry, is a means of storing much more music in a smaller space than on records or tapes. The recorded music is read by a laser beam. The discs are expected eventually to replace records. The first disc produced at Terre Haute was *Born in the USA* by Bruce Springsteen. Digital Audio Disc Corporation is a subsidiary of CBS/Sony.

BY all odds the Hoosier who *wrote the most songs* was Harry Von Tilzer of Indianapolis, the man who was responsible for coining the term Tin Pan Alley for the section in New York to which writers of popular music were attracted. Von Tilzer is said to have written 8,000 songs before his death in 1930, including "Wait 'Til the Sun Shines, Nellie," and "I Want a Girl Just Like the Girl That Married Dear Old Dad." His brother Albert, also a prolific composer, wrote the melody to "Take Me Out to the Ball Game," to accompany words by Jack Norworth.

THE *Indiana march king* was Fred A. Jewell of Worthington, a contemporary of John Philip Sousa. Jewell composed and published nearly 200 musical pieces, many of them long standard with circus bands. Among his works were "Pageant of Progress," the official march of the Chicago Worlds Fair in 1933, and "Checkered Flag," written in 1928 for the Indianapolis 500-Mile Race. More than 100 Jewell works were purchased after his death by Purdue University's music department. Jewell started his own publishing house in Iowa in 1918. He returned to Indianapolis in 1926 and directed the Murat Shrine Band and taught music at Worthington and Martinsville. He died in 1936 at the age of 58.

THE *debut of singer Frank Sinatra* was in Indianapolis in the Lyric Theater February 2, 1940, when he appeared with the Tommy Dorsey Orchestra.

THE Indianapolis Symphony Orchestra was the *first in the nation to provide industrial concerts* in which businesses "brought out" a performance. The idea was instituted in 1942 with a concert for employees of the P. R. Mallory Company in Indianapolis, followed by concerts for Indianapolis Railways and L. S. Ayres employees, and four concerts for workers at Radio Corporation of America.

THE most extensive *collection of material on Stephen Foster*, the noted Southern song writer, was that amassed by Josiah K. Lilly, Sr., who gave the collection to the University of Pittsburgh.

HOLDERS of the *most Indiana State Fair high school band contest titles* are Ben Davis High School of Indianapolis and Wapahani High School of Delaware County, with 5 crowns each. Ben Davis won in 1960, 1961, 1964, 1966, and 1967, and then stopped competing. Wapahani won in 1975, 1978, 1981, 1982, 1983.

THE *last public performance by singer Elvis Presley* was

in Market Square Arena, Indianapolis, on June 26, 1977, an event marked by a plaque and photo enshrined in the arena showcase.

MICHAEL JACKSON of Gary holds the record for the *number of Grammys won in a single year* with eight, presented February 28, 1984, for recordings in 1983. The previous record had been held by Paul Simon with seven in 1970. Jackson's album *Thriller* was named top LP of the year, his "Beat It" was named record of the year, and his "Billie Jean" was picked as best new rhythm and blues song. He also was awarded three best male vocalist awards for "Beat It" in the rock category, "Billie Jean" in the rhythm and blues category, and "Thriller" in the pop category. His non-musical narration on *E.T., the Extra-Terrestrial* was chosen the best children's recording and he was named producer of the year along with Quincy Jones. The former Hoosier had been nominated for 12 Grammys for his work in 1983.

THE *world record for the most Top* 10 *singles* from one album was set in 1984 by Michael Jackson of Gary with the six from his album *Thriller*. Jackson also is the sole Hoosier singer to twice have four singles from the same album make the Top 10. The first time was when four of his singles from the album *Off the Wall* made the list, and the second time was when four of his singles from *Thriller* made the top of the chart in 1983.

IN early 1984 the sale of 23 million copies of the album *Thriller* by Michael Jackson of Gary made it the *biggest selling solo album of music ever*.

INDIANA'S *largest school of music* is the Indiana University School of Music, which annually trains more than 1,500 students and has about 1,000 concerts, recitals, operas, and ballets.

THE *largest music hall in the world* is Elliott Hall at Purdue University, dedicated in 1940 and seating 6,073. It acquired the undisputed title with the closing of Radio City Music Hall in New York, which also seated about 6,000.

THE state's *largest college marching band* is the Purdue University All-American Marching Band, with approximately 380 members; it is among the largest in the nation.

THE *largest pipe organ* in Indiana is that in the Paramount Music Palace, an Indianapolis pizza restaurant, which has 42 pipes and may be the second largest in the world. It started playing in January 1979.

FOX PRODUCTS at South Whitely is the *largest supplier of bassoons in the world*, turning out more than 700 of the instruments annually, each costing $2,000 to $7,000. The firm was founded in 1949 by Hugo Fox, former bassoonist with the Chicago Symphony Orchestra, and also makes oboes and contrabassoons.

THE Hoosier *expert on recorded music* is William Schwann of Gas City, whose *Schwann Record and Tape Guide* has been the bible of music dealers since 1949. Schwann operated a music store and found he couldn't keep up with releases after the long-playing records came out in 1948. The next year he compiled a listing of releases, noting 674 selections on 26 pages, and gave it to music dealers. Eventually his guide was used throughout the U.S. and in 25 other countries.

[SEE ALSO *Collections; Governors; Photography; Inventions; Televison.*]

N

NEWSPAPERS

THE *first printing press* in Indiana was one which arrived June 21, 1803, at Vincennes, brought by Elihu Stout.

THE first *professional journalist* in Indiana was Elihu Stout, by virtue of the *Indiana Gazette* of Vincennes, 1804, the first newspaper in the state. Stout, from Kentucky, printed an inaugural issue July 31 to announce a referendum on whether people wanted representative government in the territory (they did). The *Gazette* lasted until a fire in 1806 and then became the *Western Sun*.

BY all odds the *most unusual newspaper* in Indiana, at least by modern standards, was the *Dog Fennel Gazette* of Rushville, circa 1819. It was printed on one side of the page and sent to subscribers, who read it and returned it to the publisher so the next edition could be printed on the back side of the pages.

Courses in printing, lithography, and engraving were taught for the first time in Indiana at New Harmony in 1826 in the social community school founded there by Robert Owen. This also was the nation's first printing instruction; an apprentice system had been used.

FRANCES WRIGHT became the *first woman editor* in Indiana when she took command of the *New Harmony Gazette* in 1826. A native of Scotland, she came to the U.S. in 1816 and traveled in England and France before becoming an editor.

THE first *daily newspaper at a college* in Indiana was *The DePauw*, which started at DePauw University at Greencastle in 1852.

THE *Sunday newspaper* in Indiana is believed to have begun with an edition of the old *Muncie News* in 1876.

THE Indiana *city with the most foreign-language newspapers* since newspapers became common in the state in the 1840s was Evansville, which has had 21, most of them in German. Indianapolis has had 14 foreign-language newspapers and Fort Wayne 11.

THE *man who published the most newspapers* in Indiana was W. B. Harris of Ellettsville. He is credited with putting out 138 newspapers, usually weeklies, usually five or fewer at any one time. He used the same general-interest stories in all the papers, adding local news and advertising for the town where the publication would circulate.

THE *first daily high school newspaper in the U.S.* was the *Shortridge Daily Echo*, which put out its first edition September 26, 1898. It was founded by a senior, Fletcher Barnard Wagner. The first issue was three columns on one side of a single page, the back used for advertising. After 31 issues the paper flopped, but it was revived January 16, 1899, after the school board approved $250 for a press.

THE *first Jewish newspaper* in Indiana was the *Indiana Jewish Chronicle*, published in Indianapolis from 1923 to 1969 by Morris Strauss.

SIGMA DELTA CHI, the first *national fraternal society* advocating excellence in journalism, was *founded in* 1909 at DePauw University, Greencastle, by these 10 men, all students there: Gilbert Clippinger, Charles A. Fisher, Billy Glenn, Marion Hedges, Aldis Hutchins, Edward Lockwood, Leroy Millikin, Eugene C. Pulliam, Paul Riddick, and Laurence Sloan.

THE first daily newspaper in Indiana to establish a department for news of women's clubs was the *Indianapolis Star* in 1911 with Grace Julian Clarke as the editor.

THE *right of the press to photograph the President* was established by Paul Shideler who, as chief photographer for *The Indianapolis News*, was stopped by Secret Service men from taking a picture of President Herbert Hoover as he entered a hotel in Indianapolis. Complaints by Shideler and the newspaper legally established the presidential photography precedent.

THE first Indiana *newspaper to win a Pulitzer Prize* was *The Indianapolis Times* in 1928, honored for meritorious public service for a campaign against the Ku Klux Klan; the second was won in 1932 by *The Indianapolis News* for a campaign for tax reform; the third was won in 1975 by *The*

Indianapolis Star for stories on police corruption in Indianapolis.

THE *first newspaper in the country completely prepared by computer* was the *South Bend Tribune* using International Business Machines equipment in late 1963.

THE *oldest active newspaperman* in Indiana is believed to have been Smiley Fowler of Greensburg, a columnist who wrote on the subject of humor until his death February 5, 1980, at the age of 97. Fowler had once served as editor of the Greensburg newspaper.

CORBIN PATRICK of *The Indianapolis Star* is believed to hold the *national record for continuous service* as a reviewer of music and drama: 56 years, as of 1983. He started reviewing in 1927.

[SEE ALSO *Inventions; Presidents.*]

N U R S I N G : SEE *Medicine.*

O

O I L

THE first oil well in Indiana was drilled on the farm of D. A. Beyson near Keystone in Wells County in 1889.

THE earliest *big-time long-producing oil well* was the Phoenix, brought in at 1,614 feet August 1, 1889, in downtown Terre Haute with a disappointing 120 barrels a day. It continued at about 1,000 barrels a month over long periods of time, however, and produced 140,000 barrels in 37 years of operation.

THE oil well in Indiana with the *largest initial production* started yielding 2,828 barrels of oil a day in 1950. It remained in production for more than 33 years. It was in the Spencer pool in Posey County, operated by Carter Oil Company, part of Exxon.

THE first *fully automated process control system for refining* was put into operation in mid-1961 by the American Oil Company at Whiting; it used an IBM computer to monitor and control instruments.

ORGANIZATIONS

THE *first women's club* in Indiana is believed to have been the Clionian Society, based on documents found in Vernon which referred to the club's existence on both July 17, 1855, and July 17, 1858. The documents were found in cornerstones in the town, but there has been little discovered to corroborate the dates.

THE *first structured women's club in the nation* was organized at New Harmony by Constance Fauntleroy Runcie, granddaughter of Robert Owen. The club, which had a constitution and bylaws, held its first meeting September 29, 1859, and enrolled 13 charter members. Born in Indianapolis, Constance, a world traveler, moved to New Harmony when she was 22, and organized the Minerva Society for the purpose of "self-improvement and mental cultivation."

THESE Greek-letter organizations were all *founded at DePauw University* at Greencastle: Kappa Alpha Theta, 1870; Alpha Chi Omega, 1855, and the Indiana chapter of Phi Beta Kappa, 1888.

THE *champion female organizer* in Indiana was Mary Wright Sewall, credited with being the founder or cofounder of 50 groups, local, state, and national. Born in Milwaukee in 1844, she came to Indianapolis in the early 1870s. She was *chairperson of the first National Council of Women* in Washington.

THE *first chapter of the Daughters of the American Revolution* was the General de Lafayette chapter, organized April 21, 1894, at Lafayette. The first *national president of the Daughters of the American Revolution*, founded October 11, 1890, was Caroline Scott Harrison, wife of Benjamin Harrison of Indianapolis.

THE *oldest Masonic lodge* in Indiana is Vincennes Lodge No. 1, F. & AM, organized in 1895 as Lodge No. 15, and redesignated No. 1 June 11, 1918.

THE first Indiana *university in the Big Ten* was Purdue, which joined the fledgling organization in 1896. Indiana University joined the football circuit in in 1899. The Big Ten grew out of a meeting in Chicago January 11, 1895, of seven schools called together by Purdue President James Smart to consider regulation and control of athletics. The conferees were called the Intercollegiate Conference of Faculty Representatives.

THE first man and probably the only male ever *elected president of an Indiana federation of clubs* was Prof. John B. Wisely of Terre Haute Teachers College (now Indiana State University), chosen in 1898 as president of the Indiana Union of Literary Clubs, forerunner of the Indiana Federation of Clubs.

THE *first Knights of Columbus Council* in Indiana was what is now Council 437, founded June 25, 1899, in Indianapolis; it is now located at 13th and Delaware streets in the capital city.

JOHN F. HAINES of Noblesville originated a boys corn club, the predecessor of 4-H clubs, in 1904. A total of 93 boys got seed corn, which they planted, tended, and harvested for prizes awarded in December. There were 53 entries in the first contest at the Walnut Grove School. The club, believed to be the first in the nation, ended in 1912 when 4-H became popular.

THE *oldest and largest predominantly black fraternity* in the nation is Kappa Alpha Psi, founded in 1911 at

Bloomington with a chapter on the campus of Indiana University.

THE crown for the *shortest-lived and most ridiculous club* in Indiana probably belongs to the St. Paul Anti-Spooning Society, organized in the summer of 1912 to ban flirting, bussing, and spooning. The only kissing allowed was a smack of the club constitution to join. The society lasted one meeting; at the second gathering girls complained that the principles were contrary to the advancement of American civilization and the organization was dissolved.

WHEN the *Ku Klux Klan* came into being in 1920, the first group, or Klavern, in Indiana was organized at Evansville by Joe M. Huffington.

INDIANA had the *largest membership* in the Ku Klux Klan of any state, an estimated 240,000 in the mid-1920s. Indianapolis led all the cities in membership with about 38,000; Gary and Hammond each had about 10,000.

THE *nation's first organization of nursing homes* was the Indiana Association of Licensed Nursing Homes, organized in 1945. By 1947 there were 78 member homes.

THE first *Young Men's Christian Association reorganized for family activities* was the Eastside Family YMCA in Indianapolis, which opened in 1958 near the Eastgate Shopping Center. Parents and children of both sexes could participate in the programs, for the first time in the history of the YMCA.

THE *John Birch Society*, an ultraconservative political organization, was *founded in Indianapolis* in 1958, although its organizer, Robert Welch, was from Massachusetts. According to the national headquarters of the group at Belmont, Mass., Welch invited 50 friends to meet to found an organization to "fight communism and work for conservative principles." He needed a meeting place for two days for the founding meeting and was offered the home of a friend of his, Margarite Dice, who lived at 3650 Washington Boulevard in Indianapolis. "Only 11 persons showed up for the two days, but the society was founded and then Welch went back to his home in Massachusetts and incorporated it there," a society spokesman explained. In 1984 there were 12 chapters of the society in the greater Indianapolis area.

THE first Hoosier and the first coach chosen to *head a national athletic organization* was Herman F. Keller, chosen as chief officer in 1959 of the National Federation of State High School Athletic Associations, most of whose members were administrators. The association represented 20,000 high schools across the U.S. Keller was basketball coach of Evansville Bosse at the time.

THE *most boy scouts at one spot* in Indiana was an estimated 4,300 who camped at Lincoln State Park for the Lincoln Camporall late in the summer of 1959 to commemorate the Lincoln Sesquicentennial. The scouts consumed more than 18,000 quarts of milk, perhaps a camping record.

THE *first Jaycee chapter behind bars* was the Wabash Valley Jaycees at the U.S Penitentiary at Terre Haute, which began March 10, 1967, with Bert Scott as president. The chapter, still active, is supervised by Francis Bever, a correctional officer.

THE first *organization of black engineers* in Indiana was the National Society of Black Engineers, founded at Purdue University in 1973.

THE *oldest motorcycle gang member* to die in Indiana probably was Harold D. (Old Man) Scroggans, the oldest members of the Outlaws at 75 when he passed away in St. Francis Hospital in Indianapolis in February 1983. He was national treasurer of the group. Burial was at New Palestine.

THE first Hoosier to become *president of the Chamber of Commerce of the United States* was Van P. Smith of Muncie, who took over the post in May 1984. Smith, at 55, was chairman of the Ontario Corporation, a holding company for eight small businesses employing from 3 to 385.

MURAT SHRINE in Indianapolis is the *largest Shrine* in Indiana and the second largest in the nation with about 25,000 members.

GEORGIANNE NEAL of Noblesville is Indiana's *sole member* of the Mount Vernon Ladies Association of the Nation, appointed to the lifetime position in 1983 to replace Mrs. Benjamin Hitz, who died. The association has 33 members, no more than one per state, and is the *smallest and oldest women's organization* in the nation. Its purpose is to run Washington's home, Mount Vernon, which is privately owned.

THE *most consecutive meetings of a high school alumni association* in Indiana is claimed by the Morristown High School Alumni Association, which has met since 1911; all graduates of the high school are members and the annual meetings attract an average of 300.

THE *sole sorority in the U.S. doing all its activities within one state* is Tri Kappa, headquartered in Indianapolis, which confines its activities to Indiana, and has done so since it was founded in 1901 at Mae Wright Sewall's Classical School for Girls in Indianapolis.

THE *first international council meeting of Kiwanis* was held in Indianapolis when 150 Kiwanis leaders from around the world met in January 1985.

[SEE ALSO *Colleges and universities.*]

P

PARACHUTING: SEE *Aviation.*

PARKS: see *Land*.

PEACE CORPS

INDIANA was the *first state to schedule tests* for Peace Corps volunteers, in May and June 1961, with testing at Indianapolis, Bloomington, Evansville, Lafayette, Vincennes, Muncie, South Bend, Fort Wayne, Terre Haute, and the University of Notre Dame.

PHONOGRAPH

THE *largest collection of sound recording devices* is that of E. T. Drake, retired physician, who operates the Midwest Phonograph Museum at Martinsville. The doctor has more than 700 phonographs and recordings, the earliest dating from 1877 when the record was invented. It also is believed to be the largest and most complete collection in the world. Drake has 600 different machines.

THE *oldest recording device* in Indiana is a phonoautograph, invented in 1858, which is part of the Drake collection. The phonoautograph was invented by Leon Scott of France to prove his assertion that sound makes vibrations. It produces a paper printout of sound vibrations similar in appearance to a cardiogram.

THE *largest and smallest phonograph records* in the state are in the Drake collection. The largest is a 20-inch recording and the smallest record is about two inches in diameter.

[SEE ALSO *Music*.]

PHOTOGRAPHY

THE first *color photograph* in Indiana probably was taken by Lester Nagley, Sr., and Frank Hohenberger, who used imported Lumier-Autochrome film from Paris to take a picture of an arbutus on Arbutus Hill east of Bloomington in April 1915.

THE *first person to photograph the Rockettes*, famed dancers of Radio City Music Hall in New York, during a performance was Noble Bretzman of Indianapolis, who was the first publicity photographer for the hall during a five-year stay in New York in the early 1930s.

THE *first sequence photographs of sports action* in Indiana *without the use of auxiliary lighting* is that done by James L. Mahler, a former Associated Press photographer and instructor in press photography at Indiana University. Mahler began experimenting with a motor-driven camera and extraordinary film-developing procedures to capture Indiana University basketball action in the old I.U. Fieldhouse at Bloomington circa 1953. Among his first efforts was a last-second long shot by James DeKyne which won a Big Ten game; Mahler recorded the shot on three separate frames of film, the last frame with the ball in the basket. His efforts were published in the *Bloomington Herald-Telephone* and the *Indiana Daily Student*.

[SEE ALSO *Newspapers; War, Civil.*]

P L A N E S : SEE *Aviation.*

P L A N T S

THE *loganberry was developed* by James Harvey Logan, born near Rockville, who experimented in his garden in California with crosses between blackberries and raspberries, perfecting the berry which carries his name in 1861. Logan, born December 1841, died July 16, 1928.

THE *largest rose ever grown* in Indiana was the American Beauty, which had stems 6 to 12 feet long and huge blossoms. It was developed at New Castle in 1901 by Myer and Herbert Heller, leading to the title "The Rose City" for New Castle. The rose was difficult to grow elsewhere, however, and in 1916, due to a combination of the death of Herbert Heller, a gas failure which affected greenhouses in New Castle, and a devastating tornado, the fame of New Castle and the supremacy of the American Beauty waned.

THE *champion grower of onions* in Indiana was Andrew W. Milnar of Kimmel, named the "monarch of onion growers" at a 1936 convention in Kalamazoo, Mich., for producing 1,471 bushels on one acre.

INDIANA'S first and last *national corn husking champion* won in the final year of that competition, 1939. He was Lawrence Pitzer, who lived near Newton; November 9, at Lawrence, Kansas, he husked more net corn in 80 minutes than competitors from other states. The pace, up to 55 ears a minute, bloodied Pitzer's hands.

A stalk of corn 24 feet 3 3/4 inches tall, grown by Raymond Francis of Jasonville in 1969, is believed to be the *tallest corn stalk* ever produced in Indiana. From special seed, the corn stalk is the tallest ever shown at the Indiana State Fair.

THE *largest squash* reported in Indiana weighed 513 pounds; it was grown in 1977 by Harold Fulp, Jr., at Ninevah. Mike Jovanovich of LaPorte reported growing 1,851 pounds of *squash from a single seed* in 1979.

BY all odds the *oldest large piece of native American wood* in Indiana is a piece of redwood more than 3000 years old in the headquarters of Kiwanis International in Indianapolis. Measuring about 6 by 18 feet and 4 inches thick, the wood was used for a conference table top. It was moved to its present location in the past president's room when the association outgrew the conference table. It was exhibited in the 1893 World's Columbian Exposition at Chicago before being acquired by Kiwanis, which had its headquarters in the Windy City before coming to Indiana.

THE *oldest nursery* is C. M. Hobbs & Sons, Inc., of

Bridgeport, which traces its beginnings to 1812 in Washington County, where trees were planted by Quakers. An orchard owned by Dr. Benjamin Albertson was moved to Bridgeport in 1875. C. M. Hobbs married a daughter of Albertson and the firm eventually assumed its present name. Today the nursery covers about 430 acres, approximately 100 acres of which are in fruit trees.

CROPS

Indiana Production Records

CROP	MOST ACRES HARVESTED	BEST ACREAGE YIELD	MOST PRODUCED
Corn	6,320,000 in 1982	129 bushels, 1982	815,280,000 bushels in 1982
Corn for silage	225,000 in 1974	17.5 tons, 1976–1982	3,045,000 tons in 1976
Soybeans	4,600,000 in 1981	40 bushels, 1982	183,200,000 bushels in 1982
Wheat	3,150,000 in 1884	49 bushels, 1980	62,100,000 bushels in 1981
Oats	2,337,000 in 1928	65 bushels, 1980 & 1981	88,469,000 bushels in 1928
Rye	450,000 in 1918	27 bushels, 1971	6,750,000 bushels in 1918
Barley	110,000 in 1942	50 bushels, 1970	2,958,000 bushels in 1955
Sorghum for grain	63,000 in 1971	80 bushels, 1971	5,040,000 bushels in 1971
Sorghum for silage	25,000 in 1971	14 tons, 1969	338,000 tons in 1971
All hay	2,534,000 in 1922	3.06 tons, 1982	3,066,000 tons in 1918
Alfalfa	775,000 in 1955 & 1956	3.80 tons, 1982	1,726,000 tons in 1965
Popcorn	50,000 in 1979	3,400 pounds, 1973	148,050,000 pounds in 1981
Tobacco	23,000 in 1886	2,700 pounds, 1970	24,900,000 pounds in 1910
Potatoes	116,000 in 1891	268 cwt*, 1971	5,746,000 cwt in 1889
Apples, commercial			123,264,000 pounds in 1937

CROPS, cont.

CROP	MOST ACRES HARVESTED	BEST ACREAGE YIELD	MOST PRODUCED
Peaches			62,064,000 pounds in 1931
Cabbage	4,000 in 1941	295 cwt, 1976	548,000 cwt, 1932
Cantaloupes	10,300 in 1939	150 cwt, 1977	710,000 cwt, 1941
Onions	9,200 in 1932	420 cwt, 1965	1,988,000 cwt in 1930
Peppermint	18,500 in 1947	45 pounds, 1969	595,000 pounds in 1942
Spearmint	15,200 in 1948	47 pounds, 1970	532,000 pounds in 1948
Strawberries	4,400 in 1940	56 cwt, 1975	121,000 cwt in 1939
Tomatoes for market	6,600 in 1931	140 cwt, 1973 & 1979	428,000 cwt in 1925
Watermelon	8,900 in 1954	170 cwt, 1965 & 1970	1,228,000 cwt in 1954
Cucumbers for processing	12,500 in 1930	10.26 tons, 1981	20,400 tons in 1930

* hundredweight

THE *largest apple-breeding program in the world* is conducted at Purdue University at West Lafayette.

WESSELMAN WOODS, sometimes called Stockwell Woods, is the *largest tract of virgin timber in the U.S. inside a city limits.* The 205 acres are part of the 400-acre Wesselman Park in Evansville.

THE *largest collection of orchids* in Indiana and one of the five largest in the world is at Ball State University at Muncie, containing 3,000 specimens found in the wild and 7,000 plants. It is part of the botany department and its presence prompted the Muncie city council to proclaim the town the Orchid Species Capital of the World.

THE *largest rose display garden* in Indiana is Lakeside Rose Garden at Fort Wayne, which has an estimated 2,500 rose bushes and is the only garden in the state approved for display of the flowers by the All-American Rose Selection committee.

No *grower of roses in the U.S.* surpasses Hill Floral Products at Richmond, operated by Joseph H. Hill and E. G. Hill. With 39 acres under glass, the firm produces about 21 million cut flowers a year and is where Forever Yours, the rose generally associated with Valentine's Day, was developed.

INDIANA is the sole state to have had *four varieties* of flower, at one time or another, as the *state flower*: the zinnia, poplar blossom, carnation, and peony. The carnation was declared the state flower by the legislature March 15, 1913; the blossom of the tulip poplar tree replaced it March 1, 1923; and the zinnia became the state flower March 3, 1931. In 1957 a bill to name the dogwood the state flower was passed by the senate, but the house insisted on the peony because the sponsor of the bill was a peony grower. It became the state flower March 3, 1957.

INDIANA is the *top popcorn-producing state* in the nation, growing a fourth of the national total; Indiana grows an estimated 148 million pounds (unpopped).

THE *tallest tree* of record in Indiana is a Shumard oak which towers 136 feet tall, owned by Philip Meltzer of Shelbyville. The tree is part of Meltzer Woods about 5 miles southeast of Shelbyville.

THE *most expensive tree* ever sold in Indiana was a black walnut on the property of the Indiana School for the Deaf in Indianapolis; it brought $13,200 from the Alexandria Walnut Company of Delaware, Ohio, in 1982.

THE *largest tulip tree*, the state tree, known to exist, is one on the Gladys Shanks farm two miles south of Washington in Daviess County, 90 feet tall, with a crown spread of 80 feet and a trunk circumference of 19 feet, 6 inches.

THE Indiana Department of Commerce program for registering *largest trees* involves a point system which adds the circumference in inches of the trunk 4 1/2 feet above the ground, the height in feet, and a measurement on the crown obtained by subtracting the narrowest measurement of the crown in feet from the widest and dividing by four. Thus, a tree with a trunk 20 inches in circumference, with a crown figure of 40, and a height of 60 feet would have a registration figure of 120—the total of these figures.

These are the state's largest registered trees.

Ash
>   *Blue ash*; a tree owned by Mrs. Nellie Wolfe, Brownsville, rating of 227.
>   *Green ash*; Nelson D. Jones, Whiteland, 294.5.
>   *White ash*; Mr. and Mrs. Dean Stead, Scottsburg, 331.

Aspen
>   A *big-tooth aspen*; J. Timothy Bettis, Monrovia, 207.25.

Basswood
>   *American linden*; Crown Hill Cemetery, Indianapolis, 240.

Beech
>   *American Beech*; John H. Schlundt, Michigan City, 285.

Birch
>   *Paper birch*; University of Notre Dame, South Bend, 129.25.
>   *River birch*; Johnson County Park Department, Franklin, 219.
>   *Yellow birch*; Indiana Division of Fish and Wildlife, Indianapolis, 139.

Box Elder
>   *Box elder*; Earl L. McCleerey, Indianapolis, 205.5

Buckeye
>   *Ohio buckeye*; Wabash College, Crawfordsville, 217.75.
>   *Yellow buckeye*; Ball State University, Muncie, 147.

Butternut
>   Mrs. Chester Kerr, Connersville, 246.

Catalpa
>   *Hardy catalpa*; Robert A. Von Allmen, Floyd Knobs, 311.25.

Cedar
>   *Eastern red cedar*; Spring Mill State Park, 174.25.
>   *Northern white cedar*; Walter E. Catey, Peru, 128.5.

Cherry
>   *Black cherry*; Charles Roush, Columbus, 261.

Chestnut
>   *American chestnut*; George Marshall, Earl Park, 171.5.

Cottonwood
> *Eastern cottonwood*; LaSalle Fish & Wildlife Area, 411.5.
> *Swamp cottonwood*; Stanley Means, St. Joe, 139.5.

Cypress
> *Bald cypress*; Mary A. Steckler, Decker, 305.25.

Dogwood
> *Flowering dogwood*; Ellsworth Beaman, Attica, 86.5.

Elm
> *Red elm*; George Banta, Logansport, 245.25.
> *Rock elm*; Thomas Gehring, Lawrenceburg, 115.25.
> *White elm*; Claude V. Smith, Fairland, 341.75.

Hackberry
> *Hackberry*; Dr. and Mrs. George Buehler, Jeffersonville, 345.25.
> *Sugar hackberry*; Norbert Frey, Guilford, 177.

Hawthorne
> *Downy hawthorne*; Carl M. Nerding, Indianapolis, 123.

Hemlock
> *Eastern hemlock*; Louis Goens, Medora, 191.

Hickory
> *Bitternut hickory*; Crown Hill Cemetery, Indianapolis, 271.5.
> *Mockernut hickory*; William A. Duncan, Brownsburg, 255.5.
> *Pignut hickory*; Richard Davenport, Morgantown, 253.25.
> *Red hickory*; Hemmer Woods Nature Preserve, Gibson County near Mackey, 205.25.
> *Shagbark hickory*; Henry Robinson, Orleans, 261.25.
> *Shellbark hickory*; Paul Maier, Griffin, 278.

Honeylocust
> *Honeylocust*; Albert Quivey, Alamo, 256.5.
> *Thornless honeylocust*; Robert M. D. Cobb, Westfield, 227.75.

Hop Hornbeam
> *American hop hornbeam*; James E. Evans, Versailles, 132.75.

Kentucky Coffee Tree
> *Kentucky coffee tree*; Mrs. Carmen Himes, Columbus, 220.

Locust
> *Black locust*; Everett C. Foster, Seymour, 233.

Magnolia
> *Cucumber tree*; Stewart Brothers, Greensburg, 230.5.
> *Umbrella magnolia*; Indiana University, Bloomington, 113.5.

Maple
> *Black maple*; Purdue University, West Lafayette, 238.75.
> *Red maple*; Theodore Avery, Tennyson, 290.5.
> *Silver maple*; Richard F. Davisson, Anderson, 365.25.
> *Sugar maple*; Mr. and Mrs. Chester C. Schroeder, Evansville, 288.75.

Mulberry
>Red mulberry; Florence Rutherford, New Castle, 218.75.

Oak
>Black Oak; Russell E. Lomax, Evansville, 344.
>
>Blackjack oak; Victor Quebbeman, New Salisbury, 133.75.
>
>Bur oak; Noe Roadside Park, Rosewood, 404.75.
>
>Chestnut oak; Thomas J. Morton Jr., Newburgh, 315.50.
>
>Cherrybark oak; South Spencer High School, Rockport, 400.5.
>
>Chinquapin oak; Morris K. Magner, Wabash, 303.
>
>Deam oak; Department of Natural Resources, Bluffton, 207.75.
>
>Jack oak; Frank Howat, Elwood, 216.25.
>
>Overcup oak; Kenneth Seel, Madison, 362.25.
>
>Pin oak; Lewis Lortz, Hope, 369.75.
>
>Post oak; Mr. and Mrs. Ausburn T. Stephens, Mt. Vernon, 236.75.
>
>Red oak; George S. Row, Osgood, 378.5.
>
>Scarlet oak; Indiana Division of Forestry, Yellowwood State Forest, 316.25.
>
>Schneck oak; Oakland City College, 327.75.
>
>Shumard oak; Phillip Meltzer, Shelbyville, 370.5.
>
>Shingle oak; Hicks Cemetery, Perryville, 281.25.
>
>Southern red oak; Larry Beeler, Rockport, 313.25.
>
>Swamp chestnut oak; George Corne, Newburgh, 356.75.
>
>Swamp white oak; Lloyd Houghland, Scottsburg, 292.0.
>
>White oak; Elden Holsapple, Mitchell, 342.75.

Pawpaw
>Pawpaw; Indiana Division of Forestry, Martin State Forest, Shoals, 53.

Pecan
>Pecan; Wanda Sieglitz, Vevay, 301.5

Persimmon
>Persimmon; Historic New Harmony, Inc., 187.

Pine
>Jack pine; Jasper-Pulaski Nursery, Medaryville, 113.
>
>Virginia pine; Russell and Edna Pennington, Scottsburg, 185.75.
>
>White pine; Pine Hills Nature Preserve, Montgomery County, 217.75.

Redbud
>Redbud; Union County Highway Department, Liberty, 127.5.

Sassafras
>Sassafras; Ralph Phillips, Hazleton, 238.

Serviceberry
  Serviceberry; Carl and Paul Haas, Terre Haute, 142.25.
Sourwood
  Sourwood; Curtis Wathen, Lanesville, 45.
Sweetgum
  Sweetgum; Amanda Hemmer, Mackey, 300.
Sycamore
  Sycamore; Von Lee Ballentine, Elizabeth, 578.
Tamarack
  Tamarack; Paul Barbour, Aurora, 177.75.
Tulip Tree
  Tulip tree; Gladys Shanks, Washington, 344.
Tupelo
  Black gum; R. E. Hagerman, Terre Haute, 244.5.
Walnut
  Black walnut; Shrader-Weaver Nature Preserve, Bentonville,
     303.5.
Willow
  Black willow; Bremen Park Department, Bremen, 354.
Yellowwood
  Yellowwood; University of Notre Dame, South Bend, 187.5.

[SEE ALSO *Fairs and festivals; Ford and drink; Organizations.*]

POLICE

THE *first policewoman* was Annie M. Buchanan Logan of Indianapolis, who was appointed to the post in Madison in 1913. She had served as a matron in the Indianapolis police department and had been an assistant at the Indiana Women's Prison before being offered the job at Madison.

THE *first flying arrest* in Indiana occurred late in 1926 when Charles Earl Halstead, an Indianapolis policeman known as the flying cop, arrested Clyde Shockley of Kokomo for flying over Indianapolis in a civilian airplane. The arrest was a stunt to mark the opening of Mars Hill Airport. Halstead, an ex-boxer, did flying to advertise and participate in air circuses; he helped dedicate air fields at Fort Wayne, Brazil, and Muncie. He died in 1940.

THE first *Indiana State policeman killed in the line of duty* was Eugene Teague, who died December 21, 1933, during a shootout involving Edward Shouse, a member of the John Dillinger gang. Teague was among police awaiting the expected arrival of Shouse at the Francis Hotel in Paris, Ill. When Shouse showed up, Teague rammed the gangster's car from behind to stop it. Two female accomplices and Shouse tried to flee and Teague was hit in the ensuing gunfight.

THE *first female police pistol team* in the nation was organized in Indianapolis by four members of the Indianapolis Police Department who began competition in 1967. They were Mrs. Barbara Hanley, Miss Elizabeth Coffal, Mrs. Alberto Edwards, and Mrs. Flo Doty.

THE *first woman excise policeman* was Patricia D. De-Later of South Bend, a graduate of DePauw University, who reported to work January 8, 1979, and qualified to drive an unmarked car and carry a revolver January 26. She was the only one of 15 women to pass an exam for the job when ranks were opened to females.

JAMES H. VINCENT of Boonville was the *shortest policeman* in Indiana at 4 feet, 8 inches tall. He served eight years as a constable at the turn of the century and was credited with 500 arrests. Known for his fearlessness, Vincent, who weighed 80 pounds, once threatened to arrest a U.S. marshal for being too noisy.

[SEE ALSO *Health and sickness; Radio.*]

POLITICS

THE *rooster as a symbol of the Democratic Party* first appeared in the *Indiana State Sentinal*, June 2, 1841, as the result of the activities of Joseph Chapman, who arrived in Greenfield in 1834, became active in politics, and "crowed" about his party. The Whigs called his style of campaigning

"crowing." In 1840 things were going badly for the Democrats, who had nominated Martin Van Buren for president.
At that time Chapman was a candidate for the legislature.
When he was urged to "crow, Chapman, crow," the Whigs
began to ridicule this rallying cry. But the Democrats
picked it up and made it a slogan. The rooster was devised
to symbolize it. Chapman enlisted in 1847 to take part in
the Mexican War, was killed April 3, 1848, and was buried
at an unknown site in Mexico.

INDIANAPOLIS was the site November 25, 1874, when the
first national political party organized in Indiana, the Green-
back Party, was formed, advocating paying off the national
debt in greenbacks. The first national convention was held
in Indianapolis May 17, 1876, choosing Peter Cooper of New
York as a presidential candidate; he got 81,737 votes in the
1876 election.

THE *tallest pole* constructed in Indiana is believed to
have been one created in Shelbyville in 1876 by Democrats
campaigning for Samuel Tilden for president and Thomas
A. Hendricks, Indiana governor, for vice-president. The
pole, 229 feet tall and 26 inches in diameter at the base, was
made by splicing sections of hickory together. It was
erected on the third try after Republicans had put up a
120-foot pole; the Democrats wanted to better their effort.
The Democrat pole was cut up and made into canes which
were sold in December, 1876, after Tilden lost the election
to Rutherford B. Hayes.

THE first Indiana *politician to be pilloried by the press
because of an alcoholic beverage* was Charles W. Fairbanks,
who, as vice-president of the U.S., served manhattans or
martinis (historians seem to differ on the type of drink) at a
party for President Theodore Roosevelt in Indianapolis May
30, 1907. The incident may have destroyed Fairbanks's
chances of becoming president.

WHEN secessionists led by Morris Hillquit left the
Socialist Labor Party, they *founded the Socialist Party* on
March 25, 1900, in Indianapolis. They held their first con-

vention in Indianapolis May 1, 1904. They had united with the Social-Democratic Party led by Eugene V. Debs of Terre Haute and Victor Louis Berger, which was founded in Indiana in 1898.

THE first woman to vote in Indiana after passage of the Federal Suffrage Amendment was Mrs. Anna D. Monroe of Indianapolis. She voted in about 10 seconds in the first ward, fifth precinct at 529 East 17th Street at 6 a.m. November 2, 1920. Mrs. Monroe was the wife of Jesse L. Monroe, clerk of the Republican board in that precinct.

POLITICS, CITY

THE *only town in Indiana deviating from November election* is Vernon in Jennings County which, under a state charter of 1851, conducts its voting on the first Monday in March. Every uneven year Vernon chooses a mayor, clerk-treasurer, marshal, and three councilmen.

THE *first black mayor in a city of medium size* was Richard D. Hatcher, elected to the top office in Gary, a city of about 90,000, in November, 1967, defeating Joseph B. Radigan.

THE *major with the most years of consecutive service* in modern times is Elton H. Geshwiler of Beech Grove, who first was elected in 1959 and won his seventh term in 1983 after 25 years on the job. Walter R. Hagedon, mayor of Tell City, and Richard L. Vissing, mayor of Jeffersonville, both in their 24th year in office in 1983, did not seek re-election.

THE *first woman elected to a municipal office* in Indiana was Mrs. Bessie Blease Ross, winning the post of city clerk at Gary in 1922.

THE *first woman elected mayor* in modern times was Mary Bercik, who won the November 1959 election as chief executive of Whiting by 400 votes. She had served two years of the unexpired term of her husband, William.

THE *youngest Hoosier to run for mayor* was Randy Coffey, 19, who won the 1975 primary election at Angola on the Democrat ticket while a student at Tri-State College. He was defeated in the November 1975 election and after college became a lawyer in Angola.

POLITICS, STATE

THE *first state election* in Indiana was August 5, 1816, in which Jonathan Jennings was chosen governor. November 4, 1816, the *first General Assembly* convened at Corydon.

THE only Hoosier to be *governor, lieutenant governor, state senator, president pro tempore of the state senate, and a state representative* was Paris Chipman Dunning, governor from December 26, 1848, to December 5, 1849. He also was a U.S. senator. From North Carolina, Dunning lived in Bloomington. He became governor when James Whitcomb was elected to the U.S. Senate. He was a state representative from 1833 to 1836 and was a state senator from 1836 to 1840. He was elected to the senate again in 1863 and became its president.

THE *first women's suffrage group* in Indiana was called together in 1851 in Dublin at the home of Amanda Way. The next year the Women's Rights Society was formed and filed a petition with the Indiana General Assembly, which ruled that granting voting rights to women was inexpedient.

THE *first black state representative* was James S. Hinton of Marion County, elected as a Republican in 1880 and serving in the Indiana General Assembly for the 1881 session.

THE *first woman to fill an elective post* in the state was Mary Stubbs Moore, named in 1906 to fill the vacancy of state statistician created by the death of her father, Joseph H. Stubbs. Her appointer was Governor James F. Hanly.

THE *first state-wide primary* elections were conducted in Indiana in 1916, at which the Republicans gave Charles W. Fairbanks 176,000 votes in a presidential preference primary and chose James P. Goodrich to run for governor and Harry S. New to run for U.S. senator. The Democrats picked John Adair as the gubernatorial candidate and John W. Kern to run for senator.

FERN ALE was the *nation's first woman secretary of a state senate* when she served in Indianapolis during the 1927 session of the Indiana General Assembly, beginning January 6 and ending March 7.

THE *first female senator* in the Indiana General Assembly was Mrs. Arcada Stark Balz, an ex-schoolteacher who served from 1942 to 1946. She was the third female in that post in the U.S., and introduced a bill creating minimum requirements for nursing homes.

THE *first black governor of Boys State*, an American Legion program to teach the operation of a republic and politics, was Primus Johnson of East Chicago, elected June 16, 1954, on the Federalist ticket, defeating Bill Jones of Kokomo on the Nationalist ticket.

JEAN MCANULTY, when named to the post in 1967 by Governor Roger Branigin, became the *first black executive press secretary* to the governor in the state's history.

THE *first black executive assistant* to an Indiana governor was William T. Ray, named to the post in 1973 upon the entry into the office of Otis T. Bowen.

THE *first woman to run for governor* in Indiana was Virginia Dill McCarty, who entered the Democratic primary in 1984. She was defeated by Wayne Townsend.

THE *first woman to run for lieutenant governor* in Indiana was Ann DeLaney, an Indianapolis attorney, who was chosen as the 1984 running mate of Wayne Townsend on the Democrat ticket. The DeLaney-Townsend ticket was beaten by Governor Robert Orr and Lieutenant Governor John Mutz, who were re-elected.

THE *most votes ever received* by an Indiana governor is the 1,236,555 cast in 1976 for Otis R. Bowen in his election to a second term.

INDIANA'S *toughest state representative* is Ken Snider, a Democrat from Deckard; he won professional boxing bouts in late 1983 and 1984 while serving as a legislator. Snider had been a well-regarded amateur before retiring from boxing in 1971. In 1973 he was elected to the Indiana General Assembly and in November 1983 he won a unanimous decision over Billy Doyle of Terre Haute in his first professional bout after coming out of retirement. In January 1984, observed by several members of the General Assembly which was in session at the time, Snider knocked out Mike Bell of Indianapolis in the third round. His third victory came February 23, 1984, against Kenny Willis, 25, of Indianapolis on a TKO one minute into the third round. At least three dozen fellow state legislators and statehouse officials were in his cheering section. Snider, 37 at the time, was fighting in the junior welterweight division at 140 pounds. "I run five miles a day and I box 24 rounds a day," he said. By January 1985, Snider had won nine bouts without a loss.

[SEE ALSO *Governors; Plants.*]

POLITICS, U.S.

THE first Indiana *member of the U.S. House of Representatives* was William Hendricks, chosen November 8, 1816, and seated December 2, 1816.

THE first *U.S. senators* chosen in Indiana were James Noble and Waller Taylor, named to the posts November 8, 1816, and seated December 12, 1816.

THE *first political convention* in Indiana was September 16, 1824, at the courthouse at Salem, where electoral support was pledged for Andrew Jackson for president. On January 8, 1828, at Indianapolis, Republicans organized for

Andrew Jackson and January 12 that year the Democrats pledged support for John Quincy Adams.

SCHUYLER COLFAX of Indiana was the *first man to preside over both branches* of Congress. He was speaker of the House from March 4, 1863, until March 3, 1869, when, by virtue of being elected vice-president, he became chief officer of the Senate, serving from March 4, 1869, to March 3, 1873.

THE *first female on the White House staff* was a secretary from Indiana, Alice Sanger, who reported for work January 2, 1890.

THE *first and only Hoosier to be censured by Congress* was William Dallas Bynum, once mayor of Washington, Ind., who was punished in 1890 because he called a representative from Pennsylvania a liar and perjurer.

No Hoosier *ran for U.S. president more often* than Eugene V. Debs, who was a candidate in 1900, 1904, 1908, 1912, and 1920 for the Socialist Party.

THE *most votes ever received by a political candidate while in prison* were the 915,302 received by Eugene V. Debs of Terre Haute in the presidential election of 1920. Debs, running for president as a socialist, had been imprisoned on conviction of violating the Espionage Act because of a speech at Canton, O. He was released from prison December 23, 1921.

JOHN W. KERN was the *first U.S. senator from Indiana to be chosen by popular vote* in 1911. He was a Democrat from Indianapolis. Before that the Indiana senators were chosen by the General Assembly.

THE *first female in Congress* from Indiana is believed to have been Virginia Jenckes of Terre Haute, who served from 1933 to 1939 from what was then the Sixth District. She was known for her red hats and her hatred of communism.

THE *most votes ever received* by a Hoosier running for

U.S. president was the 22,000,000 cast for Wendell Willkie in the 1940 campaign in which Franklin D. Roosevelt, his Democrat opponent, was elected.

THE *first black U.S. senator* from Indiana was Robert L. Brokenburr of Indianapolis, who served from 1941 to 1948 and from 1953 to 1964. An attorney, he was admitted to the bar in 1910 and practiced before the U.S. Supreme Court in 1953. He died in March 1974 at the age of 87.

THE *record for service in the U.S. Congress* by a Hoosier is 34 years by Ray Madden of Lake County, who retired in 1976. He was a congressman 25 days longer than Charles Halleck of Rensselaer, who served from 1935 to 1968.

THE *most embarrassing slip of the tongue* in modern times by a Hoosier politician was made by Rep. Earl Landgrebe, Republican, when told in 1974 of the existence of a tape in the Watergate affair. "Don't confuse me with the facts," said Landgrebe. "I've got a closed mind." It was thought that he meant to say he had an open mind.

THE *first wedding of two incumbent members* of the U.S. House of Representatives occurred January 3, 1976, when Andrew Jacobs Jr. of the 11th District in Indiana married Congresswoman Martha Keys of Kansas. Both were Democrats. Mrs. Keys was 45 and Jacobs 43 and her four children by a previous wedding witnessed the ceremonies at Topeka, Kansas. A former marriage by Jacobs had ended in divorce. Jacobs and Mrs. Keys, who kept that name under a marriage agreement, separated in mid-1981.

[SEE ALSO *Presidents.*]

POPULATION

THE *center of U.S. population was in Indiana longer* than in any other state; it was first found in Indiana in 1890 and stayed within the state 60 years until a site in Illinois was designated in 1950. The center is chosen by mathematically calculating a spot from which the same number of people live in every direction.

THE *earliest site* was a spot in front of a farm occupied by A. M. Armstrong 10 miles south of Greensburg, chosen in 1890 as the population center of the U.S.

A spot 75 feet east of a walnut tree on the old Bailey McConnell farm three miles southeast of Carlisle was the *last center of population in Indiana,* chosen in 1940. The farm was owned by Gilbert and Ralph Corbin, managed by their father, John Corbin, and occupied by Chancy Bennett.

PROF. WILBUR A. COGSHALL of Indiana University was the *last man* to precisely locate the U.S. center of population in *Indiana,* using a mathematical formula and figures from the census.

More people of German national origin live in Indiana than any other nationality, according to the 1980 census; a total of 739,223.

THE *nationality with the fewest members in Indiana is the Portuguese* with 786, according to the 1980 census.

POST OFFICES: SEE *Mail.*

PRESIDENTS

THE *oldest Hoosier to assume the presidency* was William Henry Harrison, 68 at the time he took office in 1841. Harrison was not born in Indiana—he was a Virginian—but his appointment as governor of the Indiana Territory on May 13, 1800, gave him a Hoosier link. In 1800 few native-born Hoosiers existed with both the years and the stature to be governor. No native from Indiana was even governor of the state until some 60 years after Harrison. Although Harrison is not listed in history as a president from Indiana, he is included here as one by virtue of his years and important actions on Indiana soil.

THE *first U.S. president to die in office* was a Hoosier by background, William Henry Harrison (1773–1841), once governor of the Indiana Territory. Harrison got pneumonia after an *inaugural address that was the longest on record*, 8445 words. It took 2 hours to give on the steps of the unfinished capitol in a chill east wind. Its length and the weather were blamed for Harrison becoming ill and dying April 4, 1841, after only 31 days in office. That made Harrison the president with the *shortest term*, and the *first president to lie in state in the White House*. He also was the *only president to have studied to be a doctor*, completing 16 weeks of a 32-week course in the medical department of the University of Pennsylvania. He also was the *first president to make no significant decisions* during his term. He was the *only president whose grandson* also became president.

THE *most valuable letter* written by a U.S. president with an Indiana background was one dated March 10, 1841, over the signature of William Henry Harrison, which sold at auction in New York in April, 1983, for $132,000, more then had ever been paid for a presidential letter at auction. The buyer was publisher Malcomb Forbes. Harrison's letters are valuable because of their scarcity; he was only in office 31 days. In the letter, Harrison wrote a businessman, "The fact is that I am so harassed by the multitudes that call upon me that I can give no proper attention to any business of my own." The letter was 1 1/2 pages long.

PERHAPS the *most unusual presidential artifact* in Indiana is a cabinet in the Evansville Museum of Arts and Sciences made by Abraham Lincoln. Of walnut and poplar, the piece of furniture is 23 3/8 inches high, 16 3/4 inches long, and 14 3/4 inches deep and was given by Lincoln to a friend, John W. Lamar of Buffaloville, when the Lincoln family left Indiana.

THE *first notification on Indiana soil* of nomination for the U.S. presidency was that received July 4, 1888, when a delegation of 55 men traveled from the Denison Hotel in Indianapolis to the home of Benjamin Harrison, about 15 blocks away, to tell him he was the Republican nominee. The *second time* this occurred in Indiana was August 17, 1940, when Wendell Willkie was notified at Elwood that he was the GOP nominee for president.

THE *first Hoosier to live in the White House after the advent of the electric light* was Benjamin Harrison. The new-fangled wiring frightened the Harrisons, however; lights were left on all over because of their reluctance to touch the switches.

More states were admitted to the Union during the term of Benjamin Harrison of Indiana than during the term of any other president. North Dakota, South Dakota, Montana, Washington, Idaho, and Wyoming became states under Harrison. He also was the *only president preceded and succeeded by the same man*, Grover Cleveland, and was the *first president whose Congress appropriated more than a billion dollars* ($507,376,397.52 during the first session and $519,535,293.31 during the second session). Harrison was the *only president with two men in his cabinet having the same last names*, Charles Foster of Ohio, secretary of the treasury, and John Watson Foster of Indiana, secretary of state.

THE *first time an incumbent U.S. president attended the funeral of an ex-president* was March 17, 1901, when President William McKinley visited Indianapolis for the burial of former president Benjamin Harrison, who died of pneumonia after a week-long illness. McKinley declared a 30-day mourning period.

THE *first black candidate for U.S. president in the nation* was attorney Frank Beckwith of Indianapolis who ran in 1960 and got 20,000 votes in the preferential primary election and ran again in 1964. But his name never was placed in nomination at the Republican national convention in those years.

[SEE ALSO *Books and periodicals.*]

Q

QUINTUPLETS: SEE *Vital statistics.*

R

RADIO

THE *first radio station* in Indiana was started by the *South Bend Tribune* newspaper in 1921 with the call letters WSBT.

THE *first campus radio station* in Indiana was WBAA at Purdue University; it went on the air in 1922.

THE *first Indiana cities to have FM radio stations* were Elkhart, Terre Haute, New Castle, and Muncie; they began in 1947. The next year additional stations started at Marion, Warsaw, Washington, Connersville, and Evansville.

WHEN WGRE-FM was established at DePauw University in April 1949, it was the *first 10-watt educational FM station in America.*

THE *only radio station in Indiana operated by prison inmates* (legally) for prison inmates is WIRP at Pendleton, which takes its call letters from the institution and the town—Indiana Reformatory, Pendleton. WIRP broadcasts live programming from a room in the reformatory to inmates who are equipped with headsets. Although four other radio stations from outside the prison are monitored and broadcast to the prisoners, WIRP is popular because it airs requests using the name of the inmate instead of his number, which is the identification most often used in the reformatory. Broadcasting hours are 3 p.m. to 1 a.m. on weekdays and from 8 a.m. to 2 a.m. on weekends. In the beginning recordings were donated, but later the station's files were supplemented with 50 to 60 new recordings a month, paid for from the reformatory recreation fund.

THE *largest FM radio station in the nation operated by a private educational institute* is WAJC at Butler University in Indianapolis, at 48,000 watts. It became part of Butler in 1951 through merger with Arthur Jordan College, whose initials form the call letters of the station.

THE *first broadcast of a college football game* was made by Floyd J. Mattice of Rochester while studying law at the University of Michigan. Mattice, a telegrapher, sent some games by the wireless, but for the October 31, 1903, game between Michigan and Minnesota, the telephone company set up a line from Minnesota to Ann Arbor, where his description of the game was heard.

IN what was probably the *first Indiana radio broadcast*, Francis Hamilton, a Purdue University graduate who had built a radio transmitter in his garage at 2011 North Alabama Street in Indianapolis, asked Indianapolis Mayor Lewis Shank to speak about the coming year on New Year's Eve, 1921. The station had call letters 9ZJ and was picked up by only a few sets. Shank's initial words are said to have been: "Hamilton, do you mean to tell me people can actually hear me over this damn dingus?"

THE Christian Men's Builder Hour, broadcast from the Third Christian Church in Indianapolis, became *radio's initial Sunday school class*. It was conceived in the mid-1920s by Merle Sidener, former newspaper editor and then a partner in the Sidener–Van Riper advertising agency.

The program lasted 25 years, beaming some 1,400 broadcasts over WFBM.

THE *first radio station to broadcast the Indiana State High School basketball tournament finals* was WOWO, Fort Wayne, in 1924. The station holds the longevity record for broadcasting the tournament.

The first glass-enclosed broadcasting booth at the Indiana State Fair in Indianapolis was installed in 1926 by WFBM, Indianapolis, at the instigation of Henry S. Wood, the station's farm editor. Daily broadcasts originated from the fairgrounds.

THE *first police department* in Indiana (and the third in the world) *to get a radio license* was the Indianpaolis department in 1928, although the police didn't go on the air until 1935, a year after the Indiana State Police radio network began using donated space at Culver Military Academy to broadcast.

THE funeral at South Bend of Knute Rockne, football coach of the University of Notre Dame, on April 4, 1931, was the *first funeral to be covered by an international radio hookup*. The coast-to-coast broadcast was sent overseas by shortwave; this is reported in the book *Permanent Addresses* by Jean Arbeiter and Linda Cirino. Rockne had died in a plane crash.

THE *push-button radio,* so common in automobiles, was first produced in 1938 by the Delco Radio Division of General Motors in Kokomo.

THE *nation's first signal-seeking car radio* was the work of the Delco Radio Division of General Motors at Kokomo, and was first produced in 1947.

THE Regency Division of Industrial Development Engineering Associates, Inc., of Indianapolis was the *first firm in the nation to mass-produce transistor radio receivers,* sending out the first shipment in October 1954. The receiver was 12 ounces, measured 3-by-5-by-1 1/4 inches, and was powered by a 22 1/2-volt B battery. It was called Regency Radio.

THE *first all-transistor car radio* was produced by Delco Radio Division of General Motors at Kokomo in 1957.

ELSIE MACGORDON of Anderson is credited with *creating more roles on radio* than any other Hoosier. At least 1,000 parts were done by her, starting about 1922. She appeared with Rudy Vallee, among other radio stars of the day.

THE *voice of Tarzan* in 364 radio broadcasts was James Hubert (Babe) Pierce of Freedom in Owen County. He also *played Tarzan* in the last silent film for that character, "Tarzan and the Golden Lion," in 1927. Pierce survived to become the oldest living actor to have played Tarzan. An All-American football center at Indiana University, Pierce went to the University of Southern California to study law, was seen by Edgar Rice Burroughs, creator of Tarzan, appeared in the films, and married Burroughs's daughter, Joan, in 1932. She played Jane on the radio. Pierce's last film was "Showboat"; he retired from real estate in 1963.

RED SKELTON, born in Vincennes July 18, 1913, compiled the *longevity record* for Indiana comics on radio. Skelton had his own show for 30 straight years.

THE *tallest trophy* in Indiana is the Buzzard Cup, awarded by Indianapolis radio station WNAP to the winner of its annual White River raft race. The trophy, done by Scott Liose of the Broad Ripple Trophy Center, is 21 feet, 1/4 inch tall, weighs 400 pounds, and has 5,000 parts in four sections.

RAILROADS

THE *first railroad "line"* in Indiana is believed to be 1 1/2 miles of wooden rails covered with strap iron, completed at Shelbyville July 4, 1834. When the owner, Judge W. J.

Peasley, could find no steam engine, he had a farmer hitch a horse to a single-passenger coach to give rides.

A length of track 7,021 feet long outside Madison is the *steepest Indiana railroad grade*, dropping 311 feet in one mile, a descent rate of 6 percent. Laid in 1836 as part of the line to Indianapolis, the first commercial track in Indiana, it was modified to accept a cog system for pulling trains after the Civil War. The first coal-burning engine climbed the hill in 1892. During the days of steam, trains backed down into Madison and engines mounted the grade pushing the cars, seldom more than eight at a time.

THE *first railroad overpass requiring elevation of the track* was at Vernon where the Madison-Indianapolis line was taken over Pike Street in 1837. The overpass also was the *first west of the Alleghenies*.

THE *first commercial railroad* was the Madison-to-Indianapolis line, begun in 1836 with rails shipped from England at $70 a ton. The first 28 miles, costing $58,000 a mile, where in place before the state was compelled to sell to private interests. The first train took to the tracks October 1, 1847. The railroad was sold to private investors in 1858.

THE first *train to cross the Wabash River* in Indiana was the one on the New Albany and Salem (Monon) Line on August 20, 1853, when guests were taken on a courtesy tour over the new bridge north of Lafayette. The run was to Battle Ground and back to Lafayette.

THE Knightstown and Shelbyville Railroad, 26 miles long, was completed about 1850. It was built to connect with a line at Shelbyville so goods could reach Indianapolis via the Madison and Indianapolis railroad. Upkeep costs and lack of business caused the line to cross in 1854, the *shortest-lived railroad* in the state and the fourth built in Indiana.

THE first railroad to *link the Ohio River with the Great*

Lakes through Indiana was the Monon, which reached from Madison to Chicago in 1854.

THE *first mule-drawn streetcars* in Indiana were those pulled up Illinois Street from Union Station in Indianapolis, beginning in June 1864. Indianapolis also eventually had the *largest mule-drawn-streetcar company* in the state, Citizens Street Railway Company, with 500 mules towing 75 cars over 20 miles of track.

THE *first refrigerated rail car* was successfully used at Hammond by George H. Hammond and Marcus Towie in 1869. The development came after the Davis brothers of Detroit invented a refrigerator box to ship fish from Lake Huron and Lake Superior to Detroit. Hammond, a Detroit butcher, thought a similar principle could be applied to beef; he purchased a site in Hammond (then called Hohman) and founded a slaughterhouse. This was the start of industry in the city, later renamed in Hammond's honor. He died in 1886 and the slaughterhouse was purchased from his widow by an English syndicate for $6 million. It burned in 1901. Hammond was able to use the rails for refrigerated shipments because the Erie and Nickel Plate railroads had arrived in Hammond in 1882, and the Monon a year later.

THE *first apprentice school for railway mechanics* was established at Elkhart in 1872 by the New York Central Railroad.

THE *first belt railroad*, that is, one circling the midsection of a city, was built in Indianapolis in 1873 and is still in use.

THE first *practical electric street railway* in the nation was installed at South Bend under a patent granted August 11, 1885, to Charles Joseph Van Depoele, the "father of the trolley." Similar systems were installed in eight cities that year. Depoele held 249 patents solely in his name and shared almost as many with other inventors.

THE *most rails put in place in a single day* was on the

old Clover Leaf line from near Decatur to Frankfort, part of an effort in which 206 miles of track were laid June 26, 1887, from Toledo to Frankfort. The job was to convert the line from narrow to standard gauge with practically no interruption to scheduling. An estimated 2,500 men took part, receiving $2.50 for the day, up from the normal pay of $1.50 a day because it was a Sunday. Work began at sunrise and trains were on the new track beginning at 4 P.M.

THE *highest railroad trestle* ever in Indiana was the steel structure over Lost River Valley near Paoli, which rose to 870 feet. It was on the Monon line.

THE *most powerful locomotive* ever built in Indiana is generally considered to be the *Reuben Wells*; it used wood for fuel and was the first steam locomotive to climb the Madison hill, a function it performed for 28 years before being replaced by a coal-burner. Reuben Wells, the man, came to Indiana in 1852 and became chief mechanic at J. M. and I. Railroad, later part of the Penn Central system. His locomotive, weighing 56 tons, was a new design created to distribute the weight properly and reduce slippage. Although the locomotive traveled more than 100,000 miles in a 38-year career, the engine was seldom more than 2 miles from its Madison home.

THE *first interurban line*, providing intercity rail transportation, was an 11-mile route from Anderson to Alexandria, built in 1897 by Charles L. Henry, an Anderson attorney. Interurban tracks soon laced the state. The largest center was Indianapolis, whose Traction Terminal handled 13 lines, making it the *city with the most tracks*.

THE first, and perhaps only, Hoosier to build his own *private railroad line* was Benjamin J. Gifford, landholder at Rensselaer, who constructed a route for shipping from McCoysburg north to Dinwiddie because there were no rails available in 1900 to transport the output of his 33,000 acres of land to market. Officially called the Chicago and Wabash Valley line, the railroad was known as the Onion

Belt. It was purchased by Monon in 1914 and abandoned in 1935.

THE *longest viaduct* still standing in Indiana is that spanning a valley between Tulip and Solsberry, used by the Illinois Central Railroad. It has a span of 2,295 feet and its highest point is 157 feet. It was dedicated December 18, 1906, and is one of the three largest in the world.

THE *smallest town* in Indiana *to have electrical street-cars* was French Lick, which operated two cars over 1.09 miles of track, from 1910 to about 1924. The cars hauled passengers from the Monon station to the French Lick Springs Hotel.

THE *last horse-drawn streetcar* in Indiana was that at Brownstown. It was abandoned in 1916, leaving only a short line in Manhattan, N.Y., still operating. The Brownstown and Ewing Street Railroad Company operated two cars over two miles of track with eight horses.

THE first railroad in Indiana and the nation of Class I designation, determined by volume of business, to *go all-diesel* was the Monon, circa 1947. Then all the "giants" in railroading were rated Class I.

A railroad freight yard at Gary was the *first in the nation fully automated*, going into operation December 17, 1954, after nearly three years of manual control. The Elgin, Joliet and Eastern Railway Company called it the Kirk Yard. Equipment installed by the General Railway Signal Company of Rochester, N.Y., sorted and assembled freight cars by radar and electronic brain circuits. The equipment also could weigh freight cars and couple them into trains.

EDWARD W. McLANE, a veteran hobo and author of *The Hobo's Handbook*, picked Evansville as *one of the seven friendliest freight yards in the U.S.* when asked to make such a selection for *The Book of Lists III*.

THE *largest railroad in the nation operated by the U.S. Navy* extends 175 miles within the Naval Ammunition

Depot at Crane in the northern third of Martin County. The depot track connects with 8 miles of Chicago, Milwaukee, St. Paul and Pacific Railroad tracks which pass through the ammunition depot; they are a portion of the line between Terre Haute and Seymour.

THE *largest operating model train layout* on public display is that of the Indianapolis Children's Museum, which has 1,200 square feet of rails and scenery.

[SEE ALSO *Accidents and disasters; Collections; Interurban; Structures.*]

RECREATION

THE *first roller-coaster* in Indiana was built around 1900 by Frank Thomas in a picnic park in Rich Valley on the Wabash River midway between Peru and Wabash. The coaster had two side-by-side tracks and was called a derby racer. Thomas also was its *first accident victim*; he fell out and broke his arm when the cars overturned on the trial run.

THE *first walk-through fun house* was built in 1926 and patented by Frank Thomas at Riverside Park in Indianapolis. It was called Blue Beard's Castle.

THE sport of *parakiting* was invented in Indiana by Morris Hultz of Churubusco and Bob Fuller of Fort Wayne around 1962 when they successfully modified military parachutes, attached them to 200-foot tow ropes, and reached heights of 50 to 150 feet when pulled by a car.

THE *first nude ski resort* in Indiana was opened in the fall of 1969 at Naked City, a nudist camp near Roselawn, by the owner-operator, Dick Drost: he called it "See and Ski." The resort did not become a runaway success; perhaps it was given a cold shoulder.

THE *most square dancers dancing at one time* in Indiana was an estimated 4,500 during the 1966 National

Square Dance Convention at the Indiana State Fairgrounds in Indianapolis. The estimate is based on the fact that about a third of the registered dancers (14,500 for this convention) are dancing at any given moment.

THE *oldest person to skydive for the first time* in Indiana is believed to have been Ardath Evitt of Paris, Ill., who was 74 when she jumped from a height of 3,000 feet at Kelly Field, Mooresville, at 4 p.m. on August 7, 1978, after waiting two weeks because of recurring rain. She may also be the oldest to make a first jump anywhere.

THE *longest stair climb race* in Indiana was up the 37 stories of the American United Life Building in Indianapolis, whose 815 steps were mounted in 4 minutes, 5 seconds February 18, 1984, by Mark Carlson of Indianapolis, who thereby became the initial record-holder for this event. In the women's category, Patricia Hagen, a copy editor for *The Indianapolis Star* and writer of a column for runners, was fastest with a time of 5 minutes, 56 seconds. An estimated 600 took part in what was called the "Bop to the Top," the oldest being Judy Pike of Plainfield, 68, whose time was 15 minutes and 2 seconds. The $7 entry fee paid by participants was given to the Leukemia Society. The current records are 4 minutes for men and 5 minutes, 4 seconds for women, set in 1985.

THE *only operating antique carrousel* in Indiana is that in the Indianapolis Children's Museum, believed made in Bonn, Germany, and brought to Indianapolis in 1917. It was in operation in Broad Ripple Park for some 40 years, but it stopped going round and round August 13, 1956, was put in storage, and some parts sold. The museum was given the remaining pieces by the Indianapolis Parks Department in 1970.

THE *longest toboggan slide* in the state and the only one on state property is that of Pokagon State Park with a course of 1,700 feet.

THE *longest skiing trail* in Indiana extends one mile downhill at Ski Starlite, Sellersburg. Ski slopes cover more than 100 acres and include one slope with a 500-foot vertical drop.

RELIGION

THE *oldest religious denomination* in Indiana is Catholic; the *first church* in Indiana was St. Francis Xavier at Vincennes, built in 1732. A new building was finished in 1834. The *first church bell* brought to Indiana probably was a bell from France put in the original log chapel of St. Frances Xavier Church in 1740. The bell was later recast. The church later was the site of the archdiocesan center. Bishops were buried there. Adjoining the church is a pioneer cemetery of French and Indian graves.

THE *oldest Catholic parish* in Indiana is that of St. Francis Xavier Church (now Cathedral) at Vincennes, which dates to 1749, but not with the same church building.

THE *earliest Protestant church* in Indiana probably was the Silver Creek Baptist Church north of Sellersburg, which was organized November 22, 1798, by John Fislar, John Pittet, Sophia Fislar, and Cattern Pittet. A church was built in 1818. The most recent church building, constructed in 1861, still stands. The Baptists, the *first organized Protestants* in the state, first held services in Knox County near the falls of the Ohio in 1798.

SILVER CREEK was the site of the *first Methodist church* in Indiana, organized in the spring of 1803 by a Father Robertson.

BRINGING religion to the Indiana pioneer area by *ministers on horseback* began in 1806 with a man named Oglesby, who rode from Hamilton, Ohio, to Lawrenceburg and back via Richmond, preaching along the route.

THE Rev. Samuel D. Robertson organized the state's *first Presbyterian church* in a barn on the land of Col. Small about two miles east of Vincennes in 1806.

THE *oldest surviving Methodist church building* in the state is a log cabin structure, built in 1807 at Charleston and moved to the campus of DePauw University in 1955, where it is an historical site.

THE *oldest church in Indiana* still on its original foundation is the Little Cedar Grove Baptist Church three miles south of Brookville on U.S. 52, maintained by the Franklin County Historical Society. It was built in 1811 on the site of a cabin church erected in 1805. It later was restored and used as a dwelling before becoming historical society property.

THE *first Sunday school* in Indiana is believed to be that founded about 1818 by Isaac Reed, a Presbyterian pastor at New Albany. He started the school along with a Mrs. Austin, a Methodist. Reed later returned East and wrote about his missionary travels in a book called *The Christian Traveller*.

IN 1831 Father Badin opened the first *orphanage* in Indiana at Ste.-Maria-des-Lacs, site of present-day Notre Dame. He operated it for about a year.

THE *first Congregational church* in Indiana was formed at Terre Haute in 1834 by the Rev. Jewett, who paused there en route farther West.

THE *oldest Episcopal church* still standing in Indiana is St. John's Episcopal Church at Crawfordsville, built in 1838.

THE Indiana African Methodist Episcopal Conference was organized by free blacks who settled around Carthage in 1828. October 2, 1840, the *first conference of the AME was organized* in Mt. Pleasant Beech Church just north of Carthage. The church had been AME since June 16, 1832.

THE *most noted evangelist* in Indiana was the Rev. Billy Sunday, born near Ames November 19, 1862, and said to have preached to an estimated 100 million in 25 years without the aid of radio or television. A Presbyterian, Sunday moved to Winona Lake near Warsaw, where he built a tabernacle and received a steady stream of visitors while resting up between speaking circuits. He died November 6, 1935.

A *week-day religious education program*, in which children who wished were dismissed from school and taken to churches for Bible study, was organized in October 14, 1914, at Gary by William Wirt, school superintendent. Five churches cooperated. The program became the largest of its kind in the Protestant world, was used as a model by other states, and involved, at its zenith, more than 50,000 school children in Indiana.

THE *first woman licensed to preach* in the Methodist Church in Indiana was Mrs. Ella Kroft, licensed in 1920, who taught and handled the choir in the churches of her husband, the Rev. Charles M. Kroft, in Sunman, Hartford City, Guilford, Whiteland, Fairfield, Bloomington, and Indianapolis. She died in Indianapolis in 1947. She was a co-founder of the American Association for Women Ministers.

ESTABLISHMENT in 1947 of the Natural Law Institute at the University of Notre Dame, South Bend, marked the *nation's first meeting to study fundamental rights and the law of God*. The institute has met annually ever since, making it the *oldest continous* in the nation.

INDIANA was the *first state to have a chapel in the Capitol* with its opening in the mid-1950s of a 20-chair chapel with lectern, stained glass window, and fireplace in Room 432 of the statehouse. The chapel was created through the efforts of Roy T. Combs, Indiana auditor. In 1983 the chapel began a program of weekly religious services at 11 a.m. each Thursday.

IN 1968, when Bishop A. James Armstrong was named to his post in the United Methodist Church of Indiana, he became, at 43, the *youngest person ever to be chosen as a Methodist bishop*. He also became director of the National Council of Churches and was controversial in both jobs because of his outspoken political activism. Armstrong resigned from both posts in November 1983, terming himself "physically and emotionally depleted," and early the next year created further controversy by relinguishing his ordination in the church. He was 59 when he resigned.

THE *first woman ordained as an Episcopal priest* was Jacqueline Means, ordained January 1, 1977, in All Saints Episcopal Church in Indianapolis.

THE *largest college chapel* (Lutheran) is that of Valparaiso University, a structure which seats 3,260 and was dedicated in September 1959. It is 340 feet long, 10 stories tall (105 feet at the peak), and has an altar 24 feet wide.

THE *largest Mennonite church* in Indiana and probably the second largest in the nation is the First Mennonite Church at Berne with membership of about 1,175. A church in Nebraska is the sole challenger to size.

THE only *Greek Orthodox Cathedral* in Indiana is SS. Constantine and Helen Greek Cathedral at Merrillville. It contains 25 stained glass windows and has a rotunda 100 feet in diameter.

THE *only Quaker Seminary in the world* is in the School of Religion at Earlham College, established in 1960 and graduating about 20 a year who usually go into hospital chaplain posts or other social service work.

[SEE ALSO *Colleges and universities; Education; Music; Newspapers.*]

RESEARCH

FATHER JULIUS A. NIEUWLAND, a chemist at the University of Notre Dame, discovered the basic formula for *synthetic rubber* in 1906 and also found 14 components from which rubber could be synthesized. Said to have saved the rubber industry $350,000,000 annually, his formula went to the DuPont Company, which translated it into a product called Duprene, later renamed Neoprene.

THE *first catalytic cracking unit* by which crude oil was broken down to obtain high-octane fuel for automobiles, was constructed by Dr. Robert Humphreys and Dr. Francis Rogers at Whiting in 1912 when they were ordered to increase the amount of gasoline obtainable from oil. Success came at a pressure of 75 pounds per square inch in a crude brick still. In 1913 a battery of 12 of them went into use at Standard Oil Company. In 1958 a reconstruction of the original still was placed in the Smithsonian Institution.

THE discovery of *what makes fireflies produce light* was made by Chase S. Osborn of Huntington. Osborn also discovered iron ore ranges in North and South America and Africa; he served as governor of Michigan from 1911 to 1922.

CHARLES E. ACKER of Bourbon was the first American to *produce tin and copper tetrachlorides*. He held some 40 patents in electrometallurgy and electrochemistry.

THE world's *first germless monkey* was produced at the University of Notre Dame at South Bend in 1941 by Prof. James A. Reyniers, director of the bacteriology lab; he created a chamber in which the animal was born by Caesarean section in such a way that it never came in contact with any germs. The monkey, named Yehudi II, lived in the germ-free environment and was used in experimentation in which germlessness was an asset.

IN late 1948 Dr. Charles C. Price, head of the University of Notre Dame chemistry department, made a report of the nation's first isolation of chemical compounds capable of *neutralizing the RH antibodies* in blood in the *Journal of the American Chemical Society*.

THE *first nuclear reactor in the U.S. for student use* was that installed at Purdue University in 1961 in the electrical engineering building's Duncan Annex at a cost of $150,000. It was constructed and installed by Lockheed Aircraft Corporation, Marietta, Ga.

THE *largest consumer research operation* in Indiana is

that of Walker Research, headquartered in Indianapolis; it conducts about 1.2 million interviews annually. The firm has branch offices at Fort Wayne and St. Louis. It began doing research by telephone outside the state for the first time in 1970. It is operated by Frank Walker, son of the founder, Tommie Walker; she began it in 1939.

No *cardiology research* program in the nation has been continuously funded by the U.S. government longer than that at the Krannert Institute of Cardiology at the Indiana University Medical Center in Indianapolis; it began in 1962 and uses about $500,000 in U.S. funds annually.

THE *first research organization investigating human sexual activity* was the Alfred C. Kinsey Institute for Sex Research at Indiana University, now the Kinsey Institute for Research in Sex, Gender, and Reproduction. The institute also has the state's *largest collection of erotic material*, including a selection of sexually oriented literature second only to that of the Vatican.

ROADS

THE *first paved road* in Indiana technically was a portion of the National Road, U.S. 40, in Centerville, which was filled with stone flagging.

INDIANA was the first state to adopt *reflectorized yellow lines* for highways, installing them in 1940; adding glass beads to signs made them also reflectorized.

THE Indiana Toll Road, opened in 1956, spanning the state east to west, was the *first superhighway* opened in Indiana.

INDIANA has *more miles of interstate highways* than any other state of comparable size. Four of the interstates, I-65, I-69, I-70, and I-74, pass through Indianapolis, creating a network of seven spokes. Interstates 80 and 90 occupy the same route across the north of Indiana, Interstate 94 crosses a segment of northwest Indiana, and I-64 crosses the southern part of the state. They are part of the 91,000 miles of highways, roads, and streets in Indiana.

THE *shortest highway* in the state is Indiana 43A, which connects Ind. 26 to the north junction of U.S. 231 in West Lafayette and is .26 of a mile long.

THE *longest highway* in Indiana is U.S. 231, which begins at the Ohio River and ends at U.S. 41 near Crown Point, a total of 298.2 miles.

[SEE ALSO *Bridges*.]

S

SAILORS AND SOLDIERS

THE first *black to be commissioned* an officer in the regular Marines was John Earl Rudder, a midshipman in the Naval Reserve Officers' Training Corps at Purdue University when he was made a second lieutenant June 8, 1948. Rudder had served as an enlisted man from July 24, 1943, to June 26, 1946.

ENSIGN JOHN LEE of Indianapolis, commissioned March 15, 1947, and assigned to the USS Kearsage, was the *first black* in the U.S. commissioned a *regular officer* in the Navy.

A Hoosier, Sgt. Homer Lee of Evansville, was a member of the crew aboard the *first tank across the 38th parallel* in Korea at 3:14 p.m., October 7, 1950, on a patrol for the First Cavalry Division. With Lee were PFC James Emerich, Sgt. Walter Hill, Sgt. Charles Gissendanner, and Cpl. Clarence Johnson.

JAMES ROBERT SORDELET of Fort Wayne became the first man in the world to *re-enlist under the North Pole*, something he accomplished as an electrician's mate first class aboard the submarine *Nautilus* August 3, 1958.

BY all estimates, no man has walked *more miles around the Tomb of the Unknown Soldier* in Arlington National Cemetery than Paul Frinsthal of Southport. Frinsthal served 27 months in the mid-1960s with the Old Guard unit at Fort Myer, Va., which provides personnel for honor guards at the tomb. Since 1919, when this duty began, no one has come close to as long on the job as Frinsthal. The reason for this, said Frinsthal, was because of the hours of standing in all kinds of weather and the precise routine required of the guards. Turnover on the 12-man unit which provides the honor guard is great and competition for the spots heavy. In April 1967 Frinsthal asked for a transfer because his legs could no longer take it. After retiring from the military he became an official at American Legion National Headquarters in Indianapolis.

[SEE ALSO *Medicine; Wars.*]

SCREEN

CHARLES FRANCIS JENKINS showed a *motion picture* for the first time in Indiana June 6, 1864, in an upstairs room over a small Richmond jewelry store. Jenkins, who worked at the Treasury Department in Washington, rode his bicycle back to Indiana and took an extra week of vacation to work on his "phantoscope." The initial film was one made in Washington, using a "butterfly" dance by Annabell, a vaudevillian. Eighteen years later Jenkins got the Elliott Cresson gold medal for having achieved motion photography. In October 1895, the Atlanta Show in Georgia was opened to exhibit Jenkins's phantoscope, making it the *earliest structure* designed and used solely *for the presentation of films*.

THE *first Tarzan* in the movies was Elmo Lincoln, born Otto Elmo Linkenhelter at Rochester, Ind. Lincoln played several parts in the historic film *Birth of a Nation* in 1914 and appeared opposite Lillian Gish in *The Greatest Thing in Life*. In 1918 he filmed *Tarzan of the Apes* and *Romance of Tarzan* with Enid Markey as Jane. Although offered $75 a week for the role, he held out for $100. In 1921 Lincoln was the lead in a 15-part serial, *The Adventures of Tarzan*. Acting was curtailed for the 6-foot, 230-pound Lincoln by the arrival of the talkies. Embittered, he retired from acting in 1937 and died of a heart attack in his Los Angeles home June 27, 1957.

THE first *drive-in* movie was developed by J. Henry Meloy in Shelby County in the 1920s to sell low-voltage lighting systems for farms. Meloy installed a projector in a 1920 Model T Ford roadster, rented films and drove around the area in the evening. He would set up the equipment and show the films to assembled country folks, adding slides showing his merchandise.

THE *biggest marquee* on a movie theater in Indiana was that built for the Lyric Theater in Indianapolis during remodeling, completed in August 1926. The marquee was 10 feet high, 50 feet long, and 16 feet deep; it held 440 letters.

THE first theater to show a *nude film* was the Ohio in Indianapolis, which played *This Nude World* October 19, 1933. The same theater showed the *first sex film with sound, The 7th Commandment*, May 4, 1933.

THE Indiana Theater in Indianapolis showed the first *three-dimensional cartoon* in Indiana with presentation of Paramount's *Somewhere in Dreamland* January 31, 1936. The same theater showed the first major *three-dimensional movie, Bwana Devil*, which opened in February 1953.

THE first *so-called adult film* shown in Indiana was *Smashing the Vice Trust*, which opened May 6, 1937, in the Indiana Theater in Indianapolis. June 4, that same year, the Indiana opened *Ecstasy*, the Hedy Lamarr film which had been banned in the U.S. for six years.

THE first man to memorialize *Hollywood stars in concrete* was Sid Patrick Grauman, born in Indianapolis; while building his Chinese Theater, he got the idea for the sidewalk that became world renowned. Grauman, who also conceived the idea of the Hollywood premier for movies, had built and sold several theaters before starting the Chinese, named for his friends in San Francisco. "We were just laying the concrete between the theater and the sidewalk when all that wet cement set the wheels in my head turning," he said later. "I ran to the phone, called my friends Doug Fairbanks, Mary Pickford, and Norma Talmadge, and asked them to hurry down. When they got there they thought I was crazy, but they were game. They were the first." Sections of the sidewalk had footprints, hand prints, and other trademarks of the stars imprinted in concrete; it became a mark of success to be enshrined there. Grauman, born in an Irish section of Indianapolis, went to California at 13. He and his mother lived in the Ambassador Hotel in Los Angeles 19 years. Grauman never married. His theater is now called Mann's.

WHEN the Motion Picture Producers & Distributors Association needed someone to develop and enforce a *code of conduct* for motion pictures and their stars in answer to public complaints, they chose Will H. Hays of Sullivan. Hays, the first Hollywood czar and the man credited with starting Beverly Hills as the home of the stars, had been postmaster-general under President Warren Harding, was an elder in the conservative Presbyterian Church, and held conservative small-town Republican views. He later made Crawfordsville his home in Indiana.

Fantasia, the first film in *stereophonic sound*, was first shown in Indiana at the Lyric Theater in Indianapolis, June 11, 1942.

INDIANA'S most famous *celebrity-basketball-player* undoubtedly is James Dean, who was a guard for Fairmount during the 1949 sectional tournament at Marion and scored 15 points in a losing cause, 40–34. Dean became the state's most famous young actor with an illustrious movie career before his death in an auto crash shortly after completion of the filming of *East of Eden*.

THE first *cinemascope* feature ever produced was *The Robe*, written by Indiana minister Lloyd C. Douglas and released in 1953.

OF all the Hoosier actors and actresses nominated for Academy Award honors, Irene Dunne, a Madison native, holds the record for the *most nominations without winning*—5. She was nominated for *Goodbye, Mr. Chips*, 1939; *Blossoms in the Dust*, 1941; *Madame Curie*, 1943; *Mrs. Parkington*, 1944; and *The Valley of Decision*, 1945.

THE first actor to be *nominated for an Oscar after his death* was James Dean of Fairmount for his role in *East of Eden*, a film finished shortly before he died in an auto crash in 1954.

THE film with an Indiana connection to win the *most Oscars* was *Ben-Hur*, based on the story written by Lew Wallace of Crawfordsville. It also was the first movie ever to win *more than* 10 *Oscars*. In 1959 *Ben-Hur* was nominated for 12 Oscars and won 11. Its only loss was for the best screenplay.

THE film with a Hoosier connection to make the *most money* was *Ben-Hur*, based on the novel by Lew Wallace; it received $36,650,000 in theater rental fees after its release in 1959.

THE *longevity record* for a regular movie in Indiana is held by the Lyric Theater in Indianapolis, which showed *Sound of Music* from March 31, 1965, to January 17, 1967.

THE largest collection of *vintage movie scripts* is at the Indiana University rare book depository at Bloomington; it includes a total of 833 scripts from nearly every type of movie. Two other universities also have extensive collections. The I.U. collection includes scripts from such films as *Citizen Kane*, *The Jazz Singer*, which was the first sound movie, *Jaws*, *The Godfather*, and *Gone with the Wind*.

SEATS

THE *most seats erected* for a single performance are the 70,000 put up by the Jack K. Elrod Company of Indianapolis for a bus jump at Kings Island by motorcycle daredevil Evel Knievel in 1976. The same firm, operated by Jack and Jeff Elrod, has the *most rental seats* in the state, 76,000.

SERVICES

THE record for volunteering continuously at one place in Indiana is 50 years, achieved in 1983 by Alberta Lossin at St. Francis Hospital Center in Beech Grove, Marion County.

SHELLS: SEE *Museums*.

SPEED

THE first record for transcontinental travel on a *motorcycle* was set in 1914 by E. G. (Cannonball) Baker, a Dearborn County native, who made the trip from California to New York in 11 days, 12 hours, and 10 minutes. In 1941 Baker made the 3,047 miles from Los Angeles to New York by motorcycle in 6 days, 6 hours, and 25 minutes.

He also drove a Model T from New York to Los Angeles in 1926 in record time of 5 days, 2 hours, and 13 minutes.

As far as can be ascertained, the record speed for a *diesel truck* driven by a Hoosier is 122.85 miles an hour, achieved by Jim Bickel of Akron, Ind. on May 10, 1980, in qualifying his Liberty Belle tractor at the Texas World Speedway, College Station, Tex., for the Great Texas Truck Race. Bickel finished seventh in the race, blowing out seven tires during it.

THE fastest *elevator* in the state is that in the American United Life Building in downtown Indianapolis, which travels 1,000 feet a minute. Since the building is 533 feet tall, it takes about 30 seconds to make the elevator trip from bottom to top. Indiana has about 11,000 elevators subject to state inspection.

NOTHING accelerated by man goes faster in Indiana than *protons* being put through the Indiana University Cyclotron Facility at Bloomington, which reach speeds up to 106,000 miles a second.

THE speed record for a *turkey* over a 200-foot course is 12.5 seconds, set in September 1983 at the Turkey Trot Festival races in Montgomery, Daviess County, by Combo, sponsored by the Shenandoah turkey processing plant of Washington, Ind., and the firm's union, VFCW 1240. The "jockey" was Patty Wright. Turkey races were started with the inception of the festival in 1972.

[SEE ALSO *Automobiles and trucks; Aviation; Bicycles; Boats; Sports.*]

SPORTS

THE six Hoosiers picked among 100 champions for an exhibition by the Smithsonian Institution, making them the *top sports figures for the state* in the eyes of the historian and two curators who made the selection, were : Kenesaw (Mountain) Landis, former commissioner of baseball;

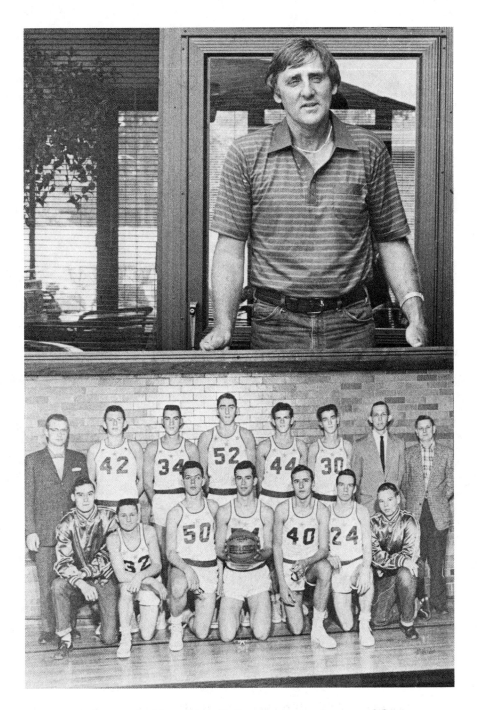

MARION PIERCE, *holder of the all-time career scoring record for an Indiana high school basketball player, displaying a picture of the New Castle team he played on as a senior. (Photo courtesy of Susan Hanafee.)*

OSCAR ROBERTSON *holds several National Basketball Association records, including career assists, and was the first Hoosier pro player to score a lifetime total of 25,000 points. (Photo courtesy of Crispus Attucks High School.)*

GORDON JOHNCOCK BEATS RICK MEARS *by .16 second in 1982,
the closest finish ever of the 500-mile Race in Indianapolis.
(Photo courtesy of Indianapolis Motor Speedway.)*

SHEILA EVANS (left) AND A. E. PITCHER *hold Senior Olympics records, she for the high jump and he for several events.*

THE ASH HOUSE on the Ohio River east of Madison is the oldest surviving brick house in Indiana. It was originally built in 1798 and a section was added later. (Photo by author.)

THE FIRST LIGHTHOUSE *built in Indiana survives at Michigan City as a museum devoted to maritime artifacts. (Photo by author.)*

THE BARN ON THE KINGEN FARM *northeast of Indianapolis is thought to be the largest round barn in the state. (Photo by author.)*

THE LARGEST NUMBER *of people to jump simultaneously in Indi-ana and the world was this group of about 3,400, organized at Ball State University in 1980 to promote the sale of the University yearbook. (Photo courtesy of* Indianapolis Star-News *library.)*

DINO DELOREAN *and* BARBARA KANE *are shown in the midst of the longest kiss in Indiana's history, done at Lafayette, but begun in New York. (Photo courtesy of radio station WXUS.)*

MAURI ROSE KIRBY *looks down from the house atop a pole in Indianapolis, where she set the world pole-sitting record. (File photo.)*

THE LARGEST SALAD *ever prepared in Indiana or the world is shown by (left to right) Deanna Regan and Sue Creech, and creators Gary Bone and Rob Packard. The salad (ingredients on poster) was assembled at Greenwood in 1978. (Photo courtesy of* Indianapolis Star-News *library.)*

SANDY ALLEN, THE WORLD'S TALLEST WOMAN *capable of standing upright, greets the crowd at an Indiana Pacer game shortly after acquiring the world title. (Photo by author.)*

Knute Rockne, Notre Dame football coach; Oscar Robertson, professional basketball player; John Wooden, basketball coach; Wilbur Shaw, auto racer; and Mark Spitz, swimmer. None was active at the time of the selection for the exhibit in the mid-1970s.

THE first Hoosier to receive the Sullivan Award for the athlete voted *tops in the nation* was Donald R. Lash of Auburn and Indiana University in 1938. Lash set several distance running records as a Big Ten competitor and was on the Olympic team.

Archery

REPRESENTATIVES of eight archery clubs met at Crawfordsville January 23, 1879, to form the *first archery association*, the National Archery Association. The first meeting and tournament was August 12–14 that year in Chicago, with 20 women and 69 men participating. The first president was Maurice Thompson and the top man in the initial tournament was Will H. Thompson. He scored 172 hits and a score of 624. Will Thompson was the author of *Alice of Old Vincennes*. He and Maurice Thompson are considered the fathers of the sport of archery.

THE only man in the nation to have earned *two* 1,300 *scores* in a single archery tournament is Richard McKinney of Muncie, 1977 world champion, 5 times national champion, and 6 times U.S. indoor champion. McKinney's best score ever is 1,329 points.

THE all-time *record score outdoors* for archers at 50 meters is held by Richard McKinney of Muncie and Arizona State University with a score of 345 in 1982.

THE outstanding Hoosier *female amateur archer* is Betty Liggett of Muncie, who holds indoor records at 18 and 25 meters for both cadet and intermediate girls classes, aggregate scores for intermediate and junior girls, and outdoor records in various classes at 30, 40, 50, and 60 meters, a total of 17 top marks.

THE record for *professional women archers* at 18 meters is held by Betty McKinney of Muncie with 548 points, set indoors in 1977.

Baseball, *Amateur*

THE *worst defeat* of an Indiana amateur baseball team was in 1867 when the Washington Nationals, a touring team of amateurs, beat Western Indianapolis 106–21. Two of the Washington players each made 14 runs.

THE *first baseball game at night* was played June 2, 1883, at Fort Wayne, where 2,000 witnessed M. E. College lose to the Quincy, Mich., Professionals 19–11. The college team was made up of boys from a club. A preliminary test of the lights at the League Park was made May 29, 1883; 11 of the 16 lights finally were used.

THE *toss* of 426 feet, 9 1/2 inches in 1910 by Sheldon LeJeune of Evansville, stood as the baseball *world record* until surpassed by a non-Hoosier in 1952.

THE first *organization for young baseball players* in which everyone got into the game, regardless of skill, was the Wildcat League of Fort Wayne, organized in 1961 by industrialist Dale W. McMillen after he learned that not all the boys who went out for Little League were accepted. The first season, in which no team standings were kept, 1,600 kids participated. Teams were shuffled throughout the season so they were as even as possible and every team recorded at least one victory.

Baseball, *College*

WHEN Indiana University met Indiana Asbury University, now DePauw, in 1883, it was the *first baseball game between colleges* in Indiana, and the first intercollegiate contest of any kind in the state. Asbury won 23–6.

BIG TEN:

These are the top marks in Big Ten play by Indiana schools in the modern era, since 1939.

SINGLE GAME:
  Most hits: 6 by Bill Gorman of Purdue against Iowa May 4, 1957
  Most runs: 5 by Bill Gorman, Purdue, against Iowa May 4, 1957
  Most doubles: 3 by Bill Eviston and John Dykes of Purdue, Eviston against Northwestern April 30, 1971, Dykes against Northwestern April 29, 1973

Most stolen bases: 4 by Reggie Woods, Indiana, against Northwestern May 6, 1966

Most putouts: 21 by Rick Tekavic, Purdue, against Illinois May 9, 1970

Most errors: 4 by Rick Voigt, Indiana, against Iowa April 22, 1979

Most strikeouts: 16 by R. E. Bailey, Purdue, against Ohio State May 12, 1939

No-hit games: Albin Hayes, Indiana, against Ohio State May 4, 1957; Larry Rosen, Indiana, against Illinois May 22, 1976

HITTING, SEASON:

Batting average: .500 by Bill Skowron, Purdue, 1950

Most hits: 28 by Terry Wedgewood, Purdue, 1971

Most total bases: 54 by Terry Wedgewood, Purdue, 1971

Most doubles: 8 by Randy Miller, Indiana, 1974

Most triples: 5 by Don Blanken, Purdue, 1941; Norm Banas, Purdue, 1951; Don Dilly, Indiana, 1964; Jamie Bucaro, Indiana, 1976

Most home runs: 6 by Terry Wedgewood, Purdue, 1971

Most runs batted in: 23 by Elam Rossy, Purdue, 1983

Fewest strikeouts: 1 by Jim Howe, Indiana, 1959

PITCHING, SEASON:

Most innings pitched: 59 2/3, Don Dunker, Indiana, 1941

Fewest bases on balls: 6 by Matt Kinzer, Purdue, 1983, and Jack Grate, Indiana, 1984

PITCHING, TOURNAMENT:

Fewest hits (9 innings): Bob Hallas, Purdue, 1981, with 2

Lowest ERA (9 innings minimum): Bob Hallas, Purdue, 1981, 0.00

NCAA: These are top marks in the National Collegiate Athletic Association tournament play by Hoosiers:

Runs in one game: 23 by Notre Dame against Northern Colorado, 1957

Single game batting average: .714 by Jim Morris, Notre Dame, 1957

3 doubles, 1 game: Dan Labhard, ISU-Evansville, against Ballarmine, May 15, 1979, Division II play

Baseball, *High School*

THE first *woman to coach a high school baseball team* in Indiana was Maureen Hight, who became head coach of the squad at North Judson-San Pierre High School in February, 1984, after a court battle with school officials. Miss Hight, 31 when awarded the post, had filed discrimination suits against the school board charging that they refused to inteview her for the coaching job, which she had applied for three years earlier. She was a physical education and health teacher at the school. Along with appointment to the job with its pay of $800 a year above her regular teaching salary, Miss Hight was awarded $2,537 in back salary and $24,000 in attorney fees. When she was a student at Nead Grade School near Peru, Miss Hight had sought and received permission from the Indiana High School Athletic Association to try out for the all-male baseball team; she played on the squad two years.

These are the records reported by Indiana high school teams in regular season play.

PITCHING

Most strikeouts, career, 518; Tom King, LaPorte, 1970–1972
Most strikeouts, season, 240; Steve Fink, Kankakee, 1973
Most no-hitters, career, 8; Marvin Jullen, Monticello Twin Lakes, 1968–1971
Lowest earned run average, 0.43; Jim Wiskotoni, Elkhart Central, 1973–1975
Most strikeouts, career, 21; Tom King, LaPorte, 1970–1972
Most strikeouts, season, 10; Tom King, LaPorte, 1972

HITTING

Most walks, career, 111; Mike Shelburne, Sheridan, 1974–1977
Most walks, season, 47; Eric Schreiber, LaPorte, 1978
Most runs batted in:
    One inning, 8; John Nonemaker, Fort Wayne Dwenger, 1977, first inning against Monroe Adams Central
    Career, 140; Don Mattingly, Evansville Reitz, 1976–1979
Most home runs, one inning, 2; John Nonemaker, Fort Wayne Dwenger, 1977, against Monroe Adams Central
Most triples, career, 25; Don Mattingly, Evansville Reitz, 1976–1979 (second best in the nation)
Most triples, season, 10; Don Mattingly, Evansville Reitz, 1978
Most runs, one game, 7; Phil Boze, Monticello Twin Lakes, 1966, against Winamac (Monticello, 34–1)
Most hits, one game, 6; Phil Boze, Monticello Twin Lakes, 1966, same game as above

TEAM RECORDS

Most double plays, season, 26; Indianapolis Chatard, 1977
Most shutouts, season, 15; Clarksville, 1968

Most strikeouts, season, 428; Clarksville, 1973

Most walks in a game, one team, 17; Indianapolis Chatard, 1976

Most walks in a game, 2 teams, 28; Morristown (16) against Hauser (12), 1980

Most grand slams, one team and 2 teams in a game and also most grand slams in an inning for one team and for two teams; Fort Wayne Dwenger and Monroe Adams Central, both getting 2 in the same inning, 1977

Most home runs, season, 45; Blackford, 1974

Most home runs, 1 game, 6; Monticello against Winamac, 1966; 6; Munster, opponent unknown, 1976

Most triples, season, 30; Evansville Reitz, 1979

Most triples, 1 game, 5, Fort Wayne Dwenger, 1977. Ties the best in the nation

Most runs by a losing team, 26; Hauser against Morristown (28), 1980

Most runs in a tie, 2 teams, 44; Fort Wayne Dwenger against Monroe Adams Central, 1977 (10 innings)

Most runs, 2 teams, 54; Morristown against Hauser (26), 1980

Most innings in a game, 28; Griffith against Highland, 1976, (Griffith, 5, Highland, 2)

Wins in a row, 59; Evansville Reitz, 1978–1979

IHSAA BASEBALL FINALS RECORDS

TEAM RECORDS

Most runs	12 by Terre Haute North, 1974
Most runs, 1 inning	7 by LaPorte, 1967
Most hits	*Tie*: 12 by LaPorte, 1973, and Terre Haute North in 1974
Most doubles	3 by LaPorte, 1973
Most triples	3 by Evansville Memorial, 1978
Most homers	*Tie*: 1 by LaPorte, 1971, and Terre Haute North, 1974
Most runs batted in	9 by Terre Haute North, 1974
Most left on base	11 by LaPorte in 1973
Fewest runs	*Tie*: 0 by Marion, 1968, and South Adams, 1972

INDIVIDUAL RECORDS

Strikeouts	12 by Kind of Evansville Memorial, 1978
Fewest hits allowed, complete game	*Tie*: 2 by Hutcheson of Marion, 1968, and by Carmichael of Bloomington, 1972

Most hits	3 by Dunlap of LaPorte, 1973
Most triples	2 by Mattingly of Evansville Memorial, 1978
Most homers	*Tie:* 1 by Yates of LaPorte, 1971, and McCabe of Terre Haute North, 1974
Most runs batted in	3-*way tie:* 3 by Packard of Logansport, 1975, Bittner of Indianapolis Marshall, 1975, Dunlap of LaPorte, 1973

Baseball, *Professional*

THE *first professional major league baseball game* was played at Fort Wayne May 4, 1871, when the Fort Wayne Kekiongas beat Cleveland 2–0. The game also included the first league double play and the first league game called by rain, although only the last half of the ninth inning remained unplayed. Fort Wayne joined a league of 10 cities formed in 1871 in which the teams made up their own schedules to play each other five games. In the league were Philadelphia, Boston, Washington, New York, Troy (N.Y.), Chicago, Rockford, Ill., Cleveland, and Fort Wayne, which chose its name from the Miami Indian Village which once occupied the site of the town.

The winning pitcher was Bob Mathews, hired from the East. The first pitch of the game was a ball, the first hit a double, the second hit a double play. The first run was scored by Fort Wayne manager and catcher Bill Lennon. The crowd was estimated at 500. By the end of the season, Fort Wayne had 7 wins and 21 losses.

THE *first game in Indiana by a team in a surviving major league* was April 28, 1887, when Indianapolis, a member of the National League, met Detroit in the Indy park at 16th Street and Capitol Avenue. Indianapolis lost 4–3 to the Wolverines, who won the pennant that year.

THE man who *developed the World Series* as we know it was John T. Brush, clothing store operator from Indianapolis, who got into baseball because of its advertising potential. In 1875 he owned a National League team in Indianapolis, brought a second National League team to Indianapolis in 1886, and in 1902 bought the New York Giants. In 1903 the Giants came in second in the league, but in 1904 they won the pennant. Brush declined a post-season game with the American League winner, but there was so much protest that he drafted rules for a mandatory post-season playoff; many of the rules still are in effect.

THE *greatest Hoosier pitcher of all time* is generally considered to be Amos Rusie, whose fast ball is credited with causing the major leagues to move the pitcher's mound in 1893 from 50 feet away from the plate to 60 feet, 6 inches. Born at Mooresville May 30, 1871, Rusie started in the National League in Indianapolis in 1889 and pitched with the Giants, Chicago, and Cincinnati, achieving a 10-year record of 245 wins and 174 losses. He won the league pitching championship in 1897 with 28 wins and 8 losses. An arm injury against Chicago in 1897 led to his departure from the game. In his prime Rusie pitched balls that batters declared they did not clearly see. He died December 4, 1942.

THE best record of *runs batted in per game* in the majors is held by Sam Thompson of Danville, who played in 1,410 games for Detroit and Philadelphia from 1885 to 1910 and batted in 1,299 runs, an average of almost one per game. Thompson was elected to the *Hall of Fame* in 1974.

AMOS RUSIE set an all-time *record for batters walked* in 1890 with 276. The same year Rusie, pitching for New York in the National League, struck out 345 batters.

THE only Hoosier players to *pitch no-hit games* in the majors were Amos W. Rusie, July 31, 1891, with New York against Brooklyn, score 6–0; Carl D. Erskine, who had two no-hitters, one June 19, 1952, for Brooklyn against Chicago, score 5–0, and the other May 12, 1956, against New York, score 3–0; and Don Larsen, who pitched the first perfect game in a World Series with New York against the Dodgers, October 8, 1956, score 2–0.

THE *first Hoosier to win three games in a seven-game* World *Series* was Charles E. (Babe) Adams of Tipton County, a hurler for the Pirates in the 1909 series against Pittsburgh. Adams, born near Groomsville, was in his rookie season when he accomplished the victories. He also held the lifetime record for the fewest walks per inning.

THE *greatest World Series* for Hoosiers surely was the 1909 clash between Pittsburgh and Detroit. Charles E. (Babe) Adams of the Pirates, a native of Tipton County, faced George Mullin, an off-season resident of Wabash, in the opening game, which Adams won. A rookie, he won three games in the series. A third Hoosier to pitch in the series was Oren Edgar (Kickapoo Ed) Summers of Ladoga, a hurler for Detroit. Shortstop for Detroit was Owen (Donie) Bush of Indianapolis, playing his first season. Hoosiers were responsible for 5 of the 7 wins in the series; the Pirates took the crown, 4 games to 3.

MAX CAREY of Terre Haute had the best success among Hoosiers in the National League in *stealing bases*. Among players who tried to steal at least 50 times, Max, who started out in life wanting to be a preacher, was caught only twice in 1922 in 53 attempts with Pittsburgh. He led the National League in stolen bases 10 times from 1910 to 1929. Only three men have stolen more bases: Ty Cobb, Lou Brock, and Eddie Collins.

THE best record for *pitching on a major league baseball team in Indianapolis* was probably that of Cy Falkenberg, who won 25 and lost 16 in the 1914 season with the Indianapolis Federals. Falkenberg's percentage was .610 and his earned run average was 2.22.

THE only Hoosier on record talented enough to *pitch with either hand* in the major leagues was Oren Edgar Summers, a native of Ladoga, who appeared in two World Series games before retiring in 1914, mainly due to rheumatism. Primarily a left-hander, he would occasionally throw right-handed to confuse batters. His record of pitching 18 scoreless innings July 16, 1909, stood unbroken for 45 years. Summers died May 12, 1953.

THE *largest crowd* ever to watch a regularly scheduled major league baseball game in Indiana is believed to be 16,462 watching in Federal Park in Indianapolis October 4, 1914, when Indianapolis, the city's participant in the Federal League, met the Kansas City Packers in a double header.

EVERETT SCOTT of Bluffton is believed to have played in *more consecutive major league games* than any other Hoosier, 1,307 starts with Boston and New York in the American League from 1916 to 1925. His record later was broken by Lou Gehrig.

THE *best season record* for a major league baseball team in Indiana was that of the Indianapolis squad in the Federal League in 1914, with 88 wins and 65 losses for a percentage of .575.

THE *first dictator* of professional baseball was Kenesaw Mountain Landis, reared at Logansport, who in 1920 took over supervision of the 16 American and National League teams, ruling with an iron hand until his death November 24, 1944.

THE first Hoosier to *manage a major league baseball team which won a pennant* was Owen J. (Donie) Bush of Indianapolis, who was at the helm when the Pittsburgh Pirates went to the World Series in 1927. They beat New York. The second and last Hoosier to manage a team to the world title was Gil Hodges of Princeton, who guided the New York Mets in 1969.

THE first time a baseball game between two professional teams was *played under lights* was in 1930 in Indianapolis when the Cincinnati Reds met the Indianapolis pro team in an exhibition game. According to accounts, the Cincinnati players misjudged the ball several times because of the glare of the lights and errors played a part in the Indianapolis 17–5 victory. "The floodlights poured a metallic glare over the baseball field and turned the field to a vividly unreal color, like grass in a postcard," said one description of the scene.

Despite this 1930 contest, some baseball histories claim that the first night game in professional ball was May 23, 1935, at Crosley Field in Cincinnati.

The professional game under the lights should not be confused with the first night baseball game ever, at Fort Wayne, which involved one amateur team. (See Baseball, Amateur.)

THE Indiana player who *set the most records* in the major leagues was Chuck (Herb) Klein of Indianapolis. He is the only Hoosier to win the triple crown, which consists of the titles in homers, runs batted in, and batting average in the same season, a feat he accomplished in 1933. Klein was four times National League home run champ, is one of only a handful to hit four homers in a single game, and is high on the lifetime home run list with 300. He was sixth highest in hits in a single season in the major leagues and fourth highest in total bases in a single season, held National League records for most games hit safely in a season, most extra-base hits in one season, and most runs produced in a season (158 in 1930). He holds the all-time record for most base runners thrown out by an outfielder, 44 in 1930.

THE *best lifetime batting average* in the major leagues by an Indiana player is the .543 of Chuck Klein during his 17 years of playing. Klein was from Indianapolis and a graduate of Southport High School. The most runs in one season for Klein was 158 in 1930.

THE *first time major league teams trained in Indiana* was the spring of 1943, when World War II restricted the usual travel to warmer climes. The Pittsburgh Pirates practiced at Muncie, Detroit Tigers at Evansville, Cincinnati at Bloomington, and Cleveland Indians at Lafayette, Chicago Cubs and White Sox at French Lick.

THE *most home runs* hit by a Hoosier in the majors is 370, the lifetime mark of Gil Hodges of Princeton. He played from 1943 to 1962.

HARRY TAYLOR of Shirkieville, pitching for the Dodgers in the 1947 World Series against the Yankees, pitched to four batters in the first inning and was *removed without ever having gotten a man out*. The first batter got a hit, the second was safe on a hit-and-run, the third man was safe when the second baseman dropped the ball, and the fourth batter, Joe Dimaggio, was walked on a 3-and-2 pitch which Taylor disputed. Although taken out of the game and also the loser in the first major league game he pitched, Taylor was National league rookie of the year for 1947. But as far as the record shows, he spent less time in his first series game than any player from Indiana.

THE first Hoosier installed in the Baseball *Hall of Fame* was Mordecai (Three Finger) Brown of Nyesville, near Terre Haute, a sensational major league pitcher who gained extra English on the ball due to having lost two fingers in a farming accident during his childhood. He was inducted in 1949.

THE Hoosier players to hit *four home runs* in a single game in the major leagues are Gil Hodges of Princeton in 1950 with the Brooklyn Dodgers, and Chuck Klein of Indianapolis in 1936 with Philadelphia.

CARL ERSKINE, while pitching for the Brooklyn Dodgers, set the *World Series strikeout record* by a Hoosier with 14 in 1952. The mark has been topped only twice since. Erskine struck out Mickey Mantle of the Yankees four times in game, and struck out Johnny Mize, the catcher, for his 14th victim; the Dodgers won, 3–2. Erskine retired in 1959 to Anderson, his home town.

A Hoosier pitched the *first perfect game in a World Series*. He was Donald James Larsen, 27, of Michigan City, whose effort October 8, 1956, retired 27 Dodgers using 97 pitches for a Yankee victory, 2–0, in the fifth game of the series.

RON KELLER of Indianapolis, who had a record of zero wins and 1 loss with the Minnesota Twins in 1966 and 1968, has the *poorest Hoosier major league pitching record*.

THE *worst batting average* in the major leagues by a Hoosier in modern time was that of Ray Oyler of Indianapolis, who batted .135 in 1968 with the Detroit Tigers. Oyler, who played shortstop for his defensive skills, was a graduate of Cathedral High School in Indianapolis. The Tigers won the pennant in 1968.

THE *Indiana city which has provided the most players* for the major leagues is Indianapolis, which was the home of 27 who made it to the big time out of a total of 204 native Hoosiers in major league uniforms since 1884.

Basketball, *Amateur*

THE Terminal Building at Crawfordsville, the first permanent home of the YMCA in that town, was the site of the *first basketball game* in Indiana in 1892. It was organized by the Rev. N. C. McCay, who had learned the game in the east from Dr. James Naismith, its inventor. Details on the team members and score are lost to history because there was not at the time a system of formal record keeping.

THE *first recorded basketball game* in Indiana was at Crawfordsville March 16, 1894, when the Crawfordsville YMCA beat the Lafayette YMCA 45–21.

THE *first wheelchair basketball team* in the state was the Whizzes of Crossroads Rehabilitation Center in Indianapolis, which posted a winning record in its debut season, 1958–59. The team won 12 of 14 exhibition games.

THE *highest scoring Indiana wheelchair basketball player* was Jack A. Hagans of Greenfield, who scored 54 points February 11, 1973, when his team, the Olympians of Indianapolis, played the Pacemakers at Chicago. Hagans hit 24 of 41 field goals and 6 of 8 free throws, all from his wheelchair. In 10 years of playing, Hagans, a victim of polio, scored 4,900 points, an average of 16 per game.

Basketball, *College*

THE collegiate *career scoring mark* in Indiana is held by Austin Carr who, at the University of Notre Dame, scored 2,560 points in 74 games.

FRANK JEAN of Hanover College holds the recod for the *most points* by a Hoosier in *one college game* with 70, scored in the 1942–43 season against the University of Louisville.

THE first Hoosier to get the *Wade Trophy*, presented to the top woman college basketball player, was LaTaunya Pollard of East Chicago, three-time all-American at Long Beach State. Miss Pollard, the fifth to receive the trophy, led the nation in scoring for the 1982–83 season with an average of 29.3 points a game.

BRANCH MCCRACKEN, a graduate of Indiana University in 1930, became the fourth coach at Ball State University and, at 22, the *youngest ever to coach a college team.* In his five years there his record was 44–40. He became basketball coach at Indiana

University in 1938, 13 years after he had entered I.U. as a student.

BIG TEN, *Men*

THE *best attendance* by an Indiana Big Ten school is enjoyed by Indiana University, which had crowds totalling 202,700 for 12 games in 1976, an average of 16,892.

THE record for being named *Big Ten basketball coach of the year* is the 5 *titles* earned by Bobby Knight, coach of Indiana University, in 1973, 1975, 1976, 1980, and 1981. Knight also was named national coach of the year in 1975 and 1976.

THE first player to be named *defensive player of the year* when the Big Ten began the category in 1984 was Ricky Hall of Purdue University. Voting was by the Big Ten Radio Association.

RICK MOUNT of Lebanon and Purdue University, holds these Big Ten basketball records:
Most points in a game, 61 against Iowa, February 28, 1970; most field goals in a season, 221; best season average, 39.4 in 14 games in 1940; best average for a career, 34.79; most field goal attempts per game, 31.1 average in 1970; most field goals in a game, 27 against Iowa, February 28, 1970, and most field goal tries, 31.1 average in 1970 in 14 games.

THE first basketball player to be *twice named most valuable player* in the Big Ten was Archie Dees of Indiana University, who received the honor in 1957 and 1958. He led the conference in scoring both years. In 1958 I.U. was a Big Ten co-champion in basketball.

PURDUE UNIVERSITY has won *more Big Ten basketball championships* than any other school in the league, 16, including its co-championship with Illinois in 1984. Indiana University ranks next with 15 titles.

INDIANA UNIVERSITY has the best record in Indiana for *consecutive Big Ten victories* and also the *most victories in a row* in all games. I.U. won 37 consecutive Big Ten victories, 1 in 1974, 18 in both 1975 and 1976; and has a record of 34 straight in all games, 3 in 1974 and 31 in 1975.

BIG TEN RECORDS

These are the best by Indiana Big Ten conference players. Those which also are the best in all the Big Ten are noted.

INDIVIDUAL

GAME

Most points, before 1960

Don Schlundt of Indiana University, 47 against Ohio State February 27, 1954, conference best.

Most field goal tries, 1 game

48 by Jimmy Rayl of Indiana against Michigan State, February 23, 1963

Best field goal average

One game: 1000 by George Faeber of Purdue against Iowa March 13, 1971 (12 of 12), tie for conference best

Most three-point goals

5 by Curt Clawson of Purdue against Minnesota, January 8, 1983

Most free throws

25 by Don Schlundt, I.U., against Ohio March 5, 1955, conference best.

Most free throws tried

30 by Don Schlundt of I.U. against Ohio State March 5, 1955, conference best.

Most free throws missed

15 by Jack Runyan of Purdue against Michigan March 2, 1953, conference record.

Best free throw percentage, 1 game

1000 by Ted Kitchel of I.U. with 18 of 18 against Illinois January 10, 1981; beaten by a Michigan State player who hit 19 of 19 against I.U. January 7, 1982. Others in Indiana equaled the percentage, but shot fewer than 18.

SEASON

Most points

552 by Rick Mount of Purdue in 1970

Most field goals tried

435 by Rick Mount of Purdue in 1970

Best field goal average

.626 by Ray Tolbert of Indiana, 1981 (107 for 171)

Most three-point tries season and career

61 by Curt Clawson of Purdue, 1983

Best three-point average

.656 by Ted Kitchell of I.U. in 1983 (21 of 32), best in conference

Most free throws

179 by Terry Dischinger of Purdue, 1962, conference best.

Most free throws tried, average

15.4 by Terry Dischinger of Purdue in 1962 (215 in 14 games), conference best.

Best free throw average per game
12.8 by Terry Dischinger of Purdue in 1967 with 179 in 14 games, conference best.
Most free throws missed, season average
6.3 by Jack Runyan of Purdue in 1953 (114 missed out of 223 tried in 18 games)
Best free throw percentage
.923 by Jon McGlocklin of I.U. with 36 of 39 in 1965 and Rick Ford of I.U. with 60 of 65 in 1970, also for .923
Most rebounds, average
17.6 by Walt Bellamy of I.U., 1961 (247 in 14 games)
Most personal fouls, average
4.36 by Harry Joyner of I.U., 1966 (61 in 14 games)
Most assists, (kept since 1975)
129 by Bruce Parkinson of Purdue in 1975 (also best average assists, 7.2 per game)

CAREER
Most points (Big Ten games only)
1,461 by Rick Mount of Purdue, 1968–1970
Most consecutive 40-point games
4 by Rick Mount of Purdue, 1969–1970 season (43, 45, 40, 53)
Most free throws in a row
34 by Jerry Sichting of Purdue in 1978–1979
Most rebounds
1,088 by Walt Bellamy of Indiana, 1959–1961

TEAM

GAME
Most points
122 by Indiana against Ohio State February 2, 1959
Most points by 2 teams
223 by Purdue-Iowa, February 11, 1974; Iowa won 112–111, conference best
Most points by a losing team
Purdue with 111 against Iowa February 11, 1974 (3 overtimes), conference record
Most points by an opponent
128 by Michigan against Purdue in 1966
Most field goals shot
114, Indiana versus Purdue February 23, 1953, most in conference
Most field goals
50 by Indiana against Ohio State February 2, 1959

Best field goal average

.755 by Purdue against Michigan January 5, 1981, 37 of 49, leads conference

Most field goals shot, 2 teams

206, Indiana (110) against Michigan State (96) January 11, 1964, second all-time high in the conference

Most field goals, 2 teams

90 by Purdue (48) against Michigan (42) January 31, 1970

Most 3-point tries

17 by Purdue against Northwestern February 12, 1983; only 2 were made

Most 3-point shots made

8 by Purdue against Minnesota January 8, 1983, in 16 tries, leads conference

Most free throws

43 by I.U. against Michigan January 3, 1955, tie for conference best

Most free throws tried, 1 team

Purdue, 65 against Michigan March 2, 1953, leads conference

Most free throws missed

30 by Purdue against Michigan March 2, 1953, leads conference

Best free throw percentage

Several with 1000, including Purdue against Wisconsin February 7, 1976

Most free throws, 2 teams

73 by Indiana (42) against Purdue (31) January 19, 1953, conference record

Most free throws tried, 2 teams

106 by Purdue versus Michigan March 2, 1953, conference record

Most free throws missed, 2 teams

46 by Purdue (30) and Michigan (16) March 2, 1953, conference record

Best free throw percentage, 2 teams

1000 by Purdue (25 of 25) against Wisconsin (22 of 22) February 7, 1976

Most personal fouls

40 by Purdue against Illinois March 1, 1952

Most personal fouls, 2 teams

73 by Purdue (40) and Illinois March 1, 1952, conference record

SEASON

Most points

1,570 by Indiana in 1975, conference best

Best point average

Purdue with 97.1 in 1969, second best in the conference

Most field goals

652 by Indiana in 1975, best in the conference

Best field goal average

37.6 by Purdue in 1969 (526 in 14 games)

Best field goal attempts average

85.7 by I.U. in 1950 (1,028 in 12 games)

Best field goal percentage

.541 by I.U. in 1981 (490 of 906), second best in the conference

Most 3-point shots

142 by Purdue in 1983, best in conference

Most 3 point shots made

52 by Purdue in 1983, best in conference

Most free throws

688 by Purdue in 1953, conference best

Best free throw attempts average

38.6 by I.U., 1954 (541 in 14 games)

Most free throws missed, average

Purdue, 15.9 in 1953, hitting 18 of 286, leads conference

Most free throws, average

25.9 by I.U., 1954 (363 in 14 games)

Best free throw percentage

.806 by Purdue in 1969, 307 of 381, best in conference

Most personal fouls

403 by Indiana in 1952, conference record

Most personal fouls, average

28.8 by I.U. in 1952 (403 in 14 games), best in the conference

BIG TEN, *Women*

These are the top marks by girls from Indiana schools in conference competition.

GAME

Most points

39 by Karma Abram of Indiana against Illinois, January 27, 1985.

Most field goals

15 by Carol Emanuel of Purdue against Wisconsin March 12, 1983; six-way tie for best in the conference

Most field goal tries

29 by Rachelle Bostic of Indiana University against Northwestern February 14, 1982; tops in the conference

Best field goal average, 1 game

.750 by Denise Jackson of Indiana University against Minnesota February 4, 1983; fifth best in the conference.

Most free throws tried

    18 by Denise Jackson of Indiana University against Wisconsin December 5, 1981; best in the conference

Most free throws made

    15 by Denise Jackson of Indiana against Wisconsin December 5, 1981; leads the conference

Most free throws missed

    7 by Denise Jackson of Indiana University against Michigan January 23, 1983; tops in the conference

Best free throw average, (9 or more shots)

    .833 by Denise Jackson of Indiana University against Wisconsin December 5, 1981; 9th in the conference

Most rebounds, 1 game

    21 by Denise Jackson of Indiana University against Michigan, January 23, 1983; second in the conference

SEASON

Best season average

    20.0 by Carol Emanuel of Purdue in 1983, 360 points in 18 games; third best in the conference

Most field goal tries per game

    18.2 by Rachelle Bostic of Indiana University in 1983, 328 in 18 games; third best in the conference

Most field goals per game

    8.3 by Rachelle Bostic of Indiana University in 1983, 149 in 18 games; fourth best in the conference

Best field goal average

    .526 by Carol Emanuel of Purdue University in 1983, 141 of 268; fifth best in the conference

Most free throws tried, average

    8.3 by Denise Jackson of Indiana University in 1983, 150 in 18 games; tops in the conference

Most free throws missed, average

    2.4 by Denise Jackson of Indiana University in 1983, 44 in 18 games; second in the conference

Best free throw average

    5.8 by Denise Jackson of Indiana University in 1983, 106 in 18 games; tops in the conference

Most rebounds, average

    12.9 by Denise Jackson of Indiana University in 1983, 233 in 18 games; tops in the conference

NATIONAL COLLEGIATE ATHLETIC ASSOCIATION, MEN

THE *first Indiana school to win* the National Collegiate Athletic Association basketball tournament was Indiana University in 1940, beating Kansas 60–42 in the second playoff year.

Steve Alford of Indiana University *led the nation in free throwing percentages* with a season mark of .913 in 1983–84, the first time an Indiana player had led in a national category since the NCAA began recording statistics in 1948. Alford hit 137 out of 150 free throws.

NCAA Marks Division I, Men

These records are held by Hoosiers in National Collegiate Athletic Association tournament play by Division I schools:

All-time scoring

Oscar Robertson of Indianapolis, 10 games in 1958, 1959, and 1960, 324 total points for an average of 32.4, playing for the University of Cincinnati (second highest of all time)

Austin Carr of the University of Notre Dame, 7 games 1969, 1970, and 1971, 289 total points for an average of 41.3 (fifth highest of all time)

Most points, single game

Austin Carr, University of Notre Dame, against Ohio State, 61 points in 1970, all-time high

Most points, 3 games

Austin Carr, University of Notre Dame, 158 points against Ohio (61), Kentucky (52) and Iowa (45) in 1970

Most points in 6 games

Joe Barry Carroll of Purdue University, 158 points in 1980 against LaSalle (33), St. John's (36), I.U. (11), Duke (26), UCLA (17), and Iowa (35)

Most field goals

1 game: Austin Carr, 25 against Ohio, March 7, 1970

3 games: Austin Carr, 68 against Ohio (25), Kentucky (22) and Iowa (21) in 1970

6 games: Joe Barry Carroll, Purdue, 63 in 1980 against LaSalle (12), St. John's (14), I.U. (5), Duke (10), UCLA (8), and Iowa (14)

Most free throws

4 games: Don Schlundt of Indiana University with 49 in 1953 against DePaul (13), Notre Dame (15), Louisiana State (13), and Kansas (8)

Most free throws, career

Oscar Robertson of Indianapolis, 90 with University of Cincinnati, 1958–60

Most team points

3 games: Notre Dame, 317 in 1970 against Ohio, Kentucky and Iowa

Most points, both teams
  227 by Notre Dame (106) against Iowa (121), 1970
Most personal fouls, 1 game
  39 with Notre Dame against Kansas, 1975
Most team free throws
  4 games: Indiana University with 108 in 1953 against Notre Dame
  (29), DePaul (30), Louisiana State (30), and Kansas (19)

NCAA, DIVISION II, MEN

These Hoosier records are held in National Collegiate Athletic
Association tournament play for Division II schools:
Most points
  4 games: Jim Thordsen of St. Joseph's, 112 in 1974 against Coe
  (33), Wisconsin-Green Bay (26), Wittenberg (25), and Southwest
  Missouri (28)
  5 games: Pete Metzelaars of Wabash, 129 in 1982
Most field goals
  Pete Metzelaars of Wabash with 54 in the tournament in 1982
Most personal fouls
  1 game: Wabash, 37 against Calvin March 1, 1980, in losing by a
  score of 88–76
Most free throws
  1 game: Evansville with 46 March 12, 1959, against North
  Carolina A & T in a game won 110–92

NCAA MARKS, WOMEN

These Hoosier scoring records are held in National Collegiate
Athletic Association tournament play for women:
Most points, 1 game
  LaTaunya Pollard, East Chicago, playing for Long Beach State
  against Howard in 1982, 40 points on 13 field goals, 14 free throws.
Most field goals, 2 games
  LaTaunya Pollard, East Chicago, playing for Long Beach State in
  1982 with 28 goals.
Most points, 2 games
  LaTaunya Pollard, East Chicago, playing for Long Beach State in
  1982 with 73 points.

Basketball, *High School, Boys*

ONLY Kokomo has won *all three mental attitude awards*
given over the years in the state basketball tournament. The
Gimbel prize was won in 1925 by Russell Walter, the IHSAA

medal was given in 1944 to Walter McFatridge, and the Trester award was given in 1955 to Jimmy Rayl.

THE first player to get the *Trester award* in the state high school basketball tournament and *also be named Mr. Basketball* for the Indiana All-Star team was Bobby Plump of Milan in 1954.

THE sole Indiana high school whose students have won the *Trester award* for mental attitude in the state basketball tournament *four times* is Marion. The winners have been Jeff Todd, 1980; Dave Colescott, 1976; Joe Sutter, 1969; and Pat Klein, 1950.

WHEN Milan Petrovic of Lake Central High School of Lake County was named the recipient of the *Trester* award in 1984, it marked the first time it was won by a *foreign-born basketball player*. Petrovic, born to Yugoslav parents in Oxford, England, while his father was stationed there, came to the U.S. when he was 4 and became an American citizen at the age of 9 on August 6, 1975.

FRANKLIN Prentice of Kendallville and Jess McAnally of Greencastle were the *only juniors to be given the Trester award* for mental attitude in the high school basketball tournament; all other recipients have been seniors. Prentice was honored in 1927, McAnally in 1932.

THE only time the *Trester award* for mental attitude in the state high school basketball tournament finals was awarded to the *same school two years in a row* was in 1973 and 1974 to players from Franklin. The 1973 winner was Garry Abplanalp, and the 1974 *award was in duplicate* to Don and Jon McGlocklin. The only other time the award was given to *two players* was in 1961 to Dick and Tom VanArsdale of Manual, Indianapolis.

ELIZABETH DIETZ became the *first woman in Indiana to coach a boys basketball team* in 1927 while principal-teacher at New Alsace High School, a two-teacher institution in Dearborn County. She joined Mrs. Blanche Steiner as the faculty of the 30-pupil school and inherited the five-man basketball squad, which played 13 games that season and won 6. When sports writers became aware of the team coached by a woman, one of them picked New Alsace to win the 1928 state basketball tournament; the team lost its first sectional game, 19–13. Miss Dietz had graduated from Indiana University with a degree in English and Latin and got a master's degree at the University of Chicago in English before taking the job at New Alsace. Later she taught at Aurora and Lawrenceburg. One of the members of her basketball team, Lewis S. Jacob, became a teacher, too, and eventually was superintendent of Dearborn County schools. Elizabeth Dietz Ogden died January 1, 1981.

THE *best winning record of a high school coach* in Indiana is that of Marion Crawley, who coached 35 years at Greencastle, Washington and Lafayette and recorded 734 victories against 231 defeats.

THE first Indiana high school to become a *"national champion"* was Wingate, invited to an interscholastic tournament at Chicago in 1920, where it beat Crawfordsville, 22–16, for the U.S. crown.

THE record for *consecutive wins* in regular season basketball games is held by Argos, which won 76 straight beginning February 4, 1978, with a victory over LaVille, and ending December 17, 1981, with a defeat by Glenn.

IN what is believed to be the *only recorded tie* in Indiana basketball, Indianapolis Tech and Frankfort called it quits in 1936 after two overtimes with the score knotted at 31. Everett Case was coach of Frankfort, which went on to win the state tournament with a record of 29 wins, one loss—and one tie.

THE *lowest score* in a regulation game is 2 February 18, 1944, when Crown Point beat Hobart 2–0.

THE *most points scored* by one team in an *overtime* in Indiana is 18, according to Gene Milner's record book for the Indiana Basketball Coaches Association. The game was February 9, 1984, between Whitko and Triton. Jeff Peters of Whitko scored 14 of the overtime points as Whitko won, 88–75. Triton scored 5 points in the overtime.

The record for *two teams in overtime* is 61 points, scored in five overtimes September 14, 1984, as Plainfield beat Mooresville, 41–34. The game was tied 7–7 at the end of regulation time. The overtime total is one point shy of the national record, set in 1977.

THE first high school basketball player in Indiana to *score* 1,000 points or more in a single season was George McGinnis of Washington High School, Indianapolis. The only others to have surpassed 1,000 are Dave Shepherd of Carmel and Steve Alford of New Castle.

DAVE SHEPHERD scored 1,079 points in a single season, 1969–1970, at Carmel High School, the record for the state. Steve Alford of New Castle had a *season total of* 1,078 in 1982–83.

THE *all-time high school career scoring record* in Indiana is held by Marion Pierce of Lewisville, who scored 3,019 points from 1957 to 1961. Pierce, No. 52 on the squad at the small Henry County school, led his team to its only sectional championship, beating New Castle in 1961. Pierce played a year at Lindsey Wilson Junior College in Kentucky, scoring 79 points in one game and averaging 32 points a game, but he left two weeks into his sophomore year. "Some people are made to go to college—I was not," he explained. He left the training camp of the Cincinnati Royals professional team after two weeks in 1963, "black and blue and fed up." Pierce took over a used auto parts business which his father had started in 1954; by 1984 it had spread to seven sites in the state, and brought in Pierce's five brothers. Pierce's scoring was 454 points in his freshman year, 797 points in his sophomore year, 796 points in his junior year, and 972 points in his senior year.

THE *most points in one game* ever scored by a high school player in Indiana is 97 points, made December 11, 1908, by Guy Barr of Rochester High School as his team defeated Bremen 139–9. Barr made 47 field goals and three free throws. He is closely followed by Snowden Hert of Newberry, who scored 90 when his team defeated Washington 140–2 in 1917, and Tim Saylor of White's Institute, who also made 90 in a game, but details are few.

THE *best record for shooting free throws* in high school in Indiana is that of Steve Alford of New Castle, who made 286 out of 303 during the 1982–83 season.

Most free throws in a row is 51, scored by Doug Winiger of Indianapolis Warren Central in the 1963–1964 season.

ALTHOUGH numbers are difficult to obtain, it is believed the *best career rebounding* in Indiana has been by George McGinnis of Indianapolis Washington with 1,638 rebounds. No. 2 appears to be Kent Benson of New Castle with 1,616 rebounds.

THE first high school in Indiana to have a *team mascot* was Logansport, according to athletic director James E. Jones. He says the use of Felix, a stuffed cat, was begun in the early 1920s.

THE *first glass backboards* in Indiana evidently were those installed in 1920 in Owensville High School by Harry L. Champ, principal and coach, put in place in the 1,400-seat gymnasium before the first sectional tournament there in the spring of 1921.

THE *largest high school gymnasium* is at New Castle, with a seating capacity of 9,325, followed by Anderson, 8,998, and Seymour, 8,422.

ONLY one high school in Indiana has *a hymn for a fight song*. Hamilton High School, whose teams are called the Marines, a name chosen years ago because of the presence of marinas in the area, uses the *Marines Hymn* to spur on the team.

STATE Tournament, *boys*

THE first man to *play on a state championship team and also coach* a team to the state championship in basketball was Burl Friddle, who played on the Franklin Wonder Five which won the tournament in 1920 and was coach of the Washington, Ind., champions of 1930 and the Frankfort champions of 1938.

THREE Indiana coaches have coached *four state basketball championship teams*, Glenn Curtis, Everett Case, and Marion Crawley. Curtis was coach of Lebanon in 1918 and Martinsville in 1924, 1927, and 1933. Crawley also coached two school teams to titles, Washington in 1941 and 1942, and Lafayette in 1948 and 1964. Case, however, holds the record for coaching the same team to four state titles, winning the championship at Frankfort in 1925, 1929, 1936, and 1939.

THE first high school basketball coach to *win state championships at two schools* was Glenn Curtis, coach of Lebanon in 1918 and coach of Martinsville when it won the title in 1924, 1927, and 1933.

THE *most free throws* shot and made in the high school basketball tournament in one game was 25 by Steve Alford of New Castle, who did not miss in the preliminary game of the semistate against Broad Ripple in 1983.

THE *most ever scored in a single game* in the high school basketball tournament was 57 by Steve Alford of New Castle in the 1983 semistate against Broad Ripple of Indianapolis. He surpassed the 49 by George McGinnis against Jac-Cen-Del in the 1969 semistate, and the 52 scored by George Kixmiller for Vincennes in the 1917 tournament.

THE biggest city in Indiana *never to have won* the state high school basketball championship is Terre Haute.

THE *longest* state high school basketball tournament was that of 1978 when storms and energy problems delayed the finals in Market Square Arena, Indianpolis, from March 25 to April 15.

THE *record long shot* in the finals of the state high school basketball tournament is one of 57 feet, made by Stacey Toran of Broad Ripple against Marion in the 1980 finals. It brought Broad Ripple victory, 71–69, and the right to play for the title, which it won.

THE first basketball player standing 7 *feet tall* to play in the state basketball tournament was Mike McCoy, center for Fort Wayne South when it won the title in 1958.

More sectional, regional, and semistate titles have been won by Lafayette than by any other school in the state basketball tournament. Sectional titles total 55, regionals 32, and semistates 10.

SECTIONALS, *boys*

THE *highest score* in a sectional game in the high school basketball tournament was the 131 scored by Jeffersonville in 1965 against 78 for Henryville.

THE seven overtimes between Camden and Delphi in 1935 made it the *longest sectional game* in high school basketball tournament history. Camden won, 22–19.

WHEN Fayetteville failed to score in its 1927 sectional game against Bedford, it achieved the *lowest score ever* in the Indiana state basketball tournament. Bedford scored 61 against the 0.

THE record for *consecutive sectional titles* is held by Lafayette with 29 from 1944 to 1972.

THE *most time outs* called in a sectional game is 17 by Jeffersonville in a game with Henryville in 1948. Coach Ed Denton called the delays to slow the start of the afternoon game by New Albany in hopes of robbing them of rest for the championship game in the evening. It didn't work. New Albany beat Jeffersonville 53–31.

THE *biggest margin of victory* in the sectionals was in 1917 when Vincennes beat Otwell 122–14, a spread of 108 points.

REGIONALS, *boys*

THE record *consecutive regional championships* in the Indiana high school basketball tournament is 11, held by Frankfort, winning titles from 1921 to 1931, and Marion, winning its 11th straight in 1985.

THE *longest regional basketball game* in the state tournament was when Swayzee beat Liberty Center 65–61 in 1964 in nine overtimes.

SEMISTATE, *boys*

No other school has been among the final 16 in the high school basketball championship more often than Lafayette, which was a Sweet 16 team 36 times.

ONLY three schools have won *three semistate titles in a row*: Lafayette, 1950–52; Crispus Attucks, 1955–57; and Terre Haute South, 1977–79.

MICHIGAN CITY has shot the *most free throws* in the last four games of the state high school tournament on the way to winning the championship: 92 in 1966.

THE *best free-throw shooting* by a state champion in the last four games of the Indiana state high school basketball tournament was that of Warsaw, the 1984 champion, which hit 73 of 90 free throws for a percentage of .811.

THE *most points scored* by a team among the Sweet 16 in the high school basketball tournament is the 103 by Gary Roosevelt against Triton in 1965.

THE 94 *points* scored by Steve Alford, New Castle, *in two games* against Indianapolis Broad Ripple and Connersville in the 1983 semistate is a record for any day of the state high school basketball tournament.

THE *highest score for both teams* in the semistate or finals of the high school basketball tournament is 194, from the South Bend Adams and Anderson game of 1973: Adams, 99; Anderson, 95.

THE *best field-goal percentage* for a team in the final 16 of the state high school basketball tournament was .585 shot by Muncie Central in 1978; the *worst field goal percentage* is .250 shot by Franklin in 1922.

THE *best free-throw percentage* as a team is 1000, by Bloomfield in 1965, which hit 7 of 7. The *worst free-throw shooting* team in the final 16 was Logansport in 1926, which hit 17 of 28 for .607.

THE *biggest margin* in a game among teams in the Sweet 16 of the high school basketball tournament was that of Roosevelt, 91, against North Miami, 30, in 1968, a difference of 61 points.

FINALS, *boys*

THE *first all-black school* to win the Indiana state high school basketball championship was Crispus Attucks, which beat Gary Roosevelt

97–74 in 1955. The score of the winner and the combined scores in that game also are records.

THE best record in the Indiana state *Catholic high school basketball tournament*, conducted from 1928 to 1942, is that of Indianapolis Cathedral High School, which won the title in 1928, 1929, 1932, and 1933, and was runnerup in 1942. The only school to win the crown three years in a row was St. Mary of Anderson, which was the champ 1936–1938.

THE first time that *four teams which already had won* state basketball crowns met in the finals was in 1962 when Evansville Bosse played Madison and Washington played Kokomo; Bosse and Washington met for the title. The final score was Bosse, 84, Washington, 81.

THE *worst free-throw shooting* in the championship game of the high school basketball tournament was that of Washington and Burris in 1942. Washington shot .222 from the charity line and Burris was zero of 3, or .000.

THE *most free throws missed* by a player in the Indiana high school basketball tournament championship game were the 6 which failed to drop for Clyde Lovellette of Terre Haute Garfield in 1947 and the 6 missed by Jimmy Webb of South Bend Adams against New Albany in 1973. Adams and Garfield both lost.

THE contest between Wingate and South Bend for the state title in 1913 was the *longest championship game* in the high school basketball tournament, lasting for five overtimes. Wingate won, 15–14.

MUNCIE CENTRAL has been in the *final game* of the high school basketball tournament 12 times, *more than any other school,* and has been among the *final four* in the tournament 16 times, also a record. Muncie Central also holds the record for being among the *final eight* teams at 23 times.

FORT WAYNE NORTHROP was the *youngest school* to win the state high school basketball crown when it took the title in 1974, three years after it came into existence. The coach was Bob Dille, 56, former coach at Fort Wayne Central, which closed. The season record for Northrop was 28–1.

THE Indiana state high school basketball tournament finals were *first broadcast* in 1924 by WOWO, Fort Wayne.

THREE schools have been *runnersup a record 5 times* in the high school basketball championships—Anderson, Lafayette Jefferson, and Muncie Central.

EAST CHICAGO WASHINGTON holds the record for the *highest total* in its final four games in capturing the state basketball championship in 1971 with 344 points. The team also scored a record number of field goals for a champion in the final four games, 144.

THE *most points ever scored by a team* in the championship game of the state high school basketball tournament was the 97 recorded by Crispus Attucks against Gary Roosevelt in 1955.

THE record for the *most total points for both teams* in the championship game of the state high school basketball tournament is 171 in the clash between Crispus Attucks (97) and Gary Roosevelt (74) in 1955.

THE *most points by one player* scored in the final game of the high school basketball tournament was 40 by Dave Shepherd of Carmel against East Chicago Roosevelt in 1970, although Roosevelt won 76–62.

THE *most points* scored in the two final games is 76 by Troy Lewis of Anderson in 1983.

THE *best field-goal shooting* in the final four games in the high school basketball tournament champions was Muncie Central's .585 in 1978 against Elkhart and Terre Haute. Muncie won the title over Terre Haute 65–64 in overtime.

The *worst field-goal shooting* in the final four games was the .174 shot by Washington in 1942 against Frankfort and Burris. Washington shot only .164 in the final game with Burris, which shot only .148.

THE 18 *field goals* scored by Oscar Robertson of Crispus Attucks in Indianapolis against Lafayette in the 1956 high school basketball tournament is a record for a title game. Attucks won 79–57.

ONLY two cities in Indiana have had *three different schools* that have won the state high school basketball crown. Indianapolis Crispus Attucks, Washington, and Broad Ripple have won; and at Fort Wayne, Central, Northrop and South high schools have been champions.

THE first high school to win *three state basketball titles in succession* was Franklin with its famed Wonder Five, which took the championship in 1920, 1921, and 1922.

THE *record for appearance* in the Indiana state basketball tournament finals is held by Muncie Central. The school won the state title a record seven times, in 1928, 1931, 1951, 1952, 1963, 1978, and 1979, and was runnerup five times, 1923, 1927, 1930, 1954, and 1960. Only two other schools, Lafayette Jefferson and Anderson, have been state runnerup as many times.

THE first team to win the high school basketball crown *without a defeat* was Crispus Attucks in 1956 with a record of 31–0.

No team has won the state high school basketball championship by a *bigger point spread* than Lebanon, which defeated Franklin in 1912 51–11, a difference of 40 points.

GEORGE CROWE, Franklin, was chosen the *first Mr. Basketball* on the first Indiana All-Star team in 1939. Crowe scored 19 points in the final game of the state high school basketball tournament although his team lost to Frankfort, 36–22. Crowe later played basketball for Indiana Central University and the Harlem Globetrotters, and played baseball with the New York Black Giants and the Milwaukee Braves.

Basketball, *High School, Girls*

STATE TOURNAMENT, *girls*

THE *first winner of the mental attitude award* in the girls state high school basketball tournament and *also selected as Miss Basketball* for the Indiana All-Star team was Judi Warren of Warsaw in 1975.

THE *first high school girl to score 2,000 points* was Jodie Whitaker, who graduated from Austin High School in 1985 with 2,073 points and a single season record of 789 points.

CROWN POINT HIGH SCHOOL became the *first to win the state title twice* with its 1985 victory and also was the first girls team to reach the state finals three times.

Team records

Total points	77 by Warsaw against Jac-Cen-Del in 1978
Field goals shot	78 by Evansville Reitz against Rushville in 1981
Field goals made	33 by Evansville Reitz against Rushville in 1981
Best field goal percentage	.564 by Warsaw against Jac-Cen-Del in 1978
Free throws shot	27 by Columbus East against Southport in 1980 and Heritage against Valparaiso in 1982
Free throws made	17 by Columbus East against Southport in 1980
Best free throw percentage	.818 by Valparaiso against Heritage in 1982

Rebounds   55 by Warsaw against Bloomfield in 1976
Personal fouls   22 by Evansville Reitz against Rushville in 1981
Errors   29 by Mt. Vernon against East Chicago Roosevelt in
                 1977
Steals   12 by Evansville Reitz against Rushville in 1981
Blocked shots   9 by Rushville against Evansville Reitz in 1981

Team Records, Final Four

Total points,
1 game   75 by Warsaw against Jac-Cen-Del in 1978
Total points,
2 games   140 by Southport in 1980
Field goals tried
1 game   81 by Evansville Reitz against Marion in 1981
Field goals made
1 game   33 by Evansville Reitz against Rushville in 1981
Field goals tried
2 games   159 by Evansville Reitz in 1981
Field goals made
2 games   60 by East Chicago Roosevelt in 1977
Best field goal
percentage,
1 game   .610 by Rushville against Chesterton in 1981
Best field goal
percentage,
2 games   .505 by Warsaw in 1978
Most free throws
tried, 1 game   35 by Rushville against Chesterton in 1981
Most free throws
made, 1 game   20 by Rushville against Chesterton in 1981
Most free throws
tried, 2 games   56 by Rushville in 1981
Most free throws
made, 2 games   34 by Heritage in 1982
Best free throw
percentage,
1 game   .818 by Valparaiso against Heritage in 1982
Best free throw
percentage,
2 games   .727 by Valparaiso in 1982
Rebounds,
1 game   62 by Evansville Reitz against Marion in 1981
Rebounds,
2 games   104 by Evansville Reitz in 1981

Personal fouls

1 game   25 by East Chicago Roosevelt against Warsaw in 1976

Personal fouls

2 games   46 by Anderson Madison Heights in 1976

Errors, 1 game 34 by Marion against Southport in 1980

Errors, 2 games 51 by Rushville in 1981

Steals, 1 game 16 by Southport against Marion in 1980

Steals, 2 games 26 by Evansville Reitz in 1981

Blocked shots,

1 game   15 by Marion against Evansville Reitz in 1981

Blocked shots,

2 games   15 by Rushville in 1981

Individual Records

Most points,

1 game   42 by Maria Stack of Columbus East against Southport
               in 1980

Most points,

2 games   70 by Maria Stack of Columbus East in 1980

Most field goals

shot, 1 game   35 by Maria Stack of Columbus East against Southport
               in 1980

Most field goals

made, 1 game 16 by LaTaunya Pollard of East Chicago Roosevelt
               against Mt. Vernon in 1977

Most free throws

shot, 1 game   20 by Maria Stack of Columbus East against Southport
               in 1980

Most free throws

made, 1 game 14 by Maria Stack of Columbus East against Southport
               in 1980.

Most free throws

shot, 2 games   27 by Maria Stack of Columbus East against Southport
               in 1980

Most free throws

made, 2 games 19 by Jody Beerman of Heritage in 1982

Most rebounds

1 game   22 by Maria Stack of Columbus East against Southport
               in 1980

Most rebounds

2 games   33 by Maria Stack of Columbus East in 1980

Most assists

1 game   10 by Judi Warren of Warsaw against East Chicago
               Roosevelt in 1976

Most assists

2 games   19 by Judi Warren of Warsaw in 1976

Most errors,

1 game   12 by Judy Burns of Marion against Southport in 1980

Most errors,

2 games   16 by Melissa Kilgore of Rushville in 1981

Most steals,

1 game   7 by Amy Metheny of Southport against Marion in 1980

Most steals,

2 games   10 by Amy Metheny of Southport in 1980

Most blocked shots

1 game   11 by Trena Keys of Marion against Evansville Reitz in 1981

Individual Records: final game

(if different from single game)

Assists   9 by Judi Warren of Warsaw against Bloomfield in 1976

Errors   7 by Melissa Kilgore of Rushville against Evansville Reitz in 1981

Steals   4 by Michelle Brand and Brenda Butler, both of Evansville Reitz against Rushville in 1981

Blocked shots   9 by Chante Stiers of Rushville against Evansville Reitz in 1981

Basketball, *Professional*

THE *best record in the American Basketball Association*, which began in 1968, was that of the Indiana Pacers; they won the eastern division in 1968–69 and 1969–70, and won the western division in 1970–71, 1971–72, 1972–73, and 1973–74.

ANN MEYER was the *first woman to try out* for a team in the National Basketball Association, attending three days of rookie camp for the Indiana Pacers September, 14, 15, and 16, 1979. Meyer, an all-American at the University of California, Los Angeles, was one of 10 (9 of them male) attempting to make the Indiana team; only seven were invited to continue seeking positions under coach Bobby Leonard. Meyer was one of those cut. Meyer, 5 feet, 9 inches tall and weighing 140 pounds, tried out in Hinkle Fieldhouse at Butler University, Indianapolis. After being cut from the team, Meyer worked as a color commentator for the Pacer games; two months later she joined the New Jersey Gems in the women's professional basketball league.

CHARLES HENRY COOPER, who was the *first black player* drafted by the National Basketball Association, played his first game for the Boston Celtics November 1, 1950, in Fort Wayne against the Pistons. Cooper was drafted April 24, 1950.

IN professional basketball, no player has *fouled out of more games* in a season than Don Meineke, playing with the Fort Wayne Pistons in 1953, who was disqualified in 26 games.

THE Fort Wayne Pistons won the *lowest-scoring game ever* in the National Basketball Association November 22, 1950, at Minneapolis, Minn., against the Lakers and their legendary center, George Mikan. The score was 18–17. Coach Murray Mendenhall decided to use stall tactics to try to draw Mikan away from the basket, and Minneapolis let the Pistons delay. The half-time score was 13–11. Fort Wayne won on a layin by Curly Johnson; Mikan let him shoot for fear of fouling him. There was so much controversy over the game that the NBA had a gentlemen's agreement not to play a stalling offense again for fear it would ruin professional basketball.

THE first Hoosier in professional basketball to reach a *lifetime total of 25,000 points* was Oscar Robertson of Crispus Attucks High School in Indianapolis and the University of Cincinnati. Robertson also was only the second professional player in history to reach that scoring plateau.

THE first Hoosier selected *most valuable player* in the National Basketball Association was Oscar Robertson, 1963–64, with the Cincinnati Royals.

THE first and only Hoosier named most valuable player in the National Basketball Association *two years in a row* is Larry Bird of the Boston Celtics, given the honor in 1984 and 1985. Bird, who played at French Lick and Indiana State University, was only the fifth player ever named most valuable two consecutive years.

THE lifetime National Basketball Association *records held by Oscar Robertson* of Crispus Attucks High School, Indianapolis, and the University of Cincinnati are:
Most free throws made, 7,694 from 1961 to 1974

Most free throws in a half, 19, December 27, 1964, playing for the
Cincinnati Royals against Baltimore
Most lifetime assists, 9,887
Highest game average in assists, 9.5 per game

BUTCH CARTER of the Indiana Pacers holds the record in the
National Basketball Association for *points scored in an overtime*
with 14 against the Boston Celtics in March 1984 in Market Square
Arena in Indianapolis. The Pacers won 123–121.

THE first basketball player in Indiana to be chosen National
Basketball Association *rookie of the year* was Don Meineke of the
Fort Wayne Pistons in 1952–53, the inaugural season of the award.
The next Hoosier so honored was Oscar Robertson of Indianapolis,
chosen for the 1961–62 season with the Cincinnati Royals.

THE record for *steals in a season* in the National Basketball
Association is 281 by Don Buse of the Indiana Pacers in 1976–77.

THE *worst basketball record* for a professional team involving
Indiana was the losing string of the Fort Wayne Pistons, later the
Detroit Pistons. In the years 1948 through 1979, when the franchise
was in both cities, the team lost 1,312 games and won 1,070, for a
percentage of .449. The Fort Wayne-Detroit franchise ranks among
the nine worst losers of all time.

Bicycling

THE first *national bicycling sprint champion* from Indiana
was Marshall (Major) Taylor of Indianapolis in 1900, although he
was riding out of Worchester, Mass. Taylor also was chosen by
Walter Bardgett, an authority on the sport until his death in 1953,
as one of the 15 best bicyclists of all time. Taylor was competing
out of Indianapolis until his mentor was forced to go to Massachusetts. Taylor accompanied him and rose to world acclaim.

DR. Robert C. Beeson, Indianapolis physician, holds the
record for the *Bike Across Missouri run*, 540 miles from St. Louis
to Kansas City and back, of 30 hours, 9 minutes, set in 1982.

MODIFIED BICYCLES

THE *International Human Powered Vehicle Association* is the governing body for racing bicycles banned from regular competitive cycling because of their streamlining or radical designs. The association held its competition in Indiana for the first time in 1983 and again in 1984. The three general classes are bicycles with two wheels, one rider; more than two wheels; and more than one rider. These are the Indiana records:

SINGLE RIDER

THE world record for 200 *meters with unlimited runup* (no restriction on the length of the course used before going through the timed section) is 57.39 miles an hour, done in September 1984 at the Indianapolis Motor Speedway by a vehicle called Lightning X2.

THE fastest Hoosier-built vehicle in human powered competition is *Moby Infinity II* of Mooresville, which won the *200-meter, limited runup* category in 1983 with a speed of 44.46 miles an hour. Rick Dregne was the rider. Only 600 yards are allowed to build up speed in this event. The *Moby Infinity* is a recumbent bicycle in which the rider reclines and steering is done with the hands at pocket level.

THE world record time for covering 4000 *meters* is 3:43.79, achieved by Fred Markham on a vehicle called *Easy Racer* in September 1984 at the Mayor Taylor Velodrome in Indianapolis during the 10th championships of the International Human Powered Vehicle Association.

THE best time in Indiana for a *six-mile race* with a LeMans start is 12.46, set October 2, 1983, at Eagle Creek Park in Indianapolis by *Lightning X2* from California.

Easy Rider of California set the Indiana record *for 12 miles*, covering the distance in 23:38.00 September 30, 1983, at Indianapolis Raceway Park.

Easy Racer, from California, holds the Indiana record *for 20 miles* of 42:46.00 on a road course at Indianapolis Raceway Park in Indianapolis in September 1984.

MULTIPLE RIDERS

THE record for a *200-meter sprint with two riders* is 55.92 miles an hour set at the Indianapolis Motor Speedway October 1, 1983, by a three-wheeled vehicle called *White Lightning*, sponsored by Northrup University. The mark is short of the world record of 58.89 miles an hour.

THE record in Indiana for a bicycle with *four riders over* 200 *meters* is 53.29 miles an hour, set in Indianapolis September, 1984, by a vehicle called *White Lightning.* The sprint permitted unlimited runup.

MULTIPLE WHEELS

THE fastest *three-wheeled vehicle over a quarter-mile drag course* is *White Lightning* from California, which went 44.59 miles an hour on October 1, 1983.

HAND POWERED

THE fastest time for 200 *meters* for a *two-wheeled vehicle powered by hand* (a category primarily for the handicapped without leg power) is 26.59 miles an hour, set in October 1983 at the Indianapolis Motor Speedway by Al House of Connecticut. There was unlimited runup.

[For other bicycling records see Senior Olympics, below.]

VELODROME MARKS

THE modern day bicycle speed records for standard racing bicycles in Indiana have been set at the Major Taylor Velodrome track in Indianapolis. The velodrome opened in 1982. Events include juniors (up to 18 years old), seniors (18 to 34), vet-35 (35 to 44), vet-45 (45 to 54), and vet-55 (55 and older) These are the records:

Men

EVENT	TIME	NAME	DATE
200 meters flying start			
seniors	0:10.888	Nelson Vails	September 1983
Vet-35	0:11.76	Joe Pignataro	July 1983
Vet-45	0:12.69	Jack Hartmann	July 1983
3 kilometer			
Junior	1:13.291	Dan Vogt	June 1984
Senior	1:06.6	Curt Harnett	May 1984
Vet-35	1:11.93	Rob Lea	July 1983
Vet-45	1:18.78	Ron Palazzo	July 1983

Flying lap

Midget	0:24.92	James Achor	May 1983
Intermediate	0:21.81	Sam Yonan	August 1983
Junior	0:21.36	Eric Scudder	August 1983

3 kilometer pursuit

Junior	3:54.810	Dan Vogt	June 1984
Vet-45	4:06.36	J. Nugent	July 1983
Vet-55	4:24.02	Bob Bergon	July 1983

4 kilometer pursuit

Senior	4:52.709	Alex Stieda	May 1983

5 kilometer pursuit

Senior	6:32.56	Paul Liebenrood	September 1984

10 kilometer pursuit

Senior	13:09.02	Paul Liebenrood	September 1984

20 kilometer pursuit

Senior	26:26.20	Paul Liebenrood	September 1984

50 kilometer pursuit

Senior	1:06.31.86	Paul Liebenrood	September 1984

4 kilometer
team pursuit

Seniors	4:37.57	Leonard Nitz	July 1982
		Vincent Maggione	
		Jay Osborne	
		Brent Emery	

1 hour record	45.425 km	Paul Liebenrood	September 1984

Women

200 meters

flying start	0:14.36	Sue Shaug	July 1983
1 kilometer	1:24.767	Lisa Sauve	June 1984
Flying lap	0:23.08	Nancy Stiller	July 1983
3 kilometers	4:12.99	Judy Layton	July 1983

Bowling

THE *first husband and wife* in the nation to *both bowl* 300 *games* in sanctioned play were Al Laureys and Mazey Laureys of New Carlisle. He bowled his perfect game October 28, 1962, and she bowled hers March 26, 1963. Since then at least 14 other couples have done the same.

Bowling, Women

THE WIBC (Women's International Bowling Congress) *best tournament lifetime average* for a Hoosier is held by Pat Dryer of Indianapolis, who played 252 games in 28 tournaments and totalled 46,391 pins for an average of 184.09.

THE record for *duplicate games* in Indiana is the three-game series of 374 which Myrtle Richards of Shelby rolled four times in a row in September 1966 in the WIBC Ladies Handicap League.

THE first woman from Indiana named to the WIBC *Hall of Fame* was Anita Rump of Fort Wayne, named in 1962.

THE only woman in Indiana to *win the state match play title twice* was Bonnie Bateman of Indianapolis, who took the crown in 1964 and 1965. The match play competition is no longer held.

THE Hoosier who has won the *most money* in a single WIBC bowling event is Margaret Lewis of Plainfield, who won $22,500 for a second-place finish in the Hoinke Classic in 1975–76 at Western Bowl in Cincinnati.

THE *record number of WIBC leagues bowled in weekly* in Indiana is 10, held by El Raye Holder of Indianapolis, who did it in 1974–75. Myrtle Fanchally of Indianapolis bowled in 9 leagues weekly in 1979–80.

No other Hoosier served *longer as secretary of a bowling league* than Pearl Switzer of South Bend, who held that post for the Regalette Monday Nite Ladies 46 years before retiring in 1976.

Records in the women's senior tournament of the Indiana Bowling Association, before competition was divided into age categories are: *Single game*: actual, 235 by Catherine Agnew of Indianapolis, 1979; with handicap, 288 by Juanite Imler, Valparaiso, 1979. *Series*: Actual, 767 by Beverly Keys, Anderson, 1982; with handicap, 961 by Alice Fisher, Angola, 1978.

CYNTHIA WHITE of Elwood holds the *singles record* in Indiana State Bowling Association tournament play with 637, bowled in 1980.

THE *best Hoosier score for a singles championship* in the WIBC tournament is Agnes Junker of Indianapolis, who won with 650 in 1947. The *first Indiana singles champion* was Alice Feeney of Indianapolis, whose 593 was victorious in 1924.

THE Indiana record holder for most games in a career in which *all frames were spares* is Ruth Vinson of Franklin with 21 games (WIBC sanctioned).

No Hoosier has won *more singles titles* in WIBC tournament play than Anita Rump of Fort Wayne, who was champion twice, in 1928 and 1930.

BOWLING, *College, Women*

THE first Hoosier bowler to win a *doubles title* in the Association of College Unions bowling tournament was Constance Groeninger of Indiana University, who won with Linda Skotnicki of Maryland in 1969 with a score of 1,040.

THE *first singles champion* from Indiana in the Association of College Unions tournament was Susie Halloway of Indiana University in 1973, who won with a score of 622. She also took the all-events title that year with a score of 1,752, fourth best since the event started in 1962. The all-events was decided by 9 games.

Bowling, *Men*

THE world record score for the 9-game *all-events title* in American Bowling Congress tournament play was set in Indianapolis in 1974 when Jim Goodman of Lorain, O., bowled 2,184 points with series scores of 731, 749, and 704.

JOE PICCIONE, JR., of Indianapolis scored 2,171 *in all-events competition* in the Indiana Bowling Association state tournament in 1980, a record in that category.

THE *world record for four games* is the 1,155 bowled by Charles Neal at Village Bowl in Indianapolis May 18, 1977, with games of 289, 290, 276, and 300.

DON MCCUNE of Munster holds the Indiana *lifetime record for the number of 300 games* in sanctioned tournament play with 7. As of 1984, McCune had bowled a total of 23 sanctioned games of 300.

THE Hoosier with the *highest lifetime pin total* in American Bowling Congress sanctioned games is Bill Doehrman of Fort Wayne, with 109,398 pins between 1908 and 1981.

THESE are the *records in the Men's Senior* Tournament of the Indiana Bowling Association, set before the competition was divided into age categories: *Single game*: actual 279 pins, Herman Muesing, Fort Wayne, 1977; with handicap, 309 pins by Carl Culberson of Marion, 1977. *Tourney total*: Actual, 973 pins by Stan Sherfick, Indianapolis, 1982; with handicap, 1,030, by Harold Tremps, Anderson, 1979.

THE *best three-game series* in league bowling in Indiana is 859, bowled by Harold Mercer of Richmond March 12, 1980, at Do-Re-Me Lanes in Richmond while bowling the Leavell and Bates Classic League. Mercer bowled games of 269, 290, and 300.

THE *record singles score* in the Indiana Bowling Association state tournament is 786 pins, set in 1978 by Joe Trombetta of Hammond.

DICK WEBER, Indianapolis native, is one of only three professional bowlers to win *three tournaments in a row*, which he did in 1961; is one of only five to roll three perfect games in one tournament, which he did in 1965; and is the first professional bowler to win the *national title in each of the last four decades*, completing the quartet September 6, 1983, with a 212–161 victory over Billy Walden at Canton, Ohio.

BILL DOEHRMAN of Fort Wayne holds the *national record for consecutive appearances* in American Bowling Congress tournaments, 71 in a row, beginning in 1908. (The tournaments were halted from 1943 to 1945.)

Bowling, *Team*

THE 1,245 pins toppled by Candace Fleet and Emma Beard of Fort Wayne in 1947 is the *highest total by a Hoosier pair* in winning the WIBC doubles tournament.

THE *highest ever scored* by an Indiana two-woman team in WIBC tournament play was 1,391, scored in 1953–54 by Jo Berkopes and Lila Lambert of Indianapolis.

THE two-woman team from Indiana with the *all-time high for four games* in the WIBC tournament is Pat Dryer and Marge Hill of Indianapolis, who scored 1,736 to win in 1953–54.

THE *most consecutive losses* in Indiana in a WIBC bowling league is 132, recorded by the team Peanuts of Hammond, which dropped 105 straight in the 1972–73 season and opened the next season with 27 straight losses.

THE all-time *high for three games* by a women's team in Indiana is 3,238, bowled in the 1949–50 season by Hickman Whirlaway at Indianapolis. The same team holds the *single-game team record* of 1,163, also in 1949–50.

THE all-time best for a *single game by a male team* in Indiana is 1,173, bowled in 1971 by Calumet Syrup at Munster.

THE *record for sponsoring teams* in a mixed league in Indiana is held by Wood Vending of Indianapolis which backed 64 teams in the 1978–79 season, closely followed by Baskin-Robbins of Indianapolis, which sponsored 52 teams the same season.

THE *record score for a two-man team* in the Indiana Bowling Association state tournament is 1,438, bowled in 1953 by Merrit Neese and Dick Weber of Indianapolis.

THE Indiana state record for *doubles in the bowling association tournament for women* is 1,464 pins, bowled in 1981 by Sue Smith and Sharon Bombeck of Michigan City in competition at South Bend.

THE *most teams ever to compete* in the Indiana state bowling tournament conducted by the Indiana Bowling Association is 1,240 teams in 1982 in Indianapolis.

THE *record score for a team* in the Indiana Bowling Association state tournament is 3,435, set in 1980 by General Business Service, Columbus, repeating its 1979 title.

THE *record three games* for a team in the Indiana State Bowling Association women's tournament is 2,952, scored by Ittes of Indianapolis in 1979.

THE Indiana team to bowl the *highest total* in winning the WIBC tournament was Hickman Oldsmobile Whirlaway of Indianapolis, which took the title in 1951 with 2,705 pins.

Boxing

THE *only Indiana female to become world champion* in boxing and retire undefeated was Pat Emerick Lancaster, who won the title in November 1949 at Council Bluffs, Iowa, by defeating Joan Hagen, and retired a few months later after receiving an auto crash injury which permanently stiffened one leg. She was 20. Born at Mishawaka and reared at South Bend, Pat had her first professional fight in May 1949. In 1955 she married and soon afterward moved to Tennessee.

THE *all-time greatest boxer* from Indiana, chosen by boxing expert Nat Fleisher, was Kid McCoy, a light-heavyweight from Shelbyville, real name, Norman Selby. McCoy, one of the first to use the name Kid in the ring, won 105 bouts and recorded 35 knockouts. He was knocked out four times.

Fishing

These are the state records for the largest fish of each species caught in Indiana through 1984:

Atlantic salmon: 14 pounds, 4 ounces, caught in Lake Michigan by Gene Tarrant of Crete, Ill., 1979.
Blue catfish: 57 pounds, caught in a Clark County lake by Raymon Ries of New Albany, 1975.
Bluegill: 3 pounds, 4 ounces, caught in a Greene County pond by Harold L. Cafey of New Castle, 1972.
Bowfin (Dogfish): 14 pounds, a tie: one caught in Tamarack Lake (Noble County) by Thomas C. Bobay of Fort Wayne, 1981, and the other in Poison Creek (Perry County) by Jim Glenn of Derby, 1984.
Brook trout: 3 pounds, 15 ounces, caught in Lake Gage (Steuben County) by Sonny Bashore of Paulding, O., 1973.
Brown trout: 22 pounds, 8 ounces, caught in Lake Michigan by Stanley Zygowicz of Whiting, 1983.
Buffalo: 48 pounds, 8 ounces, caught in Pike Lake, Warsaw, by Lowell Walls of Warsaw, 1983.
Bullhead: 4 pounds, caught in Middlefork Reservoir (Wayne County) by John Stephenson of Richmond, 1978.
Burbot: 4 pounds, 8 ounces, caught in Whitewater River (Franklin County) by Don Herron of Connersville, 1981.
Carp: 38 pounds, 1 ounce, caught in a lake in Lake County by Frank J. Drost of Hammond, 1967.
Channel catfish: 37 pounds, 8 ounces, caught in a lake in Vanderburg County by Randy Eugene Jones of Evansville, 1980.
Chinook: 38 pounds, caught in Trail Creek in LaPorte County by Rich Baker of Michigan City, 1980.
Cisco: 3 pounds, 12 ounces, caught in Big Cedar Lake in Whitley County by Phillip Wisniewski of Fort Wayne, 1980.
Coho: 20 pounds, 12 ounces, caught in Lake Michigan by John Beutner of Michigan City, 1972.

Crappie: 4 pounds, 9 ounces, a tie. One was caught in Big Chapman Lake (Kosciusko County) by Joan Draving of Kokomo, 1978, and the other in a Brown County farm pond by Dave Goodnight of Indianapolis, 1980.

Flathead catfish: 79 pounds, 8 ounces, caught in White River (Lawrence County) by Glen T. Simpson of Indianapolis, 1966; also a world record.

Flier: 3 1/2 ounces, caught in a Jackson County stream by Harold H. Otte of Seymour, 1983.

Freshwater drum (white perch): 30 pounds, White River (Martin County) by Garland Fellers of Loogootee, 1963.

Green sunfish: 1 pound, 9 ounces, caught in a Dubois County pond by Norman Fromme of Jasper, 1978.

Lake Sturgeon: 72 pounds, 8 ounces, caught in a LaPorte County lake by David L. Bays of LaPorte, 1978.

Lake Trout: 27 pounds, caught in Lake Michigan by Wayne Campbell of Anderson, 1982.

Largemouth bass: 11 pounds, 11 ounces, caught in Ferdinand Reservoir (DuBois County) by Curt Reynolds of Ferdinand, 1968.

Muskellunge: 23 pounds, 6 ounces, caught in Brookville Reservoir (Franklin County) by Lonzie Furkins of Beech Grove, 1984.

Northern Pike: 28 pounds, 14 ounces, caught in Yellow River in Marshall County by Terry Barner of Osceola, 1983.

Paddlefish: 79 pounds, 6 ounces, caught in a Posey County gravel pit by Kenneth Parker of Fort Branch, 1982.

Rainbow trout: 13 pounds, 13 ounces, caught in Pretty Lake (LaGrange County) by Charles Rasler, Jr., of LaGrange, 1983.

Redear: 3 pounds, 10 ounces, caught in a Brown County lake by R. Peckman of Nashville, 1974.

Rockbass: 3 pounds, caught in Sugar Creek (Hancock County) by David Thomas of Indianapolis, 1969.

Sauger: 6 pounds, 1 ounce, caught in Tippecanoe River (Carroll County) by Mark Bigger of Lafayette, 1983.

Smallmouth bass: 6 pounds, 8 ounces, caught in a Rush County stream by Jim Connerly of New Castle, 1970.

Spotted bass: 5 pounds, 1 1/2 ounces, caught in a Howard County lake by John William-Pio of Kokomo, 1975.

Steelhead trout: 24 pounds, 13 ounces, caught in Lake Michigan by Ron Nance of Merrillville, 1983.

Striped Bass: 23 pounds, 7 ounces in Brookville Lake (Franklin County) by Eugene Clemmens of Cincinnati, 1984.

Sucker: 10 pounds, 10 ounces in White River in Bartholomew County by Ken Rowe of North Judson, 1984.

Tiger muskie: 16 pounds, 2 ounces, caught in Lake Holiday (Porter County) by Robert Keough of Lake Station, 1982.

Tiger trout: 3 pounds, caught in Lake Michigan by Mike Ratter of Calumet City, Ill., 1978.

Walleye: 14 pounds, 4 ounces, tie: the first was caught in the Kankakee River (Lake County) by Leon Richart of Waldron, 1974; the second was caught in Tippecanoe River (Pulaski County) by Donald Tedford of Indianapolis, 1977.

Warmouth: 1 pound, .48 ounce, caught in a Clay County farm pond by John R. Hayes of Bowling Green, 1981.

White bass: 4 pounds, 3 ounces, caught in Lake Freeman (Carroll County) by James Wagner of Lafayette, 1965.

White catfish: 5 pounds, 4 ounces, caught in a Hendricks County pond by Gary R. Eggers of Plainfield, 1978.

Yellow bass: 2 pounds, 4 ounces, caught on Monroe Reservoir (Monroe County) by Don Stalker of Bedford, 1977; also a world record.

Yellow perch: 2 pounds, 8 ounces, caught in a Vigo County gravel pit by Roy W. Burkel, Jr., of Terre Haute, 1981.

Football, *College*

THE *first artificial playing surface* in Indiana was installed at Indiana State University in 1967. It covered 72,000 square feet, weighed 35 tons, and cost $175,000 installed.

THE *first football game in Indiana on artificial turf* was September 16, 1967, at Terre Haute between Indiana State University and Eastern Illinois, which the Hoosier school won 41–6 before a crowd of 10,500.

THE *largest attendance* at a Big Ten football game in Indiana was the 71,629 who saw Purdue University play host to Indiana University at West Lafayette November 22, 1980.

THE *largest crowd ever to see an Indiana football team play* probably was the 120,000 who packed Soldiers' Field in Chicago to see Notre Dame play Navy in 1927.

BIG TEN RECORDS

These are the best marks in the Big Ten by an Indiana school or player.

INDIVIDUAL

Most points, 1 game
  30, Mike Northington of Purdue against Iowa, November 3, 1973.

Most field goals, 1 game
> 5 by Rick Anderson of Purdue against Michigan State October 25, 1980 (shared by others)

Longest run from scrimmage, 1 game
> 100 yards, Mickey Erehart of Indiana University against Iowa, November 9, 1912

Longest score from scrimmage
> 94 by Mike Pruitt of Purdue against Iowa November 2, 1974

Longest pass and longest pass for a touchdown
> 95 yards by Len Dawson to Erich Barnes, Purdue versus Northwestern, November 12, 1955

Longest punt return
> 93 yards, held by both Steve Porter of Indiana against Wisconsin October 24, 1970, and Phil Mateja of Purdue against Iowa October 6, 1951

Longest run with a blocked kick
> 92 yards by Earl Falson of Indiana against Michigan State November 8, 1958, made during a field goal attempt

Most touchdowns, 1 game
> 5 by Mike Northington of Purdue against Iowa November 3, 1973 (tied by several others)

Best pass percentage, 1 game
> .857 by Dale Samuels of Purdue against Illinois October 25, 1957, with 12 of 14 attempts

Longest run with a recovered fumble
> 92 yards by Dale Kenelpp of Indiana against Minnesota November 4, 1978

Most yards per play, 1 game
> 17.9 by Mike Pruitt of Purdue against Iowa November 2, 1974

Most yards passing, 1 game
> 516 by Scott Campbell of Purdue against Ohio State October 31, 1981, completing 31 of 52 (second best in the Big Ten)

Most total yards
> 477 by Scott Campbell of Purdue against Ohio State October 31, 1981—516 yards passing and minus 39 yards rushing

Most touchdown passes, 1 game
> 4 by Reggie Arnold of Purdue against Iowa October 22, 1977

Most field goals
> 15 in the 1980 season by Rick Anderson of Purdue out of 21 attempts (second best in all the Big Ten)

Total net yards, season
> 1,176 by Otis Armstrong of Purdue in 1972

Most passes tried
> 331 by Scott Campbell in 1982 (5th best in all the Big Ten)

Best pass-completion percentage, season
.682 by Mark Herrmann of Purdue in 1980, 174 of 259
Most net yards gained passing
2,350 by Mark Herrmann of Purdue in 1980
Most touchdown passes, season
16 by Scott Campbell of Purdue, 1981
Most yards rushing and passing, season
2,356 by Scott Campbell of Purdue in 1981, 93 rushing
Most passes caught, season
51 by Dave Young of Purdue in 1980
All-time best receiving
180 passes caught by Dave Young of Purdue, 1977–1980
Most passes completed
181 by Scott Campbell of Purdue in 1982
Most passes intercepted
4 by Paul Berry of Purdue against Wisconsin October 9, 1976
Most touchdowns from kickoffs
3 by Stan Brown of Purdue in 1970 (100, 98 and 93 yards)
Best kickoff-return average
41.1 yards by Stan Brown of Purdue in 1970 (12 for 493 yards)
Most plays, individual
393 by Scott Campbell of Purdue in 1982 (62 rushes, 331 passes)

TEAM

Most plays
103 by Purdue against Michigan October 25, 1980
Highest losing score
38 by Purdue against Wisconsin (42) November 12, 1983
Most rushes
92 by Purdue against Iowa October 26, 1968
Best average per rush
10.33 by Purdue against Illinois October 2, 1943
Most first downs rushing
31 by Purdue against Iowa October 26, 1966
Fewest first downs rushing
0 by Indiana against Michigan November 12, 1949
Fewest yards gained rushing
59 by Indiana in 1948
Most first downs
34 by Purdue against Michigan State October 25, 1980
Most yards gained passing
304.9 by Purdue in 1980 (8 games)
Highest pass completion percentage
.673 by Purdue in 1980 (177 of 283)

Highest pass completion percentage by opponents
  .625 by Purdue in 1982 (9 games)
Most yards gained passing by opponents
  493.9 by Indiana in 1983 (9 games9)
Most opponent first downs
  27.0 by Indiana in 1946 (6 games)
Most fumbles, season average
  5.5 by Indiana in 1946 (6 games); tied by others
Fewest fumbles, season
  1 by Purdue in 1875 (8 games)
Fewest yards gained, season
  118.6 by Purdue in 1942 (5 games)
Lowest fumble average
  .25 by Purdue in 1975
Most opponents' fumbles recovered
  3 by Purdue in 1943 (6 games); tied by others
Fewest fumbles recovered per game
  .22 by Purdue in 1983 (9 games)
Fewest penalties
  2.0 by Indiana in 1946 (6 games)

THE Indiana school with the record for *appearances in bowl games* is the University of Notre Dame, the first Hoosier school to appear in the Rose Bowl (1925), the Orange Bowl (1975), the Sugar Bowl (1973), the Cotton Bowl (1970), and the Gator Bowl (1976).

THE first college to have a *black player* in Indiana was Indiana University, which played Preston Eagleston at halfback in 1893.

THE only *Big Ten football coach-of-the-year* from Indiana has been Jim Young, chosen for the honor in 1978 while coaching Purdue University. Two Indiana coaches have been national coaches of the year: Alvin N. (Bo) McMillan of Indiana University in 1945 and John Pont of I.U. in 1967.

THE *best football coaching percentage* at an Indiana college or university is that of Knute Rockne of Notre Dame with a mark of 105 wins, 12 losses, and 5 ties. Rockne teams won 20 straight, all the games in 1919 and 1920 and the first two games of 1921.

JOHN W. ESTERLINE, a fullback at Purdue University in 1894, devised a way to take the ball from the quarterback while in the midst of a leap and kick it before coming down, thus making the *first quick kick* in Indiana, if not the nation. Its first use was against Minnesota, the second opponent of the 1894–95 season. Esterline played three more years, one as a graduate student.

CREDIT for the *first successful forward pass* in football generally goes to Knute Rockne, a back for Notre Dame, and quarterback Gus Dorias, who threw the passes to Rockne in 1913 in a game against Army. The passes were the result of summer practice by Rockne and Dorias.

THE only Indiana University to be chosen *national football champion* on the basis of news wire polls is the University of Notre Dame, which was named tops in the ratings in 1943, 1946, 1947, 1949, 1966, 1973, and 1977. Selection of such mythical champions was not begun until 1936.

National Collegiate Athletic Association—These Hoosier records are held in National Collegiate Athletic Association (NCAA) tournament play among Division II schools:

Completion percentage
Frank Houk of Ball State, completing 12 of 15 passes in 1965 for a percentage of .800
Most passes tried
Dave Harvey of Wabash, throwing 47 against Widener December 3, 1977, in losing 39–36
Most passes caught
Randy Mellinger of Wabash, catching 11 against Widener, December 3, 1977
Longest pass play
Dave Harvey to Tom Conway for an 82-yard Wabash touchdown November 19, 1977, against St. John's

THE first college quarterback to *pass more than 9,000 yards in a career* was Mark Herrmann of Purdue University, who completed for 9,946 yards, 1978–81, averaging 210 per game. Herrmann was a graduate of Carmel High School.

THE Butler University football team *held its opponents scoreless* for 51 quarters, 12 3/4 games, a national record. The bulldogs were finally scored on October 15, 1983, by Georgetown of Kentucky to end the streak.

THE *collegiate career scoring record* by a Hoosier is 468 points by Elmer Oliphant of Linton, an all-American halfback. In the days before eligibility rules, he played four years at Purdue University and three years for Army.

THE *greatest scorer in football in one season* in Indiana was Ed McGovern, who scored 165 points in 1942 playing for Rose Poly Institute (now Rose-Hulman Institute).

THE *best win percentage* among major colleges in Indiana is that of Notre Dame, which in 93 years won 621 games, lost 172, and tied 39 for a winning mark of .770.

Football, *High school*

THE *first high schools to have football teams* were Indianapolis High School and Terre Haute High School in 1892. Their opponents were college teams of the time; they did not play each other.

These are the reported records in Indiana high schools during regular season play:

TEAMS

Most points in a game
  128 by Kirklin against Waveland (o), 1921
  (115 by Batesville against Decatur, o, in recent times, October 8, 1983)
Most touchdowns in a season
  42 by Hamilton Southeastern, 1981
Most yards gained, season
  5,582 by Hamilton Southeastern, 1981 (14 games)
Longest undefeated string and most consecutive wins
  60 by Bloomington South, 1967–1973 (60-0-0)

INDIVIDUALS

Longest field goal
  61 yards by Jerry Spicer of Hobart, 1975

SEASON

Most points in a season
  265 by Burt Austin of Franklin Central, Marion County, 1982
Most rushes, season
  440 by Pete Buchanan of Plymouth, 1977
Most passes, season
  353 by Ron Moyer, Hamilton Southeastern, 1981

Most yards passing, season
   3,250 by Ron Moyer of Hamilton Southeastern, 1981
Most receptions in a season
   96 by Doug Stis of Hamilton Southeastern, 1981
Most yards receiving, season
   1,665 by Doug Stis of Hamilton Southeastern, 1981
Best reception average per game
   118.9 yards by Doug Stis of Hamilton Southeastern, 1981 (14 games)
      (75 catch minimum)
Best reception percentage, season
   17.3 by Doug Stis of Hamilton Southeastern, 1981

CAREER

Most points in a career
   587 by Burt Austin of Franklin Central, Marion County, 1980–1982
Most yards rushing, career
   4,666 by Burt Austin of Franklin Central, Marion County, 1980–1981
Most touchdown passes
   41 by Ron Moyer of Hamilton Southeastern, 1978–1981
Most passes, career
   740 by Ron Moyer of Hamilton Southeastern, 1978–1981
Most yards passing, career
   6,167 by Ron Moyer of Hamilton Southeastern, 1978–1981

IHSAA Football Championships, Final Games

SCORING, TEAMS

Most points	44 by Tippecanoe Valley against Hamilton Southeastern (Division A), 1979
Most touchdowns	7 by Tippecanoe Valley against Hamilton Southeastern (Division A), 1979
Most touchdowns, rushing	6 by Tippecanoe Valley against Hamilton Southeastern (Division A), 1979
Most touchdowns passing	3-way tie: 3 by Carmel against Fort Wayne Dwenger (Division AAA), 1978; Sheridan against North Judson (Division A), and Warren Central against Hobart (Division AAAA), 1984
Most field goals	2 by Indianapolis Ritter against Tippecanoe Valley (Division A), 1977

Longest run	79 yards by Dave Slater of Fort Wayne Luers against Indianapolis Chatard (Division AA), 1983
Best average per carry	8.3 (19 carries for 157 yards) by Nick Barnes of Mishawaka Marian against Providence (Division A), 1973

PASSING

Most attempts	43 by Tim O'Brien of Hobart against Warren Central (Division AAAA), 1984
Most completions	24 (of 43) by Tim O'Brien of Hobart against Warren Central (Division AAAA), 1984
Most yards	250 by Tim O'Brien of Hobart against Warren Central (Division AAAA), 1984
Best average	29.5 by Mike Loftus of Jasper against Mishawaka Marian (Division AA), 1973
Most touchdown passes	3-way tie: 3 by Jeff Parker of Merrillville against Indianapolis Cathedral (Division AAA), 1976; David Broecker of Carmel against F. W. Dwenger (Division AAA), 1978; Jeff George of Warren Central against Hobart (Division AAAA), 1984
Longest pass	59 yards by Jeff Parker to Tom Szmagaj of Merrillville against Indianapolis Cathedral (Division AAA), 1976
Most receptions	Tie: 7 by Jon Ogle of Carmel against Valparaiso (Division AAA), 1975; Bob Stephenson of Evansville Reitz against Portage (Division AAA), 1977
Most yards	132 by Steve Braun of Jasper against Mishawaka Marian (Division AA), 1976
Longest pass reception play	61 yards by Rick Packard of Oak Hill against Southbridge (Division A), 1982
Best average pass reception	Tie: 35 by Burt Austin of Franklin Central against McCutcheon (Division AA), 1982; Rick Packard of Oak Hill against Southridge (Division A), 1982
Most passes tried	43 by Hobart against Warren Central (Division AAAA), 1984
Fewest passes tried	0 by Blackford against Noblesville (Division AA), 1979

Most yards gained	219 by Merrillville against Indianapolis Cathedral (Division AAA), 1976
Most interceptions	5 by Indianapolis Chatard against West Lafayette (Division AA), 1984
Interceptions by individuals	2 in a game by 9 players from 1975 to 1984
Most yards returned on interceptions	88 by Tippecanoe Valley against Hamilton Southeastern (Division A), 1979
Most yards gained on interceptions	72 by Bill Jamison of Tippecanoe Valley against Hamilton Southeastern (Division A), 1979
Longest interception run	60 yards by Bill Jamison of Tippecanoe Valley against Hamilton Southeastern (Division A), 1979

PUNTING

Most punts	Tie: 7 by Greenfield-Central against Mishawaka Marian (Division AA), 1975; Brownsburg against Goshen (Division AA), 1978
Best average	43.8 by Fort Wayne Dwenger against Roncalli of Indianapolis (Division AA), 1983
Most returned	4 by Fort Wayne Dwenger against Carmel (Division AAA), 1978
Most yards returned	48 by Northwood against Franklin Central (Division AA), 1980
Best return average	24 by Northwood against Franklin Central (Division AA), 1980
Longest punt	69 yards by Blair Kiel of Columbus East against Hobart (Division AAA), 1979
Most punt returns	5 by Kevin Shomber, of Concord against Brownsburg (Division AAA), 1984
Most yards on a punt return	63 by Mark Allen of Valparaiso against Carmel (Division AAA), 1975
Best average punt return	22 (2 returns) by Mark Drobac of Hobart against Carmel (Division AAA), 1980

SCORING, INDIVIDUAL

Most points	30 by Tim Alspaugh of Tippecanoe Valley against Hamilton Southeastern (Division A), 1979

Most touchdowns	5 by Tim Alspaugh, Tippecanoe Valley against Hamilton Southeastern (Division A), 1979
Most touchdowns rushing	Same as above
Most touchdowns passing receptions	3 by Lanch Scheib of Warren Central against Hobart (Division AAAA), 1984
Most field goals	2 by Paul Loviscek of Indianapolis Ritter against Tippecanoe Valley (Division A), 1977
Most extra points	4-way tie: 4 by Eric Stauffer of Warren Central against Hobart (Division AAAA) and Karl Selander of Indianapolis Chatard against West Lafayette (Division AA), 1984; Tom Male of Mishawaka Marian against Greenfield Central (Division AA), 1975, and Chuck Hansen of Merrillville against Indianapolis Cathedral (Division AA), 1976
Longest touchdown run	80 yards by Rod Coffey of Hamilton Southeastern against Tippecanoe Valley (Division A), 1979
Longest touchdown pass reception	54 yards by Tom Szmagaj of Merrillville (Division AAA), 1976
Longest field goal	41 yards by Mike Budzielek of Hobart against Castle (Division AAA), 1982

FIRST DOWNS

Most	27 by Mishawaka Marian against Jasper (Division AA), 1976
Most rushing	16 by Portage against Evansville Reitz (Division AAA), 1977
Most passing	14 by Hobart against Warren Central (Division AAAA), 1984

RUSHING

Most attempts	40 by Tim Alspaugh of Tippecanoe Valley against Hamilton Southeastern (Division A), 1979
Most yards	241 by Burt Austin of Franklin Central against Goshen (Division AA), 1981

KICKOFFS

Most returns	3-way tie: 4 by Tom Bowling of Indianapolis Cathedral against Merrillville (Division AAA), 1976; Orlando Guest of Evansville Reitz against Portage (Division AAA), 1977; Dan Folta of West Lafayette against Indianapolis Chatard (Division AA), 1984
Most yards on kickoff returns	93 (2 returns) by Rod Coffey of Hamilton Southeastern against Tippecanoe Valley (Division A), 1979; also best average of 46.5 yards per return
Longest single kickoff return	94 yards by Barry Ehle of Woodlan against Hamilton Southeastern (Division A), 1981
Most returns by a team	9 by McCutcheon against Franklin Central (Division AA), 1982
Most yards on kickoff returns	117 by Hamilton Southeastern against Tippecanoe Valley (Division A), 1979
Best kickoff-return average	29.2 by Hamilton Southeastern against Tippecanoe Valley (Division A), 1979

TOTAL OFFENSE

Most plays	72 by Sheridan against North Judson (Division A), 1984 (61 rushing, 11 passing)
Most yards	373 by Mishawaka Marian against Jasper (Division AA), 1976
Most rushes	61 by Sheridan against North Judson (Division A), 1984
Most yards rushing	349 by Portage against Evansville Reitz (Division AAA), 1977
Fewest yards lost rushing	1 by Hamilton Southeastern against Tippecanoe Valley (Division A), 1979

DEFENSE

Fewest plays allowed	3-way tie: 34 by Mishawaka Marian against Greenfield Central (Division AA), 1975; Tippecanoe Valley against Hamilton Southeastern (Division A), 1979; Hobart against Carmel (Division AAA), 1980

Fewest yards allowed	70 by Mishawaka Marian against Greenfield Central (Division AA), 1975
Fewest first downs allowed	Tie: 2 by North Judson against Sheridan (Division A), 1984; Roncalli against Fort Wayne Dwenger (Division AAA), 1983
Fewest first downs by rushing only	3 by six schools
Fewest rushing attempts	17 by North Judson against Sheridan (Division A), 1984
Fewest yards allowed rushing	23 by Sheridan against North Judson (Division A), 1984
Most yards tackled for a loss	56 by Carmel against Hobart (Division AAA), 1980
Fewest net yards allowed, rushing	25 by Castle against Hobart (Division AAA), 1982
Smallest average gain allowed, rushing	1.0 by Castle against Hobart (Division AAA), 1982
Fewest pass completions allowed	Tie: 0 by Garrett against North Knox (Division A), 1974; Fort Wayne Snider against Carmel (Division AAA), 1981
Fewest yards allowed by passing	Tie: 0 by North Knox against Garrett (Division A), 1974; Carmel against Fort Wayne Snider (Division AAA), 1981

TEAM RECORDS

Most penalties	9 by Tippecanoe Valley against Hamilton Southeastern (Division A), 1979
Most yards penalized	121 by Tippecanoe Valley against Hamilton Southeastern (Division A), 1979
Fewest penalties	0 by Carmel against Valparaiso (Division AAA), 1975
Fewest yards penalized	0 by Valparaiso against Carmel (Division AAA), 1975
Most fumbles	6 by North Judson against Sheridan (Division A), 1980
Most fumbles lost	5 by Fountain Central against Lawrenceburg (Division A), 1978

Football, *Professional*

A TEAM organized in Pine Village in 1898 decided to hire players and turn professional in 1915, thereby becoming Indiana's *first professional team.* The squad was put together by C. G. Beckett, who taught school there. This independent team was unbeaten. Their first professional game was against Wabash, which they won 7-0. That same year they played the Purdue All-Stars on Thanksgiving Day after hiring Jim Thorpe, the legendary athlete, who was coaching at Indiana University, for $250. They lost only 7 games in 20 years.

THE *most fumbles lost* by a Hoosier in professional football in a single game were the 7 dropped by Len Dawson November 15, 1964, when his Kansas City team played San Diego. Dawson, quarterback at Purdue before turning professional, also holds the career mark of 84 fumbles lost while playing for Pittsburgh, Cleveland, Dallas, and Kansas City.

PETE PIHOS, an All-American from Indiana University, is the *only player* in the National Football League to be named to the *single platoon all-league team,* the *league all-defensive team* and the *league all-offensive team.* Pihos, who was drafted by the Eagles in 1945, was on the single platoon team in 1948 and 1949, was on the defensive team in 1952 and on the offensive team in 1953, 1954, and 1955.

THE Hoosier who has led the National Football League the most often in *percentage of passes completed* is Len Dawson with eight seasons, 1962, 1964-69, and 1975. His *six seasons in a row* is also a record.

Golf, *Amateur*

THE *first black to win a golf championship* in Indiana was George Roddy of Indianapolis, who won the Indianapolis Amateur Golf Tournament in July 1967.

THE *first bona fide golf course* laid out for that purpose in Indiana is believed to have been the old Indianapolis Country Club, established in 1897. It occupied the present site of the Woodstock Country Club.

THE *oldest golfer in the nation to hit a hole-in-one* is William H. Diddel of Indianapolis, who was 93 when he dropped one on a single shot at the Royal Poinciana Course, Naples, Fla., January 1, 1978, in the 142-yard 8th hole.

Golf, *College*

THE Indiana school to win the *most Big Ten golf championships in a row* is Purdue University, which won with Joe Campbell in 1956 and 1957 and followed with victories by John Konsek in 1958, 1959, and 1960.

THE *first national intercollegiate golf champion* from an Indiana school was Fred Wampler of Purdue University, who won the title in 1950.

The first Indiana school to capture the *national intercollegiate golf team championship* was the University of Notre Dame in 1944.

IN Big ten tournament play, Fred Wampler of Purdue University holds the record for the *lowest finishing round* with 64 in 1950.

FRED WAMPLER and John Konsek, both of Purdue, lead in the *number of Big Ten titles* with 3 each, Wampler in 1948–50 and Konsek in 1958–60. Only one other Big Ten golfer has won as many.

PURDUE holds the *team record* in Big Ten tournament play with 1,417 in 1981 on these scores: Rick Dalpos, 278; Eric Dutt, 283; Mike Granger, 285; Guy Wuollet, 285; Jay Smith, 286.

Golf, *Professional*

THE *oldest member* of the Ladies Professional Golf Association tour to win *two tournaments in a season* was Sandy Spuzich of Speedway, who in 1982 captured the Corning (N.Y.) Classic and the Mary Kay Golf Classic at Dallas, Tex. Sandy was 45.

THE *leader in winnings* among active women golfers from Indiana in the LPGA is Sandra Spuzich of Speedway, whose lifetime earnings midway through the 1983 season were about $460,000. She also holds the single-year earnings record for active Indiana LPGA golfers with $89,822 in 1982.

Gymnastics

THE *most state high school boys championships* in gymnastics have been won by Columbus North High School, formerly Columbus High School, with 11 titles from 1967 to 1979. The school also has won the *most consecutive titles* with five, from 1975 through 1979.

THE sole *gymnastics record in National Collegiate Athletic Association tournament competition* held by a Hoosier is the 5 individual titles in a career, compiled by Kurt Thomas of Indiana State University, with victories in the all-around in 1977 and 1979, the horizontal bars in 1979, and the parallel bars in 1977 and 1979.

Hockey

THE *first female hockey referee* accredited by the Amateur Hockey Association was Niegel Allen of Indianapolis, who was a volunteer official in the Indianapolis Youth Hockey League in 1972 after passing the hockey association test; she was one of three females certified in the nation.

THE record number of *home victories in a row* in the Central Hockey League is the 33 games won in the 1982–83 season by the Indianapolis Checkers. The Checkers also set the league record for the *most straight losses* that same season with 14. The Central Hockey League was formed in 1961.

Hunting

THE *most deer* ever taken in Indiana *in a single hunting season* was 27,671 killed in 1984, almost 2,500 more than the previous high, which occurred in 1983 when hunters took a total harvest of 25,232.

DEER SIZE is determined by number and size of antler points and distance between antlers in typical category for ordinary antlers, and non-typical category for those with unusual configurations. Records are kept for both gun and bow-and-arrow hunters. *Gun*: The *largest deer with typical antlers* was taken by William W. Cripe, Frankfort, in Clinton County in 1974, and had an antler measurement of 197 1/8 inches. The *largest non-typical deer* was one shot by Zoltan Dobsa of Cincinnati in Switzerland County in 1977, measuring 154 1/8 inches. *Bow*: The records for bow-and-arrow hunters are: *typical*, shot by Hale Harvey of Huntington in Huntington County, 1967, measuring 189 4/8; *non-typical*, taken by Walter Sobczak, Lowell, in Lake County, 1979, measuring 193 6/8 inches.

THE *largest turkey* taken in modern-day hunting (since 1969) was one of 26 pounds, shot by Jim Tomes of Charlestown in Washington County on opening day of the 1983 season, April 20. With him on the hunt was Roy Hobbs of Pekin. Indiana biologists, the only source on turkey size, said the 26-pounder surpassed by at least 1 1/2 pounds the largest theretofore known. The number of turkeys killed in the 1985 hunting season was a record 253.

Olympics

THE *most gold medals* won in Olympic competition is 10 by Raymond Clarence Ewry of Purdue University; he was a native of Lafayette, born October 14, 1874. Ewry won the standing high jump and the standing long jump in 1900, 1904, 1906,* and 1908, and won the standing triple jump in 1900 and 1904. He became crippled later in life, was long a benefactor of Purdue sports, and died September 27, 1937. His records are unlikely to be surpassed since there no longer is competition in these events.

THE *most gold medals in a single Olympics* were seven won by Mark Spitz, swimmer for Indiana University, in 1972. His gold medals were for the 100-meter freestyle, 200-meter freestyle, 100-meter butterfly, 200-meter butterfly, 4-by-100 freestyle relay, 4-by-200 freestyle relay, and 4-by-100 medley relay. Spitz also won gold medals in the 1968 Olympics in the 100- and 200-meter relays. All his wins in 1972 were world records at the time.

MARK SPITZ, swimmer for Indiana University, holds the record for the *most medals* won in Olympic competition, 11. He won nine gold medals in two Olympics, plus a silver medal in the 100-meter butterfly and a bronze medal in the 100-meter freestyle in 1968.

THE *first Hoosier named to the Olympic Basketball Committee* was Marion K. Summers of Brownstown, who headed the men's basketball committee from 1969 to 1972 and managed the American team at the 1972 Munich games.

The *largest crowd to watch a basketball game in the U.S.* is 67,596, attending the Hoosier Dome July 9, 1984, when the U.S. Olympic team played a group of National Basketball Association players.

*The 1906 games in Athens were an exception to the games every four years and they were not recognized by the International

Olympic Committee. However, they marked the first time the U.S. had an Olympic organization and assembled a national team for the games. (*The World Almanac, Encyclopedia Americana*)

Racing, *Automobile*

THE winner of the *first Great American Race* from California to Indianapolis was a 1941 Cadillac driven by Michael G. Anderson of Tucson, Ariz., which finished the 2,800-mile competition May 28, 1983, seven days after the contest for pre-1942 autos began. Of the 69 starting cars, 59 finished.

ON the basis of performance, the *greatest drag racer* in Indiana is Bob Glidden of Whiteland, who was five times national hot rod champion, was undefeated in one season, and in another season won 10 major meet championships. With drag-strip victory October 21, 1984, in the National Hot Rod Association World Finals at Pomona Raceway at Los Angeles, Cal., Glidden brought his string of wins in national events to 37, a record for any Hoosier.

Drag racing performance is based on type of car and type of fuel being used and is divided into the time taken to go a quarter mile and the top speed recorded during the run. These are the records in Indiana (spring, 1984). *Funny car*: The record in this division (modified autos) is an elapsed time of 5.73 seconds, established in September 1982 at Indianapolis Raceway Park by Don Prudhomme of California. The top speed in this division was set by Mark Oswald September 1982 at Indianapolis Raceway Park at 257.87 miles an hour. *Pro stock*: The fastest speed in this division in Indiana is 181.81 miles an hour, achieved in September 1983 by Lee Shepherd at the National Hot Rod Association meet at Clermont. This speed was topped outside the state by Bob Glidden of Whiteland, who at the same time set a national record for elapsed time and speed, running the course in 7.53 seconds at an average speed of 185.87 miles an hour. The event was in February 1985 at Pomona Raceway, Los Angeles. *Top alcohol funny cars*: The elapsed time of 6.308 seconds and the speed of 223.88 were national bests, established May 1, 1984, by Brad Anderson of California at Indianapolis Raceway Park in the National Hot Rod Association Sportsnationals.

THE first race between an Oldsmobile and Cadillac and perhaps the *first auto race* of any kind in the state was March 24, 1903, between Indianapolis and Columbus. An Olds, driven by Earl Fisher, beat a Cadillac, driven by W. A. Carr, when the

Cadillac lost bearings 2 miles north of Columbus and could not continue. The race was to have been from Indianapolis to Columbus and return, so the competition lasted less than half the distance. The time for the Olds to complete the 43 miles from Monument Circle in downtown Indianapolis to Columbus was 3 hours, 10 minutes.

THE *fastest Indiana passenger car* of record is a 1953 Studebaker, driven over a flat course at a peak speed of 181.810 miles an hour in 1969 by B. Geisler. The car, although rebuilt, had only off-the-shelf parts. The record stood until 1983 when a Camaro driven by Andy Granatelli reached 184.238 mph.

THE *oldest speedway* in Indiana and the *fastest half-mile course in the world* is Winchester Speedway, constructed in 1915 with a race surface which ranges from flat to a bank of 34 degrees. Indiana and U.S. records at the track are: *Late model stock*: one lap in 15.741 seconds, 115.8 miles an hour by Mark Martin, Charlotte, N.C.; October 3, 1980. *Midgets*: one lap in 16.562 seconds, 108.68 miles an hour by Bob Cicconi, Prospect Park, Pa.; March 15, 1981.

THE first time crash helmets were worn in American racing was in the 1916 Indianapolis 500-Mile Race when Eddie Rickenbacker and Pete Henderson donned steel headgear.

THE 500-Mile Race in 1911 marked the *first long-distance automobile race on a closed course* or track and was won by Ray Harroun, 29 years old, in 6 hours, 41 minutes, and 8 seconds. Forty cars started, 26 finished; one contestant was killed in an accident; the crowd was estimated at 85,000

Racing, *Automobile*: THE 500-MILE RACE

LARRY BISCEGLIA of Long Beach, Calif., holds the record for being *first in line* for the opening of the Indianapolis Motor Speedway for activities leading up to the 500-Mile Race—37 straight years, as of 1985. He has used only three cars for his annual trips to Indianapolis from his homes in Chicago, Arizona, and California.

THE *first* 500-*Mile Race* in Indianapolis in 1911 was won by Ray Harroun, the 1910 American Automobile Association driving champion, who came out of retirement to compete. The Indianapolis native was an engineer and designer for Howard Marmon, president of the Nordyke and Marmon Company, which built the 6-cylinder car called the *Yellow Jacket*. It quickly was dubbed the *Wasp* by sportswriters. Said Harroun, who got $14,000 for the victory: "I wouldn't drive in another race, not even for twice as much money."

CARS

THE first racer to appear at the Speedway with *front-wheel drive* was one designed in 1925 by Harry Miller, who had 17 entries.

DAVE EVANS drove the *first diesel-powered car* to compete in the 500-Mile Race, the Cummins Diesel Special No. 8, which finished 13th in the 1931 race. Entered because of a waiver in the rules prohibiting non-gasoline cars, the Cummins was the *first car to go the distance nonstop* at an average speed of 86.107 miles an hour.

THE *first appearance of the Novi-type race car* at the 500-Mile Race was in 1941 when Ralph Hepburn drove a Bowes Seal Fast supercharged V8 designed by Bud Winfield. He finished 4th with an average speed of 113.631.

THE *only car with a number* 13 ever driven in the 500-Mile Race was the Mason Special of 1914 with Jack Mason behind the wheel. Mason was relieved by Lee Oldfield. The car went out on the 66th lap because of a broken piston.

A *rear-engine car* appeared for the 500-Mile Race in 1938, but failed to qualify. The first to make the race was in 1939, a 6-cylinder supercharged, four-wheel-drive creation driven by George Bailey, who finished 26th. The car, No. 17, went out on the 47th lap with a valve malfunction.

THE *first rocket car* tested on the Indianapolis Motor Speedway track was one driven 110 miles an hour May 21, 1946, by Duke Nalon. Sponsored by the Estee Bedding Company of Chicago, the car had twin rockets built by General Tire and Rubber Company, Aero-Jet Division. After going 80 miles an hour on gasoline, Nalon fired the 41-pound rockets one at a time. Nobody could explain clearly what the test proved.

DRIVERS

THE record number of *appearances in consecutive 500-Mile Races* is 28 by A. J. Foyt, Jr.

THE *first driver to win* the 500-Mile Race *without a relief* was Jules Goux of France, victor in 1913.

THE first time a *father and son competed* in the same 500-Mile Race was in 1983 when Al Unser qualified at a speed of 201.954 miles an hour and his son, Al Unser, Jr., 21, qualified at 202.146 miles an hour.

FRENCHMAN Jules Goux reportedly consumed 6 pints of chilled champagne during the 500-Mile Race in 1913, no doubt the first, and probably the last, to *drink and drive* in winning the race. His Peugeot averaged 86.03 miles an hour.

THE first driver given the *rookie-of-the-year award* at the 500-Mile Race was Art Cross in 1952, who finished 5th at a speed of 124.292 miles an hour.

THE *most laps run in competition* at the Indianapolis Motor Speedway was 3,996 by A. J. Foyt, Jr., in 28 races.

The record for *laps leading* the 500-Mile Race is 613, set by Ralph DePalma in races in 1911, 1912, 1915, 1919, 1920, and 1921. DePalma's greatest number of leading laps in one race was 196 in 1912.

THE *record amount won in lap prizes*, given for leading a lap in the 500-Mile Race, is $101,150, awarded to Al Unser, Sr., in his career at Indianapolis. Unser has led 595 laps, second highest number in Speedway history.

BOTH Roland Free and Cy Marshall drove in the 500-Mile Race and *did not compete again for 17 years*. In 1930 Free finished 20th after going out on the 69th lap with clutch failure, and Marshall was 26th, crashing on the 29th lap. In 1947, when both drivers returned to the race, Free was 28th and Marshall 8th.

No other driver has *covered as many miles* in competition in the 500-Mile Race as A. J. Foyt, Jr., with 9,990.

CLIFF WOODBURY, who sat in the pole position for the 1929 race, crashed in the fourth lap, then served as relief driver for three others, making him the *only driver to operate four cars* in the same 500-Mile Race.

THE *most rookies* competing in the 500-Mile Race, other than the first race in 1911, was in 1950 when 21 beginners took the driver's test, including Bill Vukovich and Bob Sweikert, later drivers of note, who did not make the 1950 race.

THE first and so far only time *two rookies of the year* were named for the 500-Mile Race was in 1961 when Parnelli Jones and Bobby Marshman shared the honors. Jones started 5th in the race and finished 12th. Marshman started last and finished 7th.

THE first man to drive the 500-Mile Race *without a stop* was Dave

Evans, who finished 13th in 1931 at the wheel of a Cummins diesel race car.

THE first race driver to *win the 500-Mile Race pole and also win the race* was Jimmy Murphy in 1922.

ONLY two winners of the 500-Mile Race have *announced their retirements* from Victory Lane—Ray Harroun, winner of the first race in 1911, and Sam Hanks, who won in 1957.

JIM MCELREATH, at 52, became the *oldest driver* to race in the 500-Mile Race in 1980. Born February 18, 1928, McElreath drove his first "500" in 1962 and was rookie of the year.

THE champion in 500-Mile Race *winnings* is Al Unser, Sr., who has collected a career total of $1,708,097.17 as of 1985. Close behind is A. J. Foyt, Jr., with $1,632.754.56.

THE *first woman to qualify* for the 500-Mile Race was Janet Guthrie in 1977. Although she completed her rookie test in 1976, she did not make the race. May 10, 1977, she crashed, but qualified in the repaired car May 22, 1977, at an average speed of 188.404 miles an hour. After completing 27 laps of the race, a broken valve seal sidelined her car, giving her a finish of 29th place. In 1978 she finished 9th, her best finish.

THE *fasted lap by a female driver* at the Indianapolis Motor Speedway is 191 miles an hour, turned in 1982 by Desire Wilson in a qualifying attempt. The 29-year-old South African did not complete qualifying, however, because the speed was feared too slow to make the race.

THE *youngest man to win* the 500-Mile Race was Troy Ruttman, 22 when he drove to victory in 1952. The oldest winner was Bobby Unser, 51 when he came in first in 1981.

THE *first black driver* to enter the 500-Mile Race was Willie T. Ribbs, who was added to the 1985 roster April 25 and quit April 26 after a circuit of the track convinced him he wasn't ready for the 200 miles per hour speeds. Ribbs, 29, of San Jose, Cal., was an experienced road-race driver.

EQUIPMENT

UNIFORMS which were *treated to retard fire* went into effect in auto racing January 1, 1960, the first year they were required in the 500-Mile Race in Indianapolis.

THE first driver *using gasoline* as a fuel to complete the 500-Mile Race without a pit stop was Cliff Bergere, who finished 5th in the 1941 race at a speed of 113.528 miles an hour.

THE first *crash helmets* in American racing, of steel, were worn in the 1916 500-Mile Race by Eddie Rickenbacker, who finished next to last, and Peter Henderson, who finished 6th.

Crash helmets were required for the first time in the 500-Mile Race in 1935.

THE *rear-view mirror* used by Ray Harroun on his *Marmon Wasp* in the 500-Mile Race in 1911 is reputed to be the first used on an automobile, at least the first used in auto racing. Harroun mounted the mirror because he carried no riding mechanic to advise him of traffic to the rear.

QUALIFICATIONS AND PRACTICE

THE sole time a one-lap record in qualifying at the 500-Mile Race was *disallowed because of darkness* was May 22, 1937, when Jimmy Snyder turned a lap at 130.492 miles an hour, only to have his attempt halted by nightfall. Thus the qualification lap record that year was 3 miles an hour slower.

THE *most consistent qualification run* at the Indianapolis Motor Speedway was by Geoge Snider in 1971, who averaged 166.652 miles an hour, with no lap varying more than .010 miles an hour from any of the others.

THE *driving test* for the 500-Mile Race was initiated in 1936 when Doc MacKenzie asked somebody to observe him while he drove on the race course. As a result, testing was begun for drivers, requiring them to do 10 laps at each of 80, 90, 100, 105, and 110 miles an hour. The first to pass was Henry Banks.

THE first time the *driver's test* at the Indianapolis Motor Speedway was *completed in a single day* was in 1956 when Eddie Sachs did his required 40 laps at speeds ranging from 110 to 125 miles an hour.

CHUCK ARNOLD holds the record for *trying to qualify in the greatest number of cars*. In 1962, Arnold got into four different cars, took the green qualifying flag in each, yet failed to make the race.

ALTHOUGH several qualification were held the morning before the 500-Mile Race over the years, the *oddest time for qualifying* on record was that of Phil Shafer, who drove the required 80 miles an hour at 5 *a.m.* on the morning of the race in 1923 event. He finished 7th.

THE first and only time *four drivers* were allowed to try to qualify at the same time was in 1947 when it was permitted because of rain delays. Mel Hanson and Emil Andres qualifed after the track officially was closed and were allowed to join the 30-car field with the permission of the other drivers.

THE *first strike* at the Indianapolis Motor Speedway was in 1947 by members of the American Society of Professional Automobile Racing. The dispute was settled largely through the efforts of Bill Fox, sports editor of *The Indianapolis News*, and membes of ASPAR were allowed to compete with the provision that they could not crowd out any of the 35 non-ASPAR drivers who were entrants. Eventually 10 ASPAR drivers made the race field of 30 cars.

RACES

GORDON JOHNCOCK beat Rick Mears by a mere .16 second in 1982, the *closest finish ever* in the 500-Mile Race.

THE record number of *cars eliminated* from the 500-Mile Race in a single accident was 11 in 1966 when the car driven by Greg Weld hit the outside wall on the main stretch during the first lap, starting a chain reaction crash.

THE *largest starting field* in the 500-Mile Race was the 42 that pulled away in the 1933 race, won by Louis Meyer.

THE *largest number of cars still in competition* at the end of 500 miles in the Indianapolis race was 26 in the first race, 1911. The starting field that year was 40.

THE *record prize* awarded in a 500-Mile Race at Indianapolis is $3,271,025, the purse for the 1985 race.

THE *first radio broadcast* of the 500-Mile Race was over WGN, Chicago, in 1924, with Quin Ryan describing the event. The winners of that race were L. L. Corum and Joe Boyer in a Duesenberg.

THE first time *rain caused a postponement* of the 500-Mile Race was in 1915 when the event was rescheduled from Saturday, May 29, to Monday, May 31. The first time two races in a row were affected by rain were 1975 and 1976. The 1975 race was stopped at 174 laps and the 1976 race halted at 102 laps.

THE first time the 500-Mile Race was *interrupted by rain* was in 1926 when the weather shut down the contest for an hour and 15 minutes. Frank Lockhart won the race, which went only 400 miles that year.

THE first and only time the last 50 laps of the 500-Mile Race was *finished in rain* was in 1940 under a yellow caution flag. Wilbur Shaw won at an average speed of 114.277.

THE *shortest* 500-Mile Race was in 1974, halted after 102 laps because of rain and won by Johnny Rutherford.

THE broadcast of the 500-Mile Race in 1949 by WFBM-TV was the *first live telecast* of the race in its entirety and was the first telecast of a sports event in Indiana.

SPEEDS

THE record for a *pit stop* during the 500-Mile Race is held by Bobby Unser, whose pause on lap 10 in the race May 30, 1976, took 4 seconds.

THE first man to win the 500-Mile Race at an *average speed of over 100 miles an hour* was Pete DePaolo in 1925, driving a Duesenberg to victory at an average of 101.127 miles an hour.

THE first 500-Mile Race driven in *less than 4 hours* was the 1951 contest, won by Lee Wallard in 3 hours, 57 minutes, 38 1/2 seconds, averaging 126.244 miles an hour.

THE *record speeds* in the 500-Mile Race for distances up to 30 laps are: 1 lap, 194.818 and 2 laps, 197.563 by Rick Mears in 1984; 4 laps, 199.208 and 10 laps, 200.649 by Bobby Rahal in 1985; 20 laps, 198.419 by Rick Mears in 1984; and 30 laps, 192.355 by Mario Andretti in 1984.

THE *longest pit stop* on record at the 500-Mile Race is 1 hour, 8 minutes, taken in 1958 by Mike Magill, whose car was red-flagged off the race course after he returned to action. He finished 17th, completing 136 laps.

THE record *speed for qualifying* for the 500-Mile Race is 212.583, accomplished by Pancho Carter for the 1985 race. Scott Brayton turned in the record qualifying lap of 214.199 in 1985.

RICK MEARS won in the *least time*, taking 3 hours, 3 minutes, 21.660 seconds on May 27, 1984, to win the 500-Mile Race in a March-Cosworth car.

THE *fastest lap* ever run during competition in the 500-Mile Race is 204.815 miles an hour, by Gordon Johncock in the 1984 race on lap 54. Johncock crashed on lap 102.

THE *fastest average speed* for the 500-Mile Race is 163.612, established in 1984 by Rick Mears, surpassing the old record of 162.962, which had survived for 12 years.

THE first man to drive a race car *200 miles an hour* at the Indianapolis Motor Speedway was Tom Sneva, who recorded a lap of

200.535 miles an hour in 1977. Mario Andretti, Johnny Rutherford, and A. J. Foyt, Jr., also turned laps at more than 200 miles an hour that year.

TRAGEDIES

THE *first death* in the 500-Mile Race was in 1911 when Arthur Greiner hit the wall on the 12th lap and his mechanic, Sam Dickson, was killed. Some had feared that driving numerous cars on the track at high speed for that great a distance would result in many injuries and deaths.

THE *first driver killed* at the Indianapolis Motor Speedway in connection with the 500-Mile Race was Herbert Jones, who hit the northeast wall on his second qualifying lap trying to make the 1926 race.

THE *first crash to occur on the pace lap* of the 500-Mile Race was in 1957 when a car driven by Elmer George bumped the car of Eddie Russo, putting both cars out of action before the race even started.

THE *first spectator killed* at the Indianapolis Motor Speedway was Bert Schoup, 16, Lafayette, fatally injured in 1923 when Tom Alley, a relief driver, crashed through the fence on the back stretch when the throttle stuck.

WOMEN

THE *first woman* to circle the Indianapolis Motor Speedway, soon after it was built, was Betty Blythe who took a ride in 1909 in a Buick which reached speeds of 60 to 70 miles an hour. Betty wrote about her experience in *The Indianapolis Star*. She really was Marie Chomel, the first women's editor of that newspaper, a girl from Loogootee known for her daring journalistic exploits and given the pen name Betty Blythe by Earl Martin, another journalist. About her tour of the Speedway, she later explained that she had been in bed with a rapid heartbeat, a recurring problem, when the races were being conducted at the Speedway. She wanted to show that a woman as well as a man could go around the course at high speed. "I was egged on, trussed up in heavy clothing topped off by a hood made of leather with an isinglass window and helped into a stripped-down stock car with just a board for a seat, driven by Bob Burman. Two drivers were killed in the 250-mile race that day and I thought I'd die before I completed the two laps at terrific speed. Gravel hit that isinglass like hailstones and when I finally was helped out of the car my legs were temporarily paralyzed and I was limp." She was driven home where she had her housekeeper heat some milk and give it to her bit by bit as she wrote about the experience, propped up to a typewriter. Afterwards, she went to bed.

THE first female officially *admitted to the garage area* at the Indianapolis Motor Speedway, a place normally restricted to men, was Mari McCloskey, assistant editor of *Woman's World*, who sued to obtain previously-denied press credentials allowing her inside Gasoline Alley before the race in 1971. (See also Drivers, above.)

Racing, *Harness*

THE *oldest active female harness-racing driver* in Indiana is Daisy Andrews of North Vernon, who raced at Shelbyville and Greensburg in 1984 at the age of 85. A driver nearly 16 years, she is in the Hall of Fame of Trotters at Goshen, N.Y.

THE Fox Stake, held annually at the Indiana State Fair in Indianapolis, is the *biggest non pari-mutuel* harness horse race in the world, offering a purse in 1984 of $188,492.

PACING

AMONG Indiana horses, Rambling Willie, a pacer from Monroeville, is the *top money-winner* with earnings of more than $2,000,000 from 1972 to 1983. In 13 years the horse won 125 races, 76 of them in 2:00; both of these are records.

THE record for *four heats, divided,* by pacers in Indiana is 8:04, set in Indianapolis by Meadow Ace in 1955. Heat times were 2:00.3, 1:59, 2:01.2, and 2:03. A divided race is one in which the field is too large for the track and has to be separated into two sections.

THE first and only horse to be chosen *Indiana Harness Horse of the Year twice in succession* is Hoosier Hotshot (real name Miss Silent Chief Tempered Yankee), who was voted the honors in 1982 and 1983 by the Indiana Trotting and Pacing Horse Association. Hotshot won 15 pacing races and had one second-place finish in 16 starts in 1982, and won all eight races she entered in 1983.

DAN PATCH holds the *fastest miles* by a Hoosier pacer with times of 1:55 1/4 at Lexington, Ky., in 1905 as a 9-year-old; 1:56 at Memphis, Tenn., in 1904 as an 8-year-old; 1:56 1/4 at the same track when he was 7; and 1:59 at Brighton Beach, N.Y., also in 1903. Patch was born at Oxford.

IN pacing on a five-eighths-mile track, Rambling Willie holds the record among Hoosier horses of all ages with a *world-record mile* time of 1:54.3 at Wilmington, Del., September 4, 1977; the mark has been equalled by a non-Hoosier horse.

THE fastest *three heats, divided,* by a 2-year-old pacer in Indiana is 5:59, set in 1969 by Truluck at Indianapolis. Heat times were 2:00.2, 1:57.4, and 2:01.4.

DAN PATCH of Oxford holds the *2-mile record* for Indiana pacers with a time of 4:17 in a time trial in 1903 at Macon, Ga. He did the first mile in 2:07 1/2.

AMONG pacers, Rambling Willie of Monroeville is the *best in history for career 2-minute miles,* with 76 between 1972 and 1982.

BORN at Oxford, Dan Patch reputedly was *never beaten* running between 1900 and 1909. Patch's first race was at Boswell, Ind., where his heat was 2:22 1/4. His best time was 1:55 1/4 at Lexington, Ky., in 1905 with H. C. Hersey driving. He ran 30 under-2-minute miles.

TROTTING

THE *fastest dead heat* for trotters in Indiana is 1:58 at Indianapolis August 22, 1980, between Tuneful Contest and Fast Tune.

Four of the 10 fastest miles of all time by trotters are by Greyhound, owned and raced by Sep Palin of Indianapolis. His 1:55 1/4 as a 6-year-old at Lexington, Ky., September 29, 1938, is the fourth fastest mile ever. Other marks are 1:55 1/2 at Lexington October 4, 1938; 1:56 at Lexington September 29, 1938; and 1:56 on the same track September 23, 1938.

AMONG 3-year-olds, the best trotting *record for three heats, divided,* by an Indiana horse is 6:07 3/4 by Greyhound is 1935 at Syracuse, N.Y. Heat times were 2:02 1/4, 2:04, and 2:01 1/2.

THE Indiana trotting horse with the *fastest mark on a mile track* is Greyhound, whose time was 1:55 1/4 in 1938 at Lexington, Ky. Greyhound, owned and raced by Sep Palin of Indianapolis, also is the best Hoosier horse on a half-mile track with a 1:59 3/4 in 1937 at Goshen, N.Y., third best in the history of that category.

THE *fastest 1 1/2 miles* by an Indiana trotter was 3:02 1/2 in a time trial by Greyhound in 1937 at Indianapolis.

THE Indiana record for *trotting 1 1/16 mile* is 2:08, set by Red Sails, noted Hoosier racer; that mark has been equalled by non-Indiana horses. The Red Sails time was in 1954 at Yonkers, N.Y. The horse, born at Crete, set *hundreds of track records* between 1948 and 1954 and is in the Harness Racing Hall of Fame.

THE *fastest mile* run by a trotter in Indiana was 1:54.8 by Nevele Pride at the Indiana State Fairgrounds August 31, 1969, in a time trial.

That time has been tied by another horse in a time trial, and by a third horse in a race outside Indiana. Nevele Pride was driven by Stanley Dancer.

THE 6:01 1/4 run by Greyhound at Goshen, N.Y., in 1936, is the best mark by a Hoosier horse in a 3-heat race for trotters of all ages. The heat marks were 2:01, 2:00 1/4, and 2 flat.

The best time for horses of any age, trotting *three heats, divided, in Indiana* is 6:03.3 set by Pronto Don in 1951 at Indianapolis. The heat times were 2:02, 1:59, and 2:02.3.

GREYHOUND holds the record for a 2-mile race in the state with a time of 4:06 at Indianapolis in 1939 in a time trial. Each mile was covered in 2:03.

THE Indiana horse with the *most 2-minute-mile records* is far and away Greyhound of Indianapolis. Greyhound is No. 1 trotter for 2-minute miles in a career with 25 from 1934 to 1940. He also holds the Hoosier record for the most 2-minute miles by a 4-year-old with 5 in 1936, an all-time high for a gelding, and is the Indiana trotter with the most 2-minute miles in a single year, 8 in 1938.

THE *fastest mile* for a *2-year-old* trotter on a mile track in Indiana is 2:00.2, run by Logan Speed August 26, 1982, at Indianapolis.

THE *2-year-old* trotter with the *fastest 3 heats, divided,* in Indiana is Noble Gesture, with a time of 6:07.4 at Indianapolis in 1970. Heat times were 2:01.1, 2:01.3, and 2:05.

INDIANA TRACK RECORDS FOR THE MILE

TRACK	HORSE	TIME-DATE
Anderson	Tim S., trotter	2:06 1/4 1939
	Coney Azoff, trotter	2:06 1/4 1943
	Miss Budlong, pacer	2:04 1939
Connersville	Neb Echo, trotter	2:06 1945
	Guinea Gold, pacer	2:02.2 1951
Converse	Kay Way, trotter	2:05 1959
	Honors Truax, pacer	2:03.4 1953
	Golden Boy Dean, pacer	2:03.4 1970
Corydon	Sis's Brother, trotter	2:05 1960
	C. J., pacer	2:02.2 1963
Frankfort	Mighty Indian, trotter	2:04.2 1960
	Guinea Gold, pacer	2:01 1951

Goshen	Brinks Donut, trotter	2:04	1979
	Raggedy Man, pacer	2:02.4	1981
Kendallville	Lakeland Albert, trotter	2:06	1935
	Ghost Ranger, pacer	2:05	1978
Kentland	Hot Dog Doc, trotter	2:10.3	1981
	Chi Town Clown, pacer	2:09.1	1979
	First Generation, pacer	2:09.1	1982
LaPorte	Highleys Joan, trotter	2:06.1	1966
	Timothy Heels, pacer	2:03.4	1973
Muncie	Curly Lambert, trotter	2:04.4	1961
	Winnipeg, pacer	2:04	1930
Portland	Coney Azoff, trotter	2:07	1944
	Miss Abbedale, pacer	2:04 1/2	1935
Shelbyville	Doctor Spencer, trotter	2:03	1946
	Adios, pacer	2:02	1944
Terre Haute	Kay Way, trotter	2:05	1959
	Gold Rise, pacer	2:03	1959

[SEE ALSO *Animals*.]

Racing, *Motorcycle*

THE *fastest recorded speed* for a motorcycle on a *closed quarter-mile course* in Indiana is 201.34 miles an hour, set by Elmer Trett of Oxford, O., competing in the National Hot Rod Association national drags at Clermont September 5, 1983.

The fastest on a *one-mile dirt track* is 102.03 mph, set August 24, 1980, at the Indiana State Fairgrounds by Hank Scott, a world record at the time.

Racing, *Running*

THE modern record for *marathon running* is 1:05.52 for 13.1 miles, set in the Indianapolis minimarathon May 27, 1983, by Gary Romesser of Greenwood. The *best time for a woman* is 1 hour, 18 minutes, 58 seconds, set May 25, 1984, by Diane Bussa of Carmel.

THE *best time by a 13-year-old* is that of Jeff Evans of Martinsville, running in the 1983 minimarathon, whose mark of 1:15.40 was a national record for that age group.

THE only Hoosier known to have competed in long-distance races in *all Indiana counties* is Rex Johnson, an Indianapolis attorney, who raced in his 92nd county November 3, 1984, at Rising Sun, Ripley County. It took him seven years to race in every county; he drove 18,250 miles to race sites. His competition per race ranged from 13 to 5,000 runners.

THREE Hoosiers were among the starting field of 300 in a race which began in Los Angeles in 1928, destination—New York, 3,665 miles away. They were John Stone, Marion, a basketball and football star; Roy McMurtry of Indianapolis, a one-armed competitor who already had run from Indianapolis to San Francisco in 20 days; and Dean Pletcher of Goshen. For professional reasons, or disguise, Pletcher called himself Mike Kelly. In Indiana the route led from Chicago to Gary, then South Bend, Ligonier, Butler, and into Ohio. Fifty-five runners finished in New York; McMurtry was 12th, Stone 33rd, and Kelly 54th. The race, held during an era of odd-ball competitions for money, was dubbed the Great Bunion Derby. The winner was Johnny Salo, with a time of 525 hours, 57 minutes, 20 seconds.

ALTHOUGH *triathlons* are difficult to compare, the best time in the largest Indiana triathlon seems to be 2 hours, 57 minutes, 37.7 seconds for a 1-mile swim, 37.3-mile bicycle segment, and a 9.3-mile run. The mark was set September 17, 1983, at the Midwest Triathlon, beginning at Lake Shafer and concluding on the Purdue University campus at West Lafayette. The victor over 703 competitors was Mac Martin of Pittsburgh.

Racing, *Ski*

THE *first professional ski race* in Indiana was held February 9, 1984, at Ski Paoli Peaks at Paoli, with a man-and-wife team from Indianapolis winning the amateur divisions. Mike Beeman won the men's 20-and-older category, and his wife Carol won the women's category. The under-20 category for men was won by Randy Viola, a student at Indiana University, and his sister Jena took top honors in the under-20 girls section. The top professional prize of $900 was won by Dave Cleveland of Lake Eldora, Colo. Jim Baker, ski school director at Paoli, was second, earning $500.

Racing, *Soap Box*

No other state has surpassed the *nine national soap box derby champions from Indiana*: Robert Turner, Muncie, 1934; Maurice

Dale, Anderson, 1935; Fred Mohler, Muncie, 1953; Terry Townsend, Anderson, 1957; James Miley, Muncie, 1958; Barney Townsend, Anderson, 1959; Fred Lake, South Bend, 1960; David Mann, Gary, 1962; and Branch Lew, Muncie, 1968.

THE Indiana *city to produce the most national soap box derby champions* has been Muncie with 4: Robert Turner in 1934; Fred Mohler in 1953, James Miley in 1958, and Branch Lew in 1968.

INDIANA holds the record for national soap box *champions in a row* with 4: Terry Townsend, Anderson, 1957; James Miley, Muncie, 1958; Barney Townsend, Anderson, 1959; and Fred Lake, South Bend, 1960.

THE *first national winner* of the soap box derby was Robert Turner of Muncie, 11 when he took the title in 1934 at Dayton, O. The second winner also was a Hoosier, Maurice Bale, Jr., of Anderson, who won at Akron, O., at the age of 13.

Racquetball

DINA PRITCHETT of Anderson at 16 became the *youngest female Indiana state racquetball champion* in the 1982 tournament at Greenbrier Racquetball Center in Indianapolis. She is the daughter of Larry and Jane Pritchett, also noted tournament racquetball players.

Senior Olympics

Senior Classic events are divided into age categories. The age of these record setters at the time of the record is shown in parentheses. Only Hoosiers holding records are shown; other records are held by out-of-state competitors.

MEN

EVENT	AGE GROUP	RECORD HOLDER	TIME-YEAR
Bicycle Racing			
2 1/2 miles	60–64	Mark Roach, Indianapolis (60)	6:40, 1981

| 10 miles | 60–64 | Mark Roach, Indianapolis (60) | 31:48, 1981 |
| | 70–74 | Hans Barz, Indianapolis (71) | 32:06, 1981 |

Swimming

50-meter freestyle	55–59	Arthur Heber, Rising Sun (56)	34.645, 1985
	60–64	Harry Hochman, Indianapolis (64)	35.84, 1982
	65–69	Fred Clute, Summitville (68)	39.60, 1982
50-meter breaststroke	55–59	Richard Mote, Indianapolis, (56)	45.08, 1982
	60–64	Harry Hochman, Indianapolis (64)	45.61, 1982
	65–69	Ed Shea, Indianapolis (66)	44.82, 1981
	70–74	Henry Ruh, Ellettsville (70)	57.28, 1982
50-meter backstroke	55–59	Robert Terry, Indianapolis (58)	43.625, 1985
	60–64	Bill Despres, Indianapolis (62)	41.963, 1985
	65–69	Harry Hochman, Indianapolis (65)	58.26, 1983
100-meter freestyle	55–59	Robert Terry, Indianapolis (58)	1:19.153, 1985
	60–64	Harry Hochman, Indianapolis (64)	1:21.84, 1982
	65–69	Harry Hochman, Indianapolis (66)	1:39.56, 1984
200-meter freestyle	55–59	Robert Terry, Indianapolis (58)	3:04.828, 1985
	60–64	Harry Hochman, Indianapolis (64)	3:07.76, 1982
	65–69	Harry Hochman, Indianapolis (65)	3:38.63, 1983
	70–74	Ed Shea, Indianapolis (70)	3:13.34, 1984
	75–79	Irv Merritt, West Lafayette (78)	4:24.57, 1982

1500-meter freestyle			
	55–59	Robert Terry, Indianapolis (57)	27:02.60, 1984
	60–64	Harry Hochman, Indianapolis (64)	28:45.80, 1982
	65–69	Ed Shea, Indianapolis (66)	27:36.97, 1981
	70–74	Ed Shea, Indianapolis (69)	27:07.22, 1984
	75–79	Irv Merritt, West Lafayette (78)	39:17.74, 1982
	80–up	Gene Moll, Indianapolis (80)	50:17.83, 1982

Track and field

50 meters			
	60–64	Charles Northrup, Indianapolis (62)	7.00, 1982
	80–up	A. E. Pitcher, Greenwood (82)	8.96, 1984 world record
100 meters	60–64	Charles Northrup, Indianapolis (61)	13.40, 1981
	70–74	Wes Ward, Indianapolis (70)	16.30, 1980
	80–up	A. E. Pitcher, Greenwood (83)	16.26, 1984 world record
200 meters	60–64	Charles Northrup, Indianapolis (61)	28.70, 1981
	65–69	Leland Erickson, Franklin (65)	36.70, 1982
	70–74	Milo Lightfoot, Warsaw (70)	34.93, 1984
	80–up	A. E. Pitcher, Greenwood (82)	36.36, 1984 world record
400 meters	65–69	Leland Erickson, Franklin (66)	1:17.16, 1983
800 meters	65–69	Leland Erickson, Franklin (66)	3:07.96, 1983
1500 meters	65–69	Leland Erickson, Franklin (65)	6:38, 1982
Mile walk	70–74	Tom Komstack, Indianapolis (71)	9:54.67, 1984

	75–79	Don Zemlock, Indianapolis (76)	10:20.64, 1984
Discus	80–up	A. E. Pitcher, Greenwood (82)	58 ft., 1 in., 1984
110-meter hurdles	80–up	A. E. Pitcher, Greenwood (81)	19.79, 1983 world record
Football throw	75–79	A. E. Pitcher, Greenwood (79)	83 ft., 10 in., 1981
	80–up	A. E. Pitcher, Greenwood (81)	68 ft., 8 in., 1983
High jump	80–up	A. E. Pitcher, Greenwood (80)	3 ft., 8 in., 1982
Javelin	65–69	Don Hummel, Indianapolis (65)	97 ft., 8 in., 1981
	80–up	A. E. Pitcher, Greenwood (80)	66 ft., 1/2 in., 1982
Pole vault	60–64	Eugene Taylor, Mishawaka (62)	7 ft., 6 in., 1985
	65–69	Don Hummel, Indianapolis (65)	8 ft., 6 in., 1981
	80–up	A. E. Pitcher, Greenwood (83)	6 ft., 0 in., 1985
Long jump	80–up	A. E. Pitcher, Greenwood (80)	9 ft., 11 in., 1982
Shot put	60–64	Harry Hochman, Indianapolis (63)	37 ft., 5 1/2 in., 1981
	65–69	Merton Porter, Indianapolis (69)	38 ft., 10 in., 1981
Softball throw	65–69	Don Hummel, Indianapolis (65)	173 ft., 7 in., 1981
	80–up	A. E. Pitcher, Greenwood (80)	93 ft., 9 in., 1982
Standing long jump	65–69	Merton Porter, Indianapolis (69)	7 ft., 3 1/2 in., 1981
	80–up	A. E. Pitcher, Greenwood (80)	6 ft., 4 3/4 in., 1982
Triple jump	80–up	A. E. Pitcher, Greenwood (80)	20 ft., 11 in., 1982

WOMEN

Bicycle racing

2 1/2 miles	70–74	Gerda Barz, Indianapolis (71)	12:14, 1984

Swimming

50-meter freestyle	55–59	Barbara Houston, Greenfield (58)	45.259, 1985
	70–74	Marcella Lammey, Indianapolis (72)	57.83, 1981
	75–79	Marcella Lammey, Indianapolis (75)	1:06.81, 1984
50-meter breaststroke	55–59	Carolyn Peet, Indianapolis (57)	1:13.314, 1985
	70–74	Marcella Lammey, Indianapolis (73)	1:13.13, 1982
	75–79	Marcella Lammey, Indianapolis (75)	1:05.37, 1984
100-meter freestyle	55–59	Barbara Houston, Greenfield (58)	1:49.082, 1985
	70–74	Marcella Lammey, Indianapolis (73)	2:08.16, 1982
	75–79	Marcella Lammey, Indianapolis (75)	2:20.73, 1984
200-meter freestyle	70–74	Marcella Lammey, Indianapolis (73)	4:27.76, 1982
	75–79	Marcella Lammey, Indianapolis (75)	4:53.51, 1984
1500-meter freestyle	55–59	Barbara Houston, Greenfield (56)	33:06.61, 1983
	70–74	Marcella Lammey, Indianapolis (73)	36:06.79, 1982
	75–79	Marcella Lammey, Indianapolis (75)	39:58.72, 1984

Track and
field

50 meters	65–69	Sheila Evans, Indianapolis (67)	8.64, 1983
Mile walk	55–59	Carolyn Peet, Indianapolis (56)	11:39.56, 1984
Football throw	65–69	Amy Robinson, Indianapolis (65)	37 ft., 5 in., 1980
High jump	65–69	Sheila Evans, Indianapolis (68)	3 ft., 7 in., 1984 world record

Shooting

A Hoosier, Lovell S. Pratt of Indianapolis, was the *first national skeet tournament champion*, winning at Solon, O., August 31, 1935, with a score of 244 out of a possible 250. The tournament was the first sponsored by the National Skeet Association.

A team of Hoosiers forming the United States International Muzzle Loading Team beat Britain at *trap shooting* in 1979 in the first such competition in more than 100 years. The Americans broke 72 birds out of 80 to 53 by the British.

The team included Bill Carmichael of Chesterton, the first shooter ever to get a perfect score in international muzzle-loading trap shooting when he won the world percussion title at Madrid in 1978; Jim Guy of Shelbyville, holder of the record for world match flintlock shooting with 18 out of 20 in 1977 at Zurich; Gary McGraw of near Connersville, and Bob Pence of Liberty.

Soccer

THE *national record for a winning string* in college soccer is 46, held by Indiana University. The team was undefeated from the opening game of the 1983 season until it lost to the University of South Florida on November 11, 1984. The team was tied twice during its unbeaten reign. The old NCAA record was 42, broken by I.U. against Purdue University in a game at Bloomington on November 3, 1984.

INDIANA UNIVERSITY is the only school in Indiana and only the second school in the nation whose soccer teams have won *national titles two years in a row*. The I.U. team won in 1982 by defeating Duke 2–1, and again in 1983 by bettering Columbia 1–0. The only other team to win the National Collegiate Athletic Association crown back to back was the San Francisco Dons in 1975–76.

INDIANA UNIVERSITY holds the record for *collegiate soccer overtimes* with the 8 extra periods played in 1982 when I.U. beat Duke at Fort Lauderdale, Fla., 2–1, for the first I.U. national title.

THE *first meeting of U.S. and Mexican collegiate championship teams* was when the Indiana University soccer team met the Mexican champs May 6, 1984, at Juarez, Mexico, in a match sponsored by El Paso–Juarez International Games, Inc.

ARMANDO BETANCOURT of Indiana holds the *record for assists* in an NCAA tournament with 6 in 1980.

Softball

THE *top softball players in Indiana history*, based on their selection to the softball Hall of Fame at Oklahoma City, Okla., are Hughie Johnson, Bill West, Ronald Kronewitter, Jim Ramage, Bernie Kampschmidt, and Clyde (Dizzy) Kirkendall.

Johnson was a first baseman for the Fort Wayne Zollner Pistons, born in Ireland and moving to Indiana in 1943. He was an all-star in 1946 and 1949, most valuable player in 1947, had a lifetime batting average of .295, played with the team until it was disbanded in 1954, and was chosen for the hall of fame in 1961.

West, a pitcher with Fort Wayne from 1946 to 1954, won 32 and lost none his first season and had a 28–6 record his last season. He pitched for the Zollner Pistons during three championships, was most valuable player in the league in 1948, an all-star 1946–49, was chosen for the hall of fame in 1963, and died in 1972.

Kronewitter, a University of Notre Dame graduate, pitched for the South Bend Bendix Brakes and had a lifetime record of 262 wins and 42 losses and 11 no-hitters. He began playing in 1928, played 5 1/2 years with Bendix, ended his career in 1941, and entered the hall of fame in 1967.

Ramage, infielder with Zollner Pistons, had a lifetime batting average of .293, held five of the 10 national fastball records, and led the league in total bases, most runs scored, and most hits in 1947. A perennial leading hitter, he tried out with three major-league baseball teams.

Kampschmidt, catcher with the Zollner Pistons beginning in 1941, was named to the all-star first team 1946–49, and played in 2,500 games and on four championship teams. He was chosen for the hall of fame in 1959.

Kirkendall pitched with the Zollner Pistons 1945–48, including three little tournaments, and was on two other world title teams—Toledo in 1935 and Cincinnati in 1937. In a career from 1932 to 1953 he had 1,144 wins and 52 losses and once pitched 33 innings in a national tournament game with 67 strikeouts and only three hits. He had a heart attack during a 1953 game, died in 1957, and entered the hall of fame in 1959.

THE *most national titles won in a row* by an Indiana team in the American Softball Association fast-pitch tournaments were the championships in 1945, 1946, and 1947 by the Fort Wayne Zollner Pistons.

THE longevity record for Indiana *commissioner* of the American Softball Association is the term of Harold G. Engelhardt of Indianapolis, who occupied the post 18 years, beginning in 1962.

WARREN CENTRAL of Indianapolis won the *first Indiana high school girls softball state tournament* June 8, 1985, with a 5–2 victory over Indianapolis North Central. The victory brought Warren Central's record for the season to 24–3. The winning pitcher was Kristyn Abel, who joined the team after completing a nine-game season at Stoneybrook Junior High School, making her not only the first pitcher to win the state tournament, but also the youngest.

Softball, *College*

THESE marks are held by women from Indiana schools in *Big Ten* softball competition in one season:

Best batting average
.404 by Sue O'Callaghan of Indiana University in 1983, best in the conference (at bat 57 times, 23 hits)

Most hits
Sue O'Callaghan of Indiana University, 23 in 57 times at bat in 1983; fourth best in the conference

Most runs
11 by Sue O'Callaghan of Indiana University in 1983; third best in the conference

Best earned run average
.356 by Sally Wood of Indiana University in 1983; best in the conference

Most doubles
3 by Terry DeLuca of Indiana University in 1983; third best in the conference

Most triples
3 by Sue O'Callaghan of Indiana University in 1983; best in the conference

Most runs batted in
8 by Brenda Thaler of Indiana University in 1983; fourth in the conference

Fewest strikeouts
Tie: 1 by Brenda Thaler of Indiana University and Linda Thayer of Indiana University; best in the conference (more than 50 times at bat)

Most stolen bases
6 by Sue O'Callaghan of Indiana University in 1983; second in the conference

Most strikeouts
36 by Amy Unterbrink of Indiana University in 1983; third best in the conference

Fewest hits permitted
32 by Sally Wood of Indiana University in 1983; leads the conference

Most victories
7 by Sally Wood of Indiana University in 1983; tied for first in the conference

Swimming

THE *first black to be best swimmer* in any age group in the Indiana Group Swimming championships was Mark Houston, 10, named best swimmer in the event in 1977 at Columbus by virtue of his five first-place finishes. Houston, a pupil at Grandview Elementary school in Indianapolis, was a member of the Indianapolis Swim Club.

JAMES EDWARD (DOC) COUNSILMAN, coach of the Indiana University swimming team at Bloomington, became the oldest to *swim the English Channel* when, at 58 years, 260 days old, he made the crossing in 13 hours, 7 minutes from Dover to Cap Gris Nez on September 14, 1979.

THE *fastest pool* is that of Indiana University Natatorium in

Indianapolis. Its design causes turbulence created by swimmers to die at the edge of the pool; in other designs, the turbulence comes back at swimmers, increasing the water resistance. The speed has been proven by the 95 meet, conference, and world records set there from its opening in 1982 through 1984.

IN 1984 Indianapolis became the first city ever to have *three Olympic trials* when competition in synchronized swimming, swimming, and diving was held in the Indiana University Natatorium.

THE *youngest person* in the U.S. ever to break a non-mechanical world record in swimming did so in Indianapolis. Gertrude Caroline Ederle broke the women's 880-yard freestyle swimming record with a time of 13 minutes, 19 seconds on August 17, 1919, when she was 12 years and 198 days old.

BOTH the men's and women's records in the 1650-yard free-style event for swimmers in the 35-to-39 age group in the *U.S. Masters YMCA Swimming Championships* are held by Hoosiers. Doug Landgraf set the men's mark at 19:56.3 and Joan Diercks set the women's mark at 20:51.84, both May 13, 1983, at Chicago. The two were swimming for the Jordan YMCA in Indianapolis.

I.U. NATATORIUM RECORDS

THESE are records set in the *Indiana University Natatorium* in Indianapolis. Records are recognized on short courses (25 meters) and long courses (50 meters) and also in yards. (Big Ten, high school, and NCAA records at the Natatorium will be found under those headings.)

WORLD RECORDS, 50 meters

MEN

100-meter breaststroke
John Moffet, June 25, 1984 — 1:02.13
100-meter butterfly
Pablo Morales, June 26, 1984 — 0:53.38
200-meter backstroke
Rick Carey, Texas, June 27, 1984 — 1:58.86

WORLD BEST, 25 meters

MEN

800-meter freestyle
Jeff Kostoff, U.S.A., January 7, 1983 — 7:44.53

WOMEN

200-meter freestyle
Brigit Meineke, Germany, January 7, 1983   1:56.35
100-meter backstroke
Kristin Otto, Germany, January 8, 1983   0:59.97
400-meter medley relay
Kristin Otto, Ute Geweniger, Ines Geissler,
    Brigit Meineke, Germany, January 8, 1983   4:02.85
200-meter backstroke
Cornelia Sirch, Germany, January 9, 1983   2:07.74
100-meter freestyle
Brigit Meineke, Germany, January 9, 1983   0:53.99
400-meter freestyle relay
Kristin Otto, Carmela Schmidt, Cornelia Sirch, Brigit
    Meineke, Germany, January 8, 1983   3:41.74

AMERICAN RECORDS, 50 meters

MEN

200-meter freestyle
Mike Heath, June 25, 1984   1:47.92
400-meter freestyle
George DiCarlo, June 28, 1984   3:51.03
800-meter freestyle
Tony Corbisiero, August 18, 1982   7:58.50
400-meter freestyle relay
Mission Viejo, August 20, 1982   3:21.89
1500-meter freestyle
George DiCarlo, June 30, 1984   15:01.51
800-meter freestyle relay
Florida Aquatics team, March 29, 1984   7:26.49
100-meter breaststroke
John Moffet, June 25, 1984 (also world mark)   1:02.13
200-meter backstroke
Rick Carey, June 27, 1984 (also world mark)   1:58.86
100-meter butterfly
Pablo Morales, June 26, 1984 (also world mark)   0:53.38

WOMEN

100-meter backstroke
Sue Walsh, August 21, 1982   1:02.48
200-meter breaststroke
Susan Rapp, June 26, 1984   2:31.54

200-meter freestyle relay
   Starlit Aquatic Club, August 21, 1982   1:44.64
200-meter individual medley
   Tracy Caulkins, June 29, 1984   2:12.78

AMERICAN RECORDS, 25 yards

MEN

100-yard backstroke
   Rick Carey, March 25, 1983   0:48.25
100-yard breaststroke
   Steve Lundquist, March 25, 1983   0:52.48
200-yard backstroke
   Rick Carey, April 6, 1983   1:44.43
400-yard medley relay
   Southern Methodist University: Mark Rhodenbaugh, Steve
      Lundquist, Bob Patten, John Spaulding, March 24, 1983   3:12.63
800-yard freestyle relay
   Florida: Eric Boyer, Geoff Gaberino, Mike Heath,
      Albert Mestre, March 25, 1983   6:25.29
1,000-yard freestyle
   Jeff Kostoff, April 6, 1983   8:48.57
1,650-yard freestyle
   Jeff Kostoff, April 9, 1983   14:46.11

WOMEN

50-yard freestyle
   Tammy Thomas, April 8, 1983   0:22.13
100-yard backstroke
   Sue Walsh, April 9, 1983   0:54.74
200-yard individual medley
   Tracy Caulkins, March 15, 1984   1:57.06
400-yard freestyle relay
   Florida, March 17, 1984   3:18.52
800-yard freestyle relay
   Florida, March 15, 1984   7:06.98
1,650-yard freestyle
   Tiffany Cohen, April 9, 1983   15:46.54

AMERICAN RECORDS, 25 *meters*

MEN

800-meter freestyle
   Jeff Kostoff, January 7, 1983   7:44.53

1,500-meter freestyle
Jeff Kostoff, January 9, 1983   14:50.37

WOMEN

50-meter freestyle
Dara Torres, January 8, 1983   0:25.37
400-meter freestyle relay
U.S.A., January 9, 1983   3:42.80
1,500-meter freestyle
Kim Linehan, January 9, 1983   15:50.96
1,500-meter freestyle
Michele Richardson, 14, became the youngest ever to win the event March 31, 1984, in the Phillips 66/U.S. Swimming Indoor Championships: time 16:12.57

Swimming, *college*

The following all-time *Big Ten records in men's swimming* are held by competitors from Indiana schools. All the swimmers are from Indiana University.

200-yard freestyle,
Jim Montgomery, 1976, 1:35.67
1,650-yard freestyle,
Rojer Madruga, March 5, 1983, Natatorium, 15:10.24
100-yard backstroke,
Mark Kerry, 1979, 0:49.78
200-yard backstroke,
Cliff Looschen, 1985, Natatorium, 1:48.01
100-yard breaststroke,
Marc Schlatter, 1979, 0:55.44
200-yard breaststroke,
John Waldman, March 3, 1984, Natatorium, 2:03.55
400-yard individual medley,
Rojer Madruga, 1983, 3:52.83
400-yard medley relay,
Arantes, Hofstetter, Hersey and Montgomery, 1977, 3:17.14

These Big Ten records were set in *conference meets at the I.U. Natatorium* in Indianapolis

50-yard freestyle,
Matt Wood, Iowa, March 1, 1984, 0:19.87
100-yard freestyle,
Matt Wood, Iowa, 1983, 0:43.96

200-yard butterfly,
  David Cowell, Ohio State, March 3, 1984, 1:46.42
100-yard butterfly,
  David Cowell, 1984, 0:47.63
100-yard backstroke
  Cliff Looschen, I.U., 1985, 0:49.93
500-yard freestyle,
  Graeme McGufficke, Illinois, March 3, 1983, 4:20.41
400-yard medley relay,
  I.U.: Cliff Looschen, John Waldman, John King, and Doug Boyd,
    1983, 3:18.33
400-yard freestyle relay,
  I.U.: Doug Boyd, Cliff Looschen, Joe Carroll, and Tony Anderson,
    1985, 2:57.26
800-yard freestyle relay,
  I.U.: Tony Anderson, Cliff Looschen, John Carlos Vellejo, and Joe
    Carroll, 1985, 6:33.68

These are the *best times by undergraduate swimmers* in Indiana, but are not conference records; all the swimmers are from Indiana University.

100-yard freestyle,
  Jim Montgomery, 977, 0:44.01 (record, 0:43.96)
500-yard freestyle,
  Chuck Sharpe, 1980, 4:22.14 (record, 4:20.41)
100-yard butterfly,
  Mark Spitz, 1972, 0:47.98 (record, 0:47.50)
200-yard butterly,
  Mark Spitz, 1972, 1:46.89 (record, 1:46.42)
200-yard individual medley,
  Fred Tyler, 1975, 1:50.62 (record, 1:50.08)
400-yard freestyle relay,
  Knox, Montgomery, Murphy, Hickcox, 1975, 2:58.42 (record,
    2:57.82)

These marks are held by *women from Indiana schools in Big Ten swimming competition:*

50-meter freestyle
  0:23:57 by Mary Beth McGinnis of Indiana University in 1980, second
    in the conference
100-yard freestyle
  0:51.69 by Jennifer Hooker of Indiana University in 1980, third in
    the conference

200-yard freestyle
   1:51.12 by Jennifer Hooker of Indiana University in 1980, fourth in
   the conference
500-yard freestyle
   4:48.92 by Jennifer Hooker of Indiana University in 1981, second in
   the conference
1650-yard freestyle
   16:32.92 by Jennifer Hooker of Indiana University in 1982, second in
   the conference
50-yard backstroke
   0:27.01 by Theresa Andrews of Indiana University in 1981, second in
   the conference
100-yard backstroke
   0:57.70 by Theresa Andrews of Indiana University in 1980, second in
   the conference
200-yard backstroke
   2:03.71 by Theresa Andrews of Indiana University in 1981, second in
   the conference
50-yard butterfly
   0:26.19 by Theresa Andrews of Indiana University in 1981, fifth in
   the conference
100-yard butterfly
   0:56.13 by Rosie Wichte of Indiana University in 1984, conference
   record
200-yard butterfly
   2:03.69 by Stephanie Porter of Indiana University in 1981, fourth in
   the conference
200-yard freestyle relay
   1:35.83 by Sattelberg, Andrews, Hooker, and McGinnis of Indiana
   University in 1981, second in the conference
200-yard medley relay
   1:46.99 by Andrews, McGinnis, Peterson, and Robbiano of Indiana
   University in 1981, second in the conference
400-yard freestyle relay
   3:28.51 by Hooker, Andrews, McGinnis, and Cremin of Indiana
   University in 1981, second in the conference
400-yard medley relay
   3:57.12 by Robbiano, Andrews, Cremin, and Aschinger of Indiana
   University in 1981, fourth in the conference
One-meter diving
   Lona Foss of Indiana University in 1981, 456.93 points, third in the
   conference

The record for *consecutive victories in National Collegiate Athletic Association* men's swimming competition is held by Indiana
University with six, 1968–1973.

The *following records* are held by Hoosiers in *NCAA swimming and diving tournament competition among men.*

Indiana University captured nine individual championships in 1969, 8 in 1971, and 6 each in 1965, 1972, and 1973, the only Indiana school to win so many.

Gary Hall of I.U. and Charlie Hickox of I.U. both captured three championships in a single year: Hall in 1971 in the 200-meter backstroke, the 200-meter individual medley, and the 400-meter medley; and Hickox in 1958 in the 100-meter backstroke, the 200-meter butterfly, and the 200-meter individual medley.

The career record for individual championships is 8 by Mark Spitz of I.U., the 100-meter butterfly in 1969, 1970, 1971, and 1972 (also an Indiana record for repeat championships), the 200-meter freestyle in 1969, the 200-meter butterfly in 1971 and 1972, and the 500-meter free-style in 1969.

These records in the *women's swimming and diving championships* of the *National Collegiate Athletic Association* all were set in the Indiana University Natatorium at Indianapolis during the 1984 competition March 15 through March 17.

100-yard breaststroke
Tracy Caulkins, Florida — 1:01.37
200-yard freestyle
Mary Beth Linzmeier, Stanford — 1:45.47
200-yard breatstroke
Susan Rapp, Stanford — 2:12.84
500-yard freestyle
Mary Beth Linzmeier — 4:38.91
200-yard butterfly
Tracy Caulkins, Florida — 1:55.55
200-yard backstroke
Sue Walsh, North Carolina — 1:58.82
200-yard individual medley
Tracy Caulkins, Florida — 1:57.06
200-yard medley relay
Libby Kinkead, Kathy Smith, Diana Zock, Krissie Bush, Stanford — 1:42.81
400-yard individual medley
Tracy Caulkins, Florida — 4:08.37
400-yard freestyle relay
Florida, also a new American record — 3:18.52

800-yard freestyle relay
    Laureen Welting, Tracy Caulkins,
    Kathy Treible, Mary Wayte, Florida
    Also an American record   7:06.98

State High School *Swimming Meet Records*

BOYS

EVENT	RECORD-YEAR	HOLDER	SCHOOL
200-yard medley relay	1:37.95, 1982	G. Anchors P. Renard C. Boneham M. Shipley	Kokomo Haworth
200-yard freestyle	1:40.668, 1983	Jeff Holowach	North Central, Indianapolis
200-yard individual medley	1:53.346, 1983	Robert Beck	Merrillville
50-yard freestyle	0:20.966, 1983	Chris Boneham	Kokomo Haworth
1-meter dive	576.05, 1978	Chris Chelich	Munster
100-yard butterfly	0:50.131, 1983	Ralph Pieniazkiewicz	South Bend Riley
100-yard freestyle	0:46.177, 1983	Kevin Hedrick	Southmont
500-yard freestyle	4:32.32, 1982	Jeff Holowach	North Central, Indianapolis
400-yard freestyle	3:45.591, 1972	Mike Kearney	Bloomington
100-yard backstroke	0:52.782 , 1981	Doug Elenz	Michigan City Elston
100-yard breaststroke	0:58.187, 1983	David Buffington	West Lafayette
400-yard freestyle relay	3:09.82, 1983	D. Whelan T. Reifeis T. Powell J. Holowach	North Central, Indianapolis

GIRLS

EVENT	RECORD-YEAR	HOLDER	SCHOOL
200-yard medley relay	1:49.26, 1983	H. Hafner J. Emerson K. Humphrey D. Daniel	Anderson
200-yard freestyle	1:51.29, 1983	Pam Hayden	Columbus East
200-yard individual medley	2:05.51, 1983	Dale Etnyre	Columbus East
50-yard freestyle	0:23.73, 1984	Heidi Hendricks	Logansport
1-meter dive	473.30, 1983	Dana Wiegand	Franklin
100-yard butterfly	0:56.27, 1983	Dale Etnyre	Columbus East
100-yard freestyle	0:51.63, 1983	Debbie Daniel	Anderson
500-yard freestyle	4:54.31, 1983	Pam Hayden	Columbus East
100-yard backstroke	0:57.47, 1983	Dorothy Linsemeyer	Michigan City Rogers
100-yard breastroke	1:07.34, 1984	Heide Hendricks	Logansport
400-yard freestyle relay	3:35.29	D. Daniel K. Watson H. Hafner J. Emerson	Anderson

For other swimming records, see Senior Olympics, below.

Table Tennis

THE *best table tennis player* in Indiana history evidently was Jimmy McClure of Indianapolis who, from 1934 until World War II, won national championships six times and world titles five times, achieving crowns in both singles and doubles play.

Tennis

THE *youngest Hoosier* ever to win the Girls 18-and-under International Grass Court Tennis championship was Shawn Foltz of Indianapolis, 15 when she triumphed August 20, 1983. She also was the second youngest in the history of the event, the youngest being Tracy Austin, who won when she was 14.

THE best record in *state individual tennis titles* is shared by Lanae Renschler of Castle at Evansville, who won her third straight title in 1985, and Courtney Lord of Brebeuf in Indianapolis, who won the title in 1978, 1979, and 1980.

Track and Field

THE Indiana *capital of pole vaulting* is probably Kokomo, which produced at least six champion vaulters: Leroy Samse, who was the 1906 Big Ten champion; Murden Hopkins, a high-school record holder in 1911; Tommy Warne, 1927 national high school record holder; Bob Babb, state champion in 1931; Harold Lees, state champion in 1937; and Paul Deschamps, state champion in 1938.

ROBERT MOUNTAIN, an executive with the Veterans Administration in Indianapolis, set *records* in the 100-meter and 200-meter dashes September 8, 1982, at the *Canadian National Amputee games*. Mountain did 100 meters in 13.1 seconds (the old record was 13.7) and did the 200 meters in 26 seconds (the old record was 28.3). Mountain lost his left leg six inches below the knee due to wounds suffered in mortar fire in 1968 in Vietnam.

Indiana AAU (by age)

BOYS
10 *and under*

EVENT	RECORD HOLDER—DATE	TIME
100 meters	Varnelle Darry, 1983	0:13.14
200 meters	Ryan Harding, 1983	0:28.58
400 meters	J. McClurg, date unknown	1:04.2
800 meters	Jeff Culbertson, 1983	2:38.2
1500 meters	Jeff Culbertson, 1982	5:07.7
Long jump	W. Spight, date unknown	14 ft., 8 1/2 in.
High jump	Mike Bragg, date unknown	4 ft., 2 in.
Shot put	Angel Scott, 1983	24 ft., 7 1/2 in.

11–12

100 meters	Mario Jackson, 1983	0:13.05
200 meters	Mike Smith, 1979	0:26.30

400 meters	J. Carlson, date unknown	1:02.9
800 meters	Ron Markezich, 1979	2:26.45
1500 meters	Mike Mundy, 1981	5:05.3
Long jump	Shawn Wall, 1980	16 ft., 2 in.
High jump	Kary Hunsberger, 1979	5 ft., 1/4 in.
Shot put	Chad Madison, 1979	38 ft., 2 1/2 in.

13–14

100 meters	John Jackson, 1982	0:11.5
200 meters	Sam Henderson, 1977	0:22.2
		(national record)
400 meters	Derrick Garner, 1980	0:52.5
800 meters	G. Walker, date unknown	2:06.8
1500 meters	Mike Mundy, 1983	4:15.75
3000 meters	Mike Mundy, 1983	9:19.98
1500-meter walk	Chris Fosse, 1979	9:04.6
80-meter hurdles	John E. Campbell, 1980	0:11.20
Long jump	T. Turner, date unknown	20 ft., 1 1/2 in.
High jump	Miles Fletcher, 1979	6 ft., 2 in.
Shot put	E. Durbin, 1980	50 ft., 10 in.
Discus	J. Shepherd, date unknown	157 ft., 11 1/2 in.
Javelin	Chris Delusky, 1981	112 ft., 9 in.
Pole vault	Todd Fishel, 1983	11 ft., 0 in.
Triple jump	Rod Parker, date unknown	28 ft., 9 3/4 in.

15–16

100 meters	Kim Coleman, 1981	0:11.5
200 meters	Jeff Jackson, 1979	0:22.0
400 meters	LeBaron Green, 1981	0:50.3
800 meters	Ken Ford, 1981	1:56.4
1500 meters	Curtis Franke, 1982	4:08.27
3000 meters	Jeff Oberlin, 1981	9:06.7
1500-meter walk	N. Stein, date unknown	8:23.8
110-meter hurdles	Ron Woodson, 1981	0:14.10
400-meter hurdles	Charles Merriweather, 1978	0:55.3
High jump	Christ Matze, 1979	
	Bill Meade, 1979	6 ft., 6 in.
Long jump	M. Cherry, date unknown	22 ft., 7 1/2 in.
Shot put	S. Hoffer, date unknown	57 ft., 1 in.
Discus	Kevin King, 1976	167 ft., 1 in.
Javelin	Andy Weintraut, 1981	163 ft., 7 in.
Pole vault	David Volz, 1977	15 ft., 8 in.
		national record
Triple jump	A. Vann, date unknown	41 ft., 7 in.
Decathlon	John Owen, 1982	5,681 points

17–18

100 meters	Kevin Martin, 1981	0:10.7
200 meters	Jeff Patrick, 1982	7
400 meters	Walter Monagan, 1981	0:21.22
800 meters	T. Martin	0:46.90
1500 meters	Jim Nagle, 1981	1:52.1
3000 meters	Stanton Temme, 1981	4:00.4
1500-meter walk	Schubert, date unknown	8:52.60
110-meter hurdles	Alex Washington, 1981	8:11
400-meter hurdles	Ronald Birchfield, 1981	0:13.9
Long jump	Eric McCarrol	0:52.7
		24 ft., 7 3/4 in.
High jump	N. Ruebel, date unknown	national record
Shot put	Dale Henderson, 1978	6 ft., 11 in.
Discus	Kevin King, 1978	60 ft., 4 1/4 in.
Javelin	John J. Smith, 1979	176 ft.
Pole vault	David Volz, 1980	174 ft., 5 in.
		17 ft.
Triple jump	Eric McCarrol, date unknown	national record
Decathlon	Robert Johnson, 1981	44 ft., 8 3/4 in.
		5,821 points

GIRLS

10–12

100 meters	Allison Gilbert, 1981	0:13.5
200 meters	Kietha Dickerson, 1979	0:29.20
400 meters	Dawn Benedict, 1976	1:08
800 meters	L. Vandersteen, date unknown	2:42.1
1500 meters	Laura Culveyhouse, 1981	5:52
1500-meter walk	Jessica Fountain, 1983	12:12.78
Long jump	Allison Gilbert, 1983	14 ft., 4 1/2 in.
High jump	Erica Ervin, 1981	
	Erin Garland, 1979	3 ft., 10 in.
Shot put	Christina Dicken, 1981	23 ft., 9 1/2 in.

11–12

100 meters	Lavette Harris, 1983	0:12.9
200 meters	Michelle Murrell, 1979	0:27.30
400 meters	Dawn Benedict, 1978	1:02.1
800 meters	Diane Bussa, 1962	2:32
1500 meters	Cindy Bradford, 1981	4:59.4
1500-meter walk	Lisa Abbott, 1981	11:02
Long jump	Lavette Harris, 1983	16 ft., 5 1/4 in.

| High jump | Nancy Hoover, 1983 | 5 ft. |
| Shot put | Robin Beasley, 1980 | 32 ft., 1/2 in. |

13–14

100 meters	Jodie Whitaker, 1981	0:12.7
200 meters	S. Smith, date unknown	
	Bianca Embry, 1976	0:25.7
400 meters	C. DeHaven, date unknown	0:58.2
800 meters	Amber Chastain, 1979	2:24.20
1500 meters	Carrie Crise, 1981	5:26.6
3000 meters	Laura Ostendorf, 1981	11:59
1500-meter walk	Christy Breeze, 1983	9:46.42
80-meter hurdles	Beth Happel, 1978	0:11.8
Long jump	Bianca Embry, 1976	17 ft., 5 1/4 in.
High jump	Angie Bradburn, 1981	5 ft., 6 3/4 in.
Shot put	Linda Able, 1978	39 ft., 1/4 in.
Discus	Angie Ryker, 1983	106 ft., 10 in.
Javelin	Angie Anderson, 1983	91 ft., 5 1/2 in.

15–16

100 meters	Crystal Carter, 1981	0:12.36
200 meters	Monique Carter, date unknown	0:24.9
400 meters	C. DeHaven, date unknown	0:55.9
800 meters	Jo Ellen Karst, 1979	2:15.63
1500 meters	Sherry Volkman, 1982	4:53.74
3000 meters	Michelle Woolsey, 1982	10:43.11
1500-meter walk	C. Brunne, date unknown	9:03.2
100-meter hurdles	Cheryl Coolie, 1979	0:14.20
400-meter hurdles	Beth Happel, 1979	1:06.80
Long jump	Jodie Whitaker, 1982	18 ft., 11 3/4 in.
High jump	Sherri Bryant, 1982	6 ft., 1/4 in. national record
Shot put	Karen Nitsch, 1979	44 ft., 8 in.
Discus	Debbie Smith, 1981	131 ft., 4 in.
Javelin	Marcia Stack, 1978	120 ft., 0 in.
Triple jump	Trisha Nichols, 1981	31 ft., 5 in.

17–18

100 meters	Sybil Perry, 1981	0:11.6
200 meters	Lorene Slerman, 1978	0:24.0
400 meters	Sheila Montgomery, 1979	0:55.40
800 meters	Lisa Allen, 1981	2:12.3
1500 meters	Diane Bussa, 1978	5:04.2
3000 meters	Cecila Peterson, 1978	11:08.9

1500-meter walk	Parke, date unknown	10:11
100-meter hurdles	Jackie Sedwick, 1979	13.93
400-meter hurdles	Beth Happel, 1981	1:00.9
Long jump	D. Smith, date unknown	18 ft., 11 in.
High jump	Bonita Harrington, 1980	5 ft., 9 3/4 in.
Shot put	Karen Nitsch, 1980	44 ft., 11 1/4 in.
Discus	Lisa Nauman, 1981	144 ft., 3 in.
Javelin	Marge Lipscomb, 1979	102 ft., 6 in.
Heptathlon	Teresa Owens, 1982	4,203 points

Track and Field, *College*

MEN

THE Indiana record for the *standing broad jump* is certainly the 11 feet, 4 7/8 inches done in the 1904 Olympics by Raymond C. Ewry of Purdue University, competing for the New York Athletic Club. Also unbroken is his record of 34 feet, 8 1/2 inches for the *hop, step, and jump* in the 1900 Olympics. Ewry was graduated from Purdue in 1894 with a degree in mechanical engineering and went to work for the board of water supply of the Catskill Aqueduct Company in New York. When the Ross-Ade Stadium was completed at Purdue, Ewry contributed soil he had brought back from Athens during the Olympics there.

THE first Indiana college athletes to win *national victories* in an official event were two Notre Dame athletes competing in the first National Collegiate Track and Field Championships in 1921 at Chicago. August Desch won the 220-yard low hurdles in 24.8 seconds. John Murphy won the high jump with a leap of 6 feet, 3 inches.

THE first Hoosier college athlete to reach *pole vaulting heights* of both 15 feet and 16 feet was Mike Hanna of Pendleton, a student at Indiana State University in 1967 and 1968. Hanna was also the first Indiana high school student to vault 14 feet.

DAVE VOLZ of Indiana University set a record for the *pole vault for athletes under 19* at 18 feet, 1/2 inch, June 12, 1981, at the University of Tennessee U.S. Junior Track and Field championships.

THE first man to run *two miles in under 9 minutes* was Donald R. Lash of Indiana University, who was timed at 8:58 in June 1936 at a meet at Princeton, N.J.

THE first Indiana school to win the *NCAA cross country title* was Indiana University, which took the crown in 1938 with 51 points.

THE record for a *standard 4-mile cross country course* in the Big Ten is 21:01.5, set in 1971 by Fred Wilt of Indiana University at West Lafayette.

DONALD R. LASH of Auburn, a graduate of Indiana University and long-time amateur runner, was *national champion in cross country seven consecutive years*, a record.

JOHN DUDECK of Indiana Univeristy set the state collegiate record for the *discus* with a toss of 184 feet, 4 inches, May 20, 1978, in a Big Ten meet at Evanston, Ill. The put broke a 30-year record of 178 feet, 11 1/2 inches.

These are the records held by Hoosiers in *Big Ten indoor men's track* **conference meets.**

60-yard dash: Larry Burton, Purdue, 1973 and 1974, and Mike McFarland, Indiana, 1975	0:05.9
300-yard dash: Mike McFarland, Indiana, 1975	0:29.6
440-yard dash: Sunder Nix, Indiana, 1984	0:46.40
400-meter dash:Sunder Nix, Indiana, 1981	0:47.93
Two-mile run: Jim Spivey, Indiana, 1980	8:35.03
60-yard high hurdles: Ron Woodson, Purdue, 1984	0:07.22
70-yard high hurdles: Phil Stapp, Indiana, 1974 (event no longer contested)	0:08.1
Mile: Terry Braham, Indiana, 1984	4:00.63
High jump: Ron Jones, Indiana, 1984	7 feet, 4 1/4 in.
Pole vault: Dave Volz, Indiana, 1982	18 feet, 1 in.

These are the best *indoor performances* **by undergraduates in Indiana Big Ten schools, but** *not in Big Ten meets*.

60 meters: tie: Larry Burton, 1973–74, Purdue University, and Mike McFarland, Indiana University, 1975, 0:05.9 (also tied by non-Hoosiers).

70-yard dash: Mike McFarland, Indiana, 1975, Mason-Dixon Games	0:06.7
Mile run: Jim Spivey, Indiana, 1982, TAC (New York)	3:57.04
Pole vault: David Volz, Indiana, 1982, Maple Leaf Games	18 feet, 6 1/2 in.
Four-mile relay: Hayes, Mandera, Heidenreich, Wysong, Indiana, 1974, All-Comers Meet	16:34.8

These are the records held by Hoosiers in *Big Ten outdoor conference meets*.

100-yard dash: Larry Burton, Purdue, 1972 and 1973 (tied by others)	0:09.4
200-meters: Albert Robinson, Indiana	20.76
Six-mile run: Pat Mandera, Indiana, 1974	28:01.4
1,500 meters: Jim Spivey, Indiana, 1980	3:38.56
400-meter high hurdles: Jon Thomas, Indiana, 1985	0:48.95
1,600-meter relay: Douglas, Thomas, Hunter, Kern, Indiana, 1985	3:04.45
Pole vault: David Volz, Indiana, 1982	18 feet, 1 in.

These are the best *outdoor performances* by undergraduates in Indiana Big Ten schools; competition is in *non-Big Ten meets*.

100-yard dash: Larry Burton, Purdue, 1973, USTFF,	0:09.2
220-yard dash (one turn): Larry Burton, Purdue, 1972, Big State Meet	0:20.3
Mile run: Jim Spivey, Indiana, 1982, UCLA-Pepsi Invitational	3:55.56
Two-mile run: Jim Spivey, Indiana, 1981, UCLA-Pepsi Invitational,	8:24.69
100-meter dash: Albert Robinson, Indiana, 1984, Dogwood Relays,	0:10.23
200-meter dash: Albert Robinson, Indiana, 1984, National Invitational	0:20.07
400-meter dash: Sunder Nix, Indiana, 1982, National Sports Festival	0:44.68
1,500-meter run: Jim Spivey, Indiana, 1981, Athletic Congress,	3:37.24
5,000-meter run: Jim Spivey, Indiana, 1982, National Sports Festival	13:33.47
400-meter hurdles: Jon Thomas, Indiana, 1983, NCAA meet	0:49.03
Pole vault: David Volz, Indiana, 1982, Durham, N.C.,	18 feet, 9 1/2 in.
440-yard relay: Indiana, Goodrich, Miller, Lundgren, Highbaugh, 1970, NCAA	0:39.9
800-meter relay: Indiana, same as above, 1970, Drake Relays	1:22.7

(In neither of the above relays did the Indiana team win.)

WOMEN

Big Ten, women—These marks are held by women from Indiana schools in Big Ten track and field competition:

INDOORS

60 meters
  07.2 by Karen Wechsler of Indiana University in 1979
Shot put
  52 feet, 5 1/2 inches (done indoors because of bad weather) by Annette Bohach of Indiana University at Bloomington, May 7, 1982

OUTDOORS

4-by-400 meter relay
  3:39.65 by Young, Watson, Ennis, and Montgomery of Indiana University in 1982
Pentathlon
  3,803 points by Maggie Woods of Purdue in 1980
3,000-meter run
  9:05.87 by Becky Cotta of Purdue University in 1984
High jump
  6 feet by Yvonne Netterville, Purdue University, May 22, 1983
400-meter hurdles
  57.75 by Sybil Perry of Purdue University, May 19, 1984
Javelin
  178 feet, 10 inches by Carla Battaglia of Indiana University, May 19, 1984

Track and Field, *High School*

THE best time for 100 meters in Indiana is 10.2 by both Don Young and Glen Moore of Gary Roosevelt, tying the national record. Among girls the Indiana record is 11.69 by Maicel Malone of Indianapolis North Central.

Cross country—THE record for high-school girls in Indiana for a 3,000-meter cross country run is 10:08, set by Marsha Grondziak of Ben Davis High School, Indianapolis, in 1982. The boys mark for 5,000 meters if 14:57.3, set in 1980 by Curt Carey, Owen Valley High School.

Hurdles—THE best time in Indiana by a high school athlete in the 300-meter low hurdles is 35.8 in 1983 by Rod Woodson of Fort Wayne Snider High School.

Pole vault—THE record pole vault for a 15-year-old is 14 feet, 6 inches, also a national record, set by James Stack of Hobart July 2, 1983, at the White River Park State Games, Indianapolis.

400-meters—THE best time in Indiana for 400 meters by a girl is 53.7, set in 1985 by Maicel Malone of Indianapolis North Central.

High jump—ANGELA BRADBURN of Norwell in 1985 jumped 6 feet, 2 inches, the best ever in Indiana for a girl.

BOYS
IHSAA tournament records

EVENT	RECORD	HOLDER DATE
100 yards	0:09.5	Clyde Peach, Brebeuf, Indianapolis, 1966
220-yard straightaway	0:20.5	Larry Highbaugh, Indianapolis Washington, 1967
220-yard curve	0:21.3	Tie: Patrick Gullet, Gary Mann, 1971 and Cornell Garret, Evansville North, 1976
440 yards	0:47.3	Kenny Head, New Albany, 1964
180-yard low hurdles	0:18.6	Jerry Saffell, LaPorte, 1963
330-yard low hurdles	0:37.0	Robert Johnson, Indianapolis Northwest, 1978
880-yard relay	1:26.6	Tie: North Central, Indianapolis, 1976 (A. Darring, B. Ervin, M. Highbaugh, D. Pipkin) and Gary Roosevelt, 1977 (C. Jones, C. Weatherspoon, J. Jones, R. Baker)
Mile Relay	3:14.8	Gary West Side, 1976 (C. Hill, W. McCallister, K. Sumbry, F. Brown)

In 1980 all track events were converted to metric distances.

100-meters	0:10.31	Jerome Harrison, Jeffersonville, 1981

200-meters	0:21.10	Jeffery Patrick, Gary Roosevelt, 1982
400-meters	0:47.1	Leon Tubbs, Fort Wayne South Side, 1978
800 meters	1:50.2	Tom Martin, Evansville Memorial, 1977
1600 meters	4:04.2	Rudy Chapa, Hammond High, 1976
3200 meters	8:55.1	Rudy Chapa, Hammond High, 1975
110-meter hurdles	0:13.4	Jerry Hill, Indianapolis Tech, 1976
300-meter low hurdles	0:35.87	Robert Kennedy, Southport, 1985 Also national record
High jump	7 feet, 1 1/4 in.	3-way tie: Jeff Woodard, New Albany, 1977; Ron Jones, Mt. Vernon, 1980; and Adam Shumpert, Peru, 1980
Long jump	24 ft., 6 3/4 in.	Kelvin Walker, Elkhart Memorial, 1983
Pole vault	16 ft., 2 in.	Dan Burton, Bloomington South, 1985
Shot put	64 ft., 3 3/4 in.	Neil Eubank, Merrillville, 1985
Discus	189 ft., 11 in.	Kevin King, Bloomington South, 1979
1600-meter relay	3:13.66	Gary West Side, 1980 (K. Carter, C. Peterson, W. Monagan, S. Burnett)
400-meter relay	0:41.02	Gary Roosevelt, 1982 (D. Young, J. Patrick, G. Moore, A. Price)

GIRLS
IHSAA Tournament records

EVENT	RECORD	HOLDER, DATE
80-yard hurdles	0:10.5	Kelly Sparks, Fort Wayne Northrop, 1977
100 yards	0:10.7	Tie: Lorene Spearman, Wawasee, 1977 and Deandra Carney, Indianapolis Arlington, 1978

440-yard relay	0:48.5	Indianapolis Arlington, 1978 (Bundles, Carney, Cunningham, Whitfield)
880-yard relay	1:42.4	Indianapolis Tech, 1978 (LaLand, S. Smith, W. Smith, Walker)
880-yard medley relay	1:46.9	Jeffersonville, 1977 (Dodd, Abell, Fitzpatrick, P. Sedwick)
Shot put 8 lbs.	50 ft., 2 1/2 in.	Eleanor Majors, Indianapolis North Central, 1978
Softball throw	239 ft.	Dru Cox, Plainfield, 1977

In 1980 all tracks were converted to metric distances.

100-meter hurdles	0:13.5	Beth Happel, Indianapolis Cathedral, 1982
100 meters	0:11.78	Maicel Malone, Indianapolis North Central, 1985
1600 meters	4:49.54	Sherry Hoover, Woodlawn, 1985
400 meters	0:54.60	Pam Sedwick, Jeffersonville, 1976
200 meters	0:23.8	3-way tie: Lorene Spearman, Wawasee, 1977, and Deandra Carney, Indianapolis Arlington, 1978, and Maicel Malone, Indianapolis North Central, 1985
800 meters	2:09.99	Kari Krehnbrink, Lafayette Jefferson, 1985
400-meter relay	0:47.91	Gary Roosevelt, 1983 (A. McClatchey, S. Nelson, D. Banks, M. Jones)
800-meter relay	1:40.92	Indianapolis Marshall, 1983 (V. Hawkins, D. Croom, B. Taylor, B. Holland)
1600-meter relay	3:48.18	Fort Wayne South Side, 1983 (C. Tyree, L. Nathan, T. McCloud, A. Goodman)

High jump	6 ft.	Angela Bradburn, Norwell, 1985
Long jump	19 ft., 7 3/4 in.	Pam Pearson, Anderson, 1982
Shot put (8 lbs., 13 oz.)	46 ft., 3 1/2 in.	Deborah Smith, Lake Station, 1984
Discus	148 ft., 9 in.	Debra Snider, Valparaiso, 1980
300-meter low hurdles	042.85	LeShundra Nathan, Fort Wayne South, 1984

[*For other Track and Field records see Senior Olympics, below.*]

Wrestling, *College*

These are records held by Indiana schools and athletes in Big Ten competition:

ARNOLD PLAZA, Purdue University, is the sole Hoosier to have been *champion four times in the conference*, in 1947, 1949, and 1950 at 121 pounds and in 1948 at 114 1/2 pounds.

BOB MARSHALL, Purdue University, held *three Big Ten titles*, in 1960 and 1962 at 157 pounds and in 1961 at 167 pounds.

INDIANA UNIVERSITY leads Purdue University in *Big Ten titles in row*, 4 to 3. I.U. won in 1931, 1932, 1933, and 1934 and Purdue was the title holder in 1948, 1949, and 1950.

BOTH Indiana University and Purdue University have had *five individual champions in one tournament*, fourth best in that category in the Big Ten. I.U. had five champions in 1933, Purdue in 1950.

Wrestling, *High School*

ONLY one high school in Indiana has won the *state wrestling title four years in a row two times*. Bloomington High School was the champion in 1941, 1942, 1943, and 1950 (there was a break in competition during World War II and immediately after) and again in 1969, 1970, 1971, and 1972. The only high school to win *five times in a row* was Delta, at Muncie, which added victory February 23, 1985, to championships in 1981, 1982, 1983, and 1985. Delta's coach was Don Patton, the *only coach of a five-in-a-row team*.

THE Indiana school to score the *most points in a dual meet* (13 classes competing) is Monroe Adams Central, scoring 78 points in 1973 against zero for Winchester.

[SEE ALSO *Automobiles; Balloons; Boats; and Speed*.]

STAGE

THE *first theatrical production* in Indiana was *She Stoops to Conquer*, staged in a large back room of Wither's Inn at Vincennes the third week of November, 1814. The play, with a curtain time of 6 p.m., was given by the Vincennes Thespian Society, which folded after two years.

ROBERT OWEN, Welsh industrialist-socialist who established New Harmony, wrote the *first play* in Indiana: *Pocahontas: a Historical Drama*, penned not long after he took over New Harmony from the Rappite sect in 1825. Most historians agree that the drama did little for the few reviewers who may have been around at the time and less for audiences.

THE first movie-vaudeville theater in the nation to be *electrically lighted* was Keiths in Indianapolis. It opened September 13, 1875, as the Grand Opera House, later being sold to Keiths. It played vaudeville until 1928 and closed July 30, 1964.

THE *oldest continuing chatauqua* and now the sole one to operate in Indiana is that at Fountain Park, Remington. It started in 1895, and presents a varied program of culture and entertainment in the original chatauqua fashion annually during the first two weeks of August.

PROBABLY the *most elaborate theatrical production* in the state was *Ben-Hur*, which came to the English Opera House in Indianapolis November 24, 1902, for a two-week run and required a crew of nine mechanics and carpenters. They spent three days remodeling the stage to handle the two carloads of special machinery. The main device was a treadmill costing $15,000 which carried the weight of two horses and chariots, made them bump and sway, and dislodged a wheel from the chariot of Messala at the proper time. "We shall have to take out the old stage at English's, which was a new stage this year, and rebuild it for the management before we leave," said an advance agent named Brady.

THE *only Hoosier to have three plays* on Broadway at the same time was George Ade, whose feat has been matched only by playwright Neil Simon. Ade's plays, performed in 1904, were *The College Widow*, *The Country Chairman*, and *Peggy from Paris*.

THE first *Broadway play* to deal with *football and college* was *The College Widow*, written by Indiana's George Ade in 1904. Although it was predicted to flop because of its subject, the play ran nearly a year and grossed $2,000,000.

THE Indianapolis Civic Theater is the *oldest continuously operating American community theater*, having been active since 1914. Its season is from September to June and it holds public auditions for its productions. It moved in 1974 to its fourth home, Showalter Pavilion at the Indianapolis Museum of Art.

PROBABLY the *most active puppeteers* have been Martin Stevens and his wife Margi, of Middlebury. Beginning with puppet shows 45 years ago, the Stevenses developed a repertoire of 20 puppet shows which were given, mainly for schools, all over the nation by various puppet companies "franchised" to give the Stevens shows.

STREETCARS: SEE *Railroads*.

STRUCTURES

THE *oldest brick house* in Indiana is said to be the Ash house along the Ohio River in Lamb near Vevay, built in

1798 by George Ash, son of a prominent Kentucky land-owner. The house sits across the Ohio from the mouth of Kentucky River.

THE *sole house of upright logs* surviving in Indiana is the Broulet French house at Vincennes, constructed in 1806 by a fur trader and one of only six such houses left in North America.

INDIANA'S *first courthouse* was a log building 31 by 25 feet, rising two stories at Salisbury in Wayne County. Constructed in 1811, a trial was held October 28th of that year while the building was underway. The courthouse is preserved at Centerville.

THE Ohio County Courthouse at Rising Sun, built in Greek Revival style in 1845, is the *oldest courthouse* still in use in Indiana. The architect is uncertain.

THE *largest columns* ever quarried and cut by hand in one piece are those of the Boone County Courthouse at Lebanon. The eight columns weigh 30 tons each and stand 38 feet tall. The same courthouse is the only public building in the world with a *meridian line* through its center (the Second Principal Meridian).

THE Decatur County Courthouse at Greensburg, probably the state's *oddest courthouse*, is widely known for the tree which grows in its tower. The building, designed by Edwin May, was completed in 1860; the tree was first probably observed July 30, 1870, evidently having taken root there by accident. So far 12 large-tooth aspens have been used to perpetuate the oddity.

WAYNE COUNTY is believed to have had *more courthouses* actually built—5—than any other county.

THE *first "skyscraper"* in Indiana was a three-story brick structure built at Walnut and High streets in Lawrenceburg in 1819, and later used as a hotel.

INDIANA'S *most unusual jail* is a two-story, cylindrical, revolving cellblock at Crawfordsville, built in 1882 and believed to be one of only six like it constructed in the nation. The jail, 21 feet in diameter, with eight wedge-shaped cells on each floor, is listed in the National Register of Historic Places and was acquired by the Montgomery County Cultural Foundation as a museum structure. Cells had to be rotated to a position in front of the exit before prisoners could be taken out; there reportedly were no escapes from it.

THE *oldest continuously operating grist mill* in Indiana is that at Bonneyville Mill Park at Bristol outside Elkhart; it has been grinding grain since the day Edward Bonney erected it in 1832. It was acquired by the Elkhart County Park and Recreation Department in 1968 and continues to grind corn, wheat, buckwheat, and rye for sale and on special contract, although most of the customers are tourists. Among things which attract them to the mill is the mill wheel, the *only horizontal wheel* in the state. A nearby stream is diverted through the basement of the mill and the wheel, completely submerged, is turned by the current pushing against propellor-like fins. In 1919 the mill was converted to electrical power, but returned to water power in 1974.

THE *earliest lighthouse* was that at Michigan City, planned with a 40-foot-high tower in 1836. A new three-story lighthouse was built in 1858; it was enlarged in 1904. When no longer used as a lighthouse, the structure became headquarters for the Coast Guard Service, then stood vacant for years until it was sold to Michigan City. It now is a museum emphasizing maritime treasures and history in that area of Lake Michigan. A small automatic warning light at Michigan City serves the purpose of a lighthouse today and is the only one in Indiana.

THE *oldest volunteer fire department* still at the same location is Washington Fire Company No. 2 at Madison, which occupies a building erected by the city in 1848. The fire company was organized January 22, 1846.

THE *first observatory* in Indiana was established in a

small brick building at Earlham College in 1861, only the second such facility west of the Alleghenies. It is equipped with a telescope installed in 1879.

THE *first prefabricated house* erected in Indiana was the Shindler Mansion at Orleans, put up in the 1880s with material cut and marked in Philadelphia. The house was a present from John B. Stetson, the hat manufacturer, to the parents of his bride, Elizabeth (Libby) Shindler.

THE round barn on the Kingen Farm near McCordsville has a diameter of 100 feet, and is believed to be the *largest round barn* in the state. Construction began around 1895.

FULTON COUNTY is the home of *round barns* in Indiana, having 15, more than any other county. There are an estimated 150 round barns in the state.

THE *largest terminal for interurban cars*, which ran on rails between cities, was the Traction Terminal in Indianapolis. It opened September 12, 1904, with the capacity for 400 arrivals and departures daily on nine tracks. An estimated 5 million passengers a year passed through the terminal, which was half a block from the Indiana Statehouse. At the time of its construction, the terminal was the largest in the world. It was razed in 1970.

THE *first skeletal-type* (steel framework) *high-rise* building in Indiana was the Majestic at Pennsylvania and Maryland streets in Indianapolis; it was designed by Oscar D. Bohlen of Indianapolis, built in 1895, and later known as the Farm Bureau Co-op Building.

WHEN a prosperous mill owner of 1914 erected the Farmers Club at Seymour as a gift, it is believed to be the only time in the nation that a place was *built specifically for farmers' wives and children* to use while their men were doing business in town. The building, recently slated for restoration, is on the National Register of Historic Places.

THE 40-foot dial at the Colgate-Palmolive-Peet Company, Jeffersonville, is the *largest clock* in Indiana; it can be seen for 2 1/2 miles, but faces Louisville, Ky., over the Ohio River. The mechanical clock came from Jersey City in 1924 and has a pendulum of 330 pounds on the end of a 76-foot rod. The minute hand is 21 feet long, the hour hand 16 feet long, and numerals for the hours are spaced 2 3/16 feet apart.

THE *largest temple in the world* used solely for Scottish Rite activities is the cathedral in Indianapolis, begun in 1927 and finished 2 years later. The building is 330 feet long, 120 feet wide, and the tower is 212 feet tall.

THE *largest fieldhouse in the U.S.* owned and operated by a private school is Hinkle Fieldhouse at Butler University in Indianapolis, which seats 14,945; it was built in 1928.

THE first *all-glass bank building* in Indiana and probably in the U.S. was Irwin Union Bank & Trust Company at Columbus. It was erected in 1956 and a three-story addition opened in 1972.

THE *Cyclotron Facility* at Bloomington is the largest such device in Indiana. It was one of a kind in the world when put into operation by Indiana University in 1974.

FOR, their dimensions, the *heaviest things* in Indiana are four magnets which are the heart of the Indiana University Cyclotron Facility at Bloomington. Used in atom-smashing activities, the magnets are each 20 feet tall and each weighs 500 tons, a total weight of 4 million pounds.

THE *largest sports arena in the state* is Market Square Arena in Indianapolis. It opened in 1974 and seats 18,000.

THE *largest Dairy Queen* in Indiana, perhaps in the world, is at Westfield on U.S. 31 at Ind. 32. It has 10,000 square feet of space, dining on two levels, and is owned by Jim Stephans of Indianapolis. It was opened in 1979.

THE first house in the U.S. built with a *wooden foundation directly on the ground* without crawl space or basement was the Sunstar, a solar-heated home built by Ivy Homes, Inc., on westside Indianapolis in 1983.

THE *largest covered stadium* in Indiana is the Hoosier Dome in Indianapolis. It opened in 1984 and seats 63,000. The dome rises 193 feet at its highest point, and covers an area of 8 acres.

WHEN the R. V. Welch Investments, Inc., building in Indianapolis was topped out late in 1984, it became the *tallest structure* in Indiana *made of precast concrete*. It is 17 stories tall. A precast building is one in which the framework is poured in concrete elsewhere and the pieces hauled to the site to be fitted together.

THE building in Indiana with the *largest ground-floor dimensions*, constructed as a single structure, is the U.S. Army Finance and Accounting Center at Fort Benjamin Harrision in Indianapolis, which is one-eighth mile long and one-fifth mile wide. It covers 14 acres. Three stories tall, it contains 1.6 million square feet of space and 80,000 square feet of windows.

THE *largest collegiate stadium* in Indiana is Ross-Ade at Purdue University, West Lafayette, which seats 69,250.

THE *largest Memorial Union building in the world* is the Indiana University Memorial Union with 475,299 square feet of space.

THE American United Life Building in downtown Indianapolis is the *tallest building* in Indiana, its 38 stories rising 533 feet, 29 feet higher than the Indiana National Bank building, also in Indianapolis.

THE *largest tent* built in Indiana is one measuring 140 by 340 feet, constructed in 1983 by Anchor Industries at Evansville and used by Hunter Mountain Recreation Area in New York for festivals and other activities.

[SEE ALSO *Counties; Education; Limestone; Museums; Music; Railroads.*]

STUNTS

APPLE PICKING—THE 365½ bushels of apples picked in eight hours by George Adrian at an orchard near Waverly September 23, 1980, is an Indiana and *world record*. Adrian began at 6:30 A.M., stopped for lunch and for two small breaks. He continued after the 8 hours to pick a total of 430 bushels of Red Delicious fruit.

Baseball—THE longest baseball game in Indiana was 56 innings, played March 19, 1983, in the gymnasium at Lawrence North High School, Indianapolis, by about 40 youths raising money for a press box for the school stadium.

Baseball cards—BASEBALL cards totalling 3,336 were made into a "house" covering an entire living room floor in July 1979 by Danny Burns, Tim Snyder, Corey Brooks, and Joe Rench, all of Muncie. The stacking was done over two days.

Beef eating—THE Indiana record for beef consumption is 51 ounces, eaten by Lester Van Bibber in one sitting at the Briarpatch restaurant in Evansville in 1975. Van Bibber moved to Seattle and the Briarpatch later became T. Twigg's.

Brick walking—THE record for continuous walking with a brick in one hand is approximately 51 miles, done in August 1976 by Indianapolis accountant David Opalak, who went from the intersection of Interstate 465 and Ind. 67 at Indianapolis to Bloomington's city hall in 22½ hours.

Burial alive—THE mark for being buried alive in Indiana, at least on purpose, is the 48 hours spent underground by Bill Shirk, who left his grave, which was equipped with a telephone, heating, and air conditioning at 2 P.M. October 31, 1976. The burial was done to raise money for the Marion County Association of Retarded Citizens.

Can piling—THE record height for piling cans probably

is 25 feet, 3 inches, reached with 7,000 cans in July 1976 by young members of the First Church of the Nazarene at Valparaiso. The cans were then sold to raise money for the church.

Card stacking—The tallest stack of cards erected in Indiana is 12 feet, 9 inches, built with 68 levels August 9, 1983, by John Sain of South Bend in the engineering school at the University of Notre Dame.

CB talking—The record for continuous talk on the CB radio in Indiana is 100 hours, set in 1976 by Pat Smith of Shelbyville, who claimed a *world record*.

Chess—THE longest recorded chess match was between Stan Zygmunt and Ilya Schwartzman in the 45th Avenue shopping center at Munster from December 28, 1979, to January 4, 1980, a total of 168 hours and a *world mark*.

Chinups—TED A. HAMILTON, Indianapolis, holds the *world's record* of 9 chinups using one finger, done in 1980 in the Indianapolis gymnasium of Fred Hoffmeister.

Cigars—LEE HYLAND, a lieutenant for the Marion County Sheriff's Department at the time, puffed 28 regulation-sized cigars simultaneously in August 1979 to set the Indiana record. A companion helped Hyland light the stogies, which were puffed for seven minutes.

Clapping—A continuous hand clapping record of 15 hours, 6 minutes was set December 24 and 25, 1973, by Suzy Fivel and Mariam Silverman, students of North Central High School in Indianapolis, in the Fivel home.

Comedy—"MIXED NUTS" performed 28 continuous hours August 6 and 7, 1982, at Broad Ripple Playhouse in Indianapolis for the Indiana record for non-stop comedy. Members included Mike Keys, Laura Guyer, Randy Montgomery, Teresa King, Cynthia Savage, Wanda Skaggs, and Mac Spears.

Dungeons and Dragons—THE Indiana record for continuous playing of the game Dungeons and Dragons is 120 hours, set from noon August 22, to 12:01 P.M. August 27, 1982, by six high-school students at Greenfield: Mark Bernhard, David Franklin, Shawn Jones, Jeff Underwood, Jon Brown, and Jeff Fink.

Escapes—No one has successfully performed more escapes than Bill Shirk, an Indianapolis radio station owner, whose record stands at 17. They have included escapes from jail and from strait jackets while suspended from helicopters. Many of his escapes were duplicated for a film in which he starred, *Modern Day Houdini*, filmed in Indianapolis.

Guitar strumming—THE record for strumming a guitar in Indiana is 200 hours, 2 minutes, set in 1978 by David Hathaway over nine days in a music store in Marion.

Group jump—THE Indiana record for jumping simultaneously, for which there seem to be few standards, is 3,400 persons, who leaped September 25, 1980, at Ball State University at Muncie. The event was arranged by editors of the *Orient*, the university yearbook.

Gum wrappers—THE longest string of gum wrappers in the state is believed to be that assembled by Teri Floyd of Indianapolis over a period of 5 years before 1978. It reached a length of 313 feet, 6½ inches.

Hitathon—THE record in Indiana for constantly hitting a baseball is 50 hours, set February 11 to February 13, 1983, in Castleton Square shopping center in Indianapolis by 40 boys from Lawrence North High School raising money for a press box at the school stadium. A pitching machine was used. The marathon began at 5 P.M. on a Friday and ended at 7 P.M. on Sunday.

Horse riding—LARRY MCKNIGHT, manager of an Indianapolis movie theater, riding at the Indianapolis Saddle Club, set a record by staying in the saddle on a horse 120 hours beginning July 8, 1975, but he left on crutches after the 5-day effort.

Hula hoop —INDIANA'S sole *national* hula-hoop champion is David Williams of Indianapolis, who won first place doing a routine to the song "Aquarius" in May 1972 against 12 other finalists at Los Angeles.

Hula hooping—THE Indiana record for non-stop hula hooping is 25½ hours, set January 27, 1979, by Toni Barrett, an Indiana University senior participating in Spirit of Sport All-Niter in Bloomington to raise funds for the Indiana Special Olympics. Toni began twirling at 9:30 A.M. on a Friday and gave it up at 11 A.M. Saturday.

Ice skating—THE ice skating record in Indiana of 100 hours was set January 1–5, 1975, at the Ice Dome Skating Rink in Indianapolis by Mark Losure and Steve Roberts; it is believed to still be the endurance mark for the state.

Immobility—MARDEANA ODOM remained motionless (except for eyelids) 5 hours, 32 minutes March 30, 1974, in the Sears Roebuck & Co. store in Castleton Square shopping center, Indianapolis. The inactivity, called freeze modeling, began at 1 P.M. and ended at 6:32 P.M. for the 16-year-old girl; she was watched at times by 120 spectators as she set the Indiana record.

Jail escape—THE record time for getting out of a jail while restrained with three pairs of handcuffs, leg irons, and 50-pound chains and behind two locked cell doors is 3 hours, 44 minutes and 42 seconds in Indiana, set by Bill Shirk, escape artist and owner of Indianapolis radio station WXLW.

Kissing—THE record for non-stop kissing in Indiana is four days, set as of June 2, 1983, by Dino DeLorean and Barbara Kane. It was part of a marathon in which the two kissed a total of 21 days. They began at Only Hearts Boutique, a New York shop, but after 17 days the boutique decided to end the stunt. The kissers were invited by WXUS-FM radio station at Lafayette to continue their marathon in Indiana. The kissing was sustained during a flight to Chicago and a trip by van to Lafayette. Rules permitted the kissers two hours of sleep every 24 hours and a five-minute break each hour.

Kite—THE altitude record for kites was set at Lake Michigan near Gary in June 1969. Using 19 kites in a train, the fliers, all of Wirt High School, reached a calculated height of 35,531 feet on their third attempt. Involved were Steve Lyman, Barry Lindstrom, Mike Galanis, Mike Nichovich, Bill Croll, Terry Retson, Carl Dreher, Dick O'Brien, Jon Trathen, Brian Ivkovich, Steve Paloncy, and Warren Hoover.

Monopoly playing—THE record for continuous playing of Monopoly is 100 hours, accomplished in October 1975 by 96 students of Brownsburg High School and some adults playing in four-hour shifts in a treehouse on the edge of property owned by Mrs. James D. Crum. The players also established some kind of altitude record for the game; the two-story treehouse was 30 feet off the ground.

Nuptials, highest—THE highest Indiana wedding was atop a 222-foot tower when Ora Williams and George P. Lenfers were married at Evansville in 1906. The tower was a smokestack newly erected by the Evansville Gas works; the manager offered $50, a bedroom suite, and a gas stove to anyone who would be married on top. Six couples applied and Ora and George were chosen by lot. As 10,000 watched, they climbed to the top of a crude ladder, where they were joined by the Rev. C. J. Armentraut, an engineer, and two reporters. The bride fainted after she returned to the ground.

Paper chain—THE Indiana record for a paper chain is 15 miles, 230 yards; it was constructed by 1,200 pupils at Craig Junior High School in Indianapolis to promote Spirit-Pride Week. It took the chain makers from 8 A.M. to 5 P.M. May 5, 1976.

Phone calls, underground—BILL SHIRK, Indianapolis, talked to a record 2,000 persons via telephone while buried

alive in Indianapolis. The site was WXLW studios in Indianapolis; the coffin was 7 feet by 35 inches by 21 inches
high. Shirk, owner of the station, suffered his greatest
hazard during the burial (done to benefit the Marion
County Association of Retarded Citizens) from the pressure
of the crowd standing on the "grave" waiting their turn on
the phone.

Pole sitting—ALTHOUGH there are no standards, the
pole-sitting champion of Indiana evidently was Mauri Rose
Kirby of Indianapolis. At 17 as a promotion stunt she
climbed into a shed 3 feet by 6 feet atop a 71-foot pole at a
small drive-in restaurant, the Southwind, on the south side
of Indianapolis and stayed aloft 211 days and 9 hours, coming down March 4, 1959. She married John Sanders, whom
she met while setting her record, and moved to Tucson,
Ariz.

Reunion—THE most unusual class reunion trip in the
state was that made by Ray Sears for the 25th reunion of
the class of 1935 at Butler University, Indianapolis; he ran
to the gathering from his Shelbyville home, a distance of
some 30 miles. Sears was 53 years old.

Salad—THE largest salad made in Indiana was one put
together in a Sailboat in August 1978 at Greenwood Park
Shopping Center by Gary Bone and Rob Packard, aided by
Deanna Regan and Sue Creech. The salad used 320 heads
of lettuce, 50 pounds of carrots, 24 heads of red cabbage, 36
bundles of broccoli, oranges, grapes, pineapple, bell pep-
pers, onions, 100 hardboiled eggs, 24 loaves of bread, 8 gallons of salad dressing, and 1,000 cherry tomatoes.

Shakespeare—A marathon in which works of William
Shakespeare were read for just over 100 hours is the record
in Indiana. The readings began April 24, 1984, at the University of Notre Dame, South Bend, and were conducted
by the Notre Dame Shakespeare Club to raise money for
the Women's Care Center and for Adam Milani, a high
school hockey player who suffered spinal damage during a
game.

Showering—THE continuous showering record in Indiana is 174 hours set by David A. Hoffman of Gary in a dormitory at Indiana University, ending Friday, January 28, 1972, after an estimated 35,000 gallons of water (worth about $35) had been used.

Shrimp eating—FRANK EMMONS, a teacher at Woodview Junior High School in Indianapolis, ate 3 pounds of shrimp in 30 minutes July 1, 1976; this is believed to be the record in Indiana. The shrimp, valued at $21, were eaten in the Durbin Junction Restaurant in Indianapolis.

Situps—THE record for continuous situps is 15,325, done in a little more than 10 hours March 17, 1973, by Tim Wood in the Jordan YMCA in Indianapolis. Wood, a lifeguard at the Y, watched college and high school basketball games on TV during the effort and was watched by an estimated 200 visitors during the day.

Spaghetti sitting—THE record for sitting in wet spaghetti in Indiana is 68 hours, set from December 18 to December 24, 1981. Lynn Helms, sports director for radio station WRBI in Batesville, sat in the store window of Halsman Company at Batesville to raise money for a rehabilitation organization. She got out of the tub of 400 pounds of spaghetti occasionally to walk around and changed clothing once in a while.

Straitjacket escape—BILL SHIRK, Indianapolis, got out of a straitjacket in 4.52 seconds, an Indiana and *world mark*.

Straitjacket, height—BILL SHIRK, Indianapolis, escaped from a straitjacket 1,610 feet in the air, suspended from a helicopter; this is believed to be an altitude record. His time for the escape, 18.83 seconds, also is considered a record.

Sundae—THE record-size ice-cream sundae in Indiana was concocted May 4, 1974, at Batesville by Gib Young of Young's Dairy Queen Brazier, using 2,056 pounds of soft ice cream and 17 gallons of syrup. Although there were only about 2,900 residents in the town, 10,000 persons showed up to eat the sundae.

Table tennis—FOUR students of Lebanon High School played table tennis doubles 72 hours and 50 minutes, concluding March 1, 1977, to set the mark in Indiana. The event was in the gymnasium at Lebanon during spring break.

Tie—THE largest necktie ever created in Indiana was one 60 feet long, hung October 1, 1984, at 2 West Washington Street in Indianapolis as part of a money-raising event for beautification of downtown Indianapolis. The tie, which weighed 250 pounds, was painted in two weeks by Mike Hebbing under commission from Melvin Simon and Associates.

Tractor trip—LARRY HARRIS and his brother Rodney of Green Forks (Wayne County) drove a regular farm tractor from Brunswick, Ga., to Oceanside, Calif., a trip of some 2,500 miles from ocean to ocean, starting January 1, 1981, and reaching the West Coast in 9 days, 25 minutes. The tractor, a Case, used 2,500 gallons of gasoline on the trip, the longest by a Hoosier tractor driver.

Teeter-totter—TWO youths from Earl Park established the Indiana record for teeter-tottering at 12½ consecutive days in 1975 while an estimated 2,000 onlookers visited the site. They were Larry Turner, 18, and John Fleming, 17. In addition to five-minute rest periods hourly, they took turns sleeping on the teeter-totter one at a time while the other kept the device in motion.

Tootsie lookalike—WHAT is believed to be the nation's first Tootsie lookalike contest was held in Indianapolis January 17, 1983, by radio station WIBC to choose a person who most resembled Dustin Hoffman in the role of a man dressed as a woman in the movie *Tootsie*. Bob Krider of Madison won the title against five others. First runnerup was a woman, Mary Rodrequez, as was the second runnerup, Susie Dodd.

Volleyball—TWELVE students at Huntington College played volleyball continuously 60 hours, 8 minutes in January 1979, the Indiana record. Those involved were Gregory Auman, Michael Chafin, Scott Dentler, Clark Wallis, Jeffrey Bennett, Michael Brown, Gary Hoobler, Charles Martindale, Jr., Martin McDonnell, Jeff Rostochack, Larry Jackson, and Walter Starrick.

SUBMARINES

THE first submarines used in Lake Michigan were four invented and built by Lodner D. Phillips of LaPorte and tried between 1845 and 1851. The first, of wood covered with copper in the shape of a whitefish, was launched from Michigan City. It used a pole through the underside to the lake bottom for propulsion and was not practical. The second, a similar design, was launched at Chicago; the third sank in Lake Erie; the fourth used a steam engine for power when not submerged, and had a cannon on deck.

[SEE ALSO *Wars, world*.]

T

TELEGRAPH

THE *first message* sent via telegraph was one chosen by a Hoosier, Annie Ellsworth of Lafayette, Ind., who gave Samuel F. B. Morse the question "What hath God wrought?" to transmit from Washington to Baltimore after Morse had perfected his invention in 1844.

THE *first telegraph office* in Indiana was opened in Vincennes in 1847.

THE O'Reilly Line was the *first telegraph route* built in Indiana, leading into the state from Dayton, Ohio, and going to Chicago via Richmond, Indianapolis, and Lafayette. A branch from Lafayette led to Terre Haute and Evansville. The line was completed in 1848 by the Ohio, Indiana and Illinois Company, principally owned by Henry O'Reilly.

THE *initial telegraph message* sent in Indiana was transmitted over the O'Reilly Line from Dayton to Indianapolis May 12, 1848. There seems to be no record of its content.

AN exchange opened in 1879 in Indianapolis for telegraph business was the *first exchange* in Indiana. It was in the Vance Block (later the Indiana Trust Company Building) at the corner of Washington Street and Virginia Avenue.

THE *first transmission of a wireless message* in the U.S. occurred in May 1899 when Dr. Jerome Green sent one from the spire of Sacred Heart Church on the University of Notre Dame campus to nearby St. Mary's College. Its content seems lost to time.

TELEPHONE

ALTHOUGH unknown to the public, witnesses have testified that Charles Reitz of Indianapolis *invented a telephone* well before the device was patented by Alexander Graham Bell. A jack-of-all-trades, Reitz operated a business for making mail boxes, appliances, and small inventions, and used his "voice over wires" to communicate between his shop and his home. Acquaintances said Reitz often was visited by Bell, Thomas Edison, and other electrical experts.

THE *first telephones* seen by the public in Indiana were two sets exhibited at the Indiana State Fair in Indianapolis in September 1877. They later were moved to the Wales Coal Company in Indianapolis to connect its office and coal yards.

THE first Indiana *schools to have a telephone* were in Evansville; in the 1870s they installed circuits with $300 worth of poles, wires, batteries, and telephones purchased by the superintendent.

THE first *telephones in public use* in Indiana are believed to have been those brought to Evansville from Boston in 1879 by William Gavitt, who started a 10-phone exchange. Gavitt obtained his phones from Theodore Vail, then president of the Bell system.

THE *world's first multiple switchboards* were installed at Evansville in 1880.

THE first *automatic telephone exchange* was installed at LaPorte in 1888 by the exchange supervisor, W. P. Cushman. The exchange, a wired box with five keys, was invented by Kansas City undertaker Almon B. Strowger. The invention never was a huge success, however, and in 1899 Strowger sold it for a small sum. He died in 1903 and was buried at Greenwood, Ind.

THE first *permanent dial telephone system* was at Richmond. Although LaPorte had the first telephone dialing system, that city went back to operators about 1900. Richmond never changed from dialing after it began on October 26, 1907.

THE *first fiber-optic line* put into telephone service in Indiana, carrying calls by light instead of electrical impulses, was an installation 2.8 miles long from the main center of the General Telephone Company in Fort Wayne to an exchange building on the north side of that city. The line, put in service in March 1979, could carry 672 simultaneous conversations.

THE *longest fiber optic telephone line* in Indiana is 37 miles long, going into service late in 1983 between Fort Wayne and North Manchester.

[SEE ALSO *Inventions.*]

TELESCOPE

THE *largest reflecting telescope* in Indiana is that of the J. I. Holcomb Observatory on the Indianapolis campus of Butler University; its mirror measures 38 inches in diameter.

TELEVISION

THE first *television transmitting station* in Indiana was W9XG, established by Purdue University December 31, 1931, to fulfill a research project into development of a TV receiver using a cathode ray tube. The project was backed by Grigsby-Grunow Company, a Chicago radio manufacturer, and was led by Roscoe H. George, research professor, and Howard J. Heim, research associate. March 29, 1932, the researchers began taking their portable TV receiver around Indiana and found that it could receive good pictures from as far away as 150 miles. The project ended in 1932. Radio Corporation of America purchased all the pending patent applications in 1934.

IN 1939 Philco dealers put on a demonstration in the Antlers Hotel in downtown Indianapolis, marking the *first public display of television* in Indiana. WLS set up a demonstration that same year at the Indiana State Fair.

THE Farnsworth Television & Radio Corporation plant at Marion is believed to be the *first to produce television receivers* in Indiana in the spring of 1947. They were 22-tube models with a 10-inch picture tube, but all sets were sent outside Indiana for distribution. The firm was that of Philo T. Farnsworth, who bought the Capehart Corporation at Fort Wayne in 1938 and expanded.

K. AND S. FILMS, operating in a building at Market and West Streets in Indianapolis, produced the *first movie for television* in Indiana, using a script by Dick Stone, a columnist for *The Indianapolis Star*, showing food preparation. It was shot in September 1948 and was marketed through Chicago. The film company was operated by Roger Sneeden, a neighbor of Stone, and Walter Krull.

THE first *commercial television station* in Indiana was WFBM-TV, Channel 6, in Indianapolis which in 1949 broadcast a baseball game from Victory Field (now Bush Stadium) in Indianapolis. One of the first live shows at WFBM was the last parade of the Grand Army of the Republic in 1949 in Indianapolis. The channel also broadcast the May 30, 1949, Indianapolis 500-Mile Race, the first time it was telecast live. It was estimated that the 500-Mile Race telecast went to about 3,000 sets, probably 15,000 persons.

WFBM-TV broadcast the 1949 500-Mile Race live in its entirety. This was the *first televised sports event* in Indiana.

THE *first television newscaster* in Indiana was Gilbert Forbes, who went on the air for Channel 6, WFBM, in 1949.

NOVEMBER 11, 1949, when WTTV, Bloomington, went on the air as the second television station in Indiana, Bloomington became the *smallest city in the nation with a television station*. The first TV station had been WFBM-TV in Indianapolis. The third TV station was WSBT-TV, South Bend.

BLOOMINGTON HIGH SCHOOL became the *first school* in Indiana *to broadcast television programs* with the telecast of the senior play at 7:30 P.M. December 8, 1949. A television cable was run into the school from WTTV, which was across the street. The initial broadcast was followed by a weekly program, "Know Your Teacher."

THE first commercial telecasts by a symphony in the U.S. were a series of seven half-hour programs begun in December 1951 and ending in February 1952 by the Indianapolis Symphony Orchestra over WFBM-TV.

EVANSVILLE became the first *city to have more than one TV station* in 1953. They were WEHT and WFIE-TV. Indianapolis did not get its second station until 1954 with the start of WISH-TV.

IN 1959 eight educational institutions, including Indiana University and Purdue University, launched the *Midwest Program on Airborne Television Instruction* in which a DC-7 flew out of Purdue to beam programs to the ground over a six-state area. The program started with seven schools in Indiana in 1961 and grew to 1,200-plus schools a year later, but when further channels were denied in 1965 by the FCC, the airborne station died.

THE highest rating of all times of a television show by a Hoosier was the Red Skelton Show on February 1, 1966, with an average audience rating of 33.3. It featured George Gobel as a guest, playing Toulouse Lautrec, who was asked by Sheriff Deadeye, played by Skelton, to autograph a painting. The Hollies, a British rock group, sang.

[SEE ALSO *Colleges and Universities; Military.*]

TOILETS

THE first *indoor bathroom* in Indiana probably was that built in the early 1800s in Indianapolis by William S. Hubbard, who pumped cistern water to the attic of a home he built at 1126 North Meridian Street and allowed it to flow by gravity to bathroom fixtures. The house later was the Indianapolis headquarters of the American Red Cross.

THE first *pay toilet* in the nation is thought to have been established in 1910 at Terre Haute by a station master trying to prevent his newly installed restrooms (a novelty at the time) from being occupied by curious townspeople when train passengers arrived. He installed nickel-operated locks to discourage use, but removed the locks for the arrival of passenger trains since toilet privileges were included in the price of the ticket. The toilet locks probably came from the Nik-o-lok Company in Indianapolis, opened by C. N. Van Cleve about the same time to merchandise coin-operated locks under rights obtained from the German inventor Emil Luden.

T O O L S : SEE *Collections.*

T O R N A D O E S

WHEN twisters struck in Indiana Palm Sunday, 1965, they caused 137 deaths and brought injury to 1,750, the *worst casualty list for tornadoes* in the state. In more recent times, 48 died and 5,500 were hurt in Indiana April 3, 1974, in tornadoes which caused half a billion dollars worth of damage.

THE *fewest tornadoes* reported in a year in Indiana is 6, the total for 1953 and 1972; the state averages 23 tornadoes sighted annually.

THE *most tornadoes* reported in Indiana in a single day were the 48 sighted on Palm Sunday, 1965. *Porter and Marion lead* all Indiana counties in tornado sightings reported since 1916, with 30 each.

THE *longest tornado* reported in Indiana was one which began at Otterbein April 3, 1974, and ended in LaGrange County, 121 miles away. In its path 18 died and 362 were hurt.

T R A I N S : see *Collections; Crime and Criminals; Museums.*

T R A N S P L A N T S : see *Medicine.*

T R E E S

THE *largest sycamore stump* in Indiana is undoubtedly the one in Highland Park in Kokomo is 12 feet high and 51 feet in circumference. It once was used as a telephone booth and can hold 24 people. The tree stood west of Kokomo on Wildcat Creek bottomland and was about 100 feet tall. The stump was moved into Highland Park, where it is displayed under a sheltering roof, in 1916.

[SEE ALSO *Plants.*]

T R U C K S : see *Automobiles and Trucks.*

U

U N D E R G R O U N D : see *Animals; Archaeology; Caves; Coal; Fossils; Gas; Gems; Graves; Limestone.*

UNDERWATER: SEE *Business; Submarines; Wars, world.*

URBAN: SEE *Cities and Towns.*

V

VITAL STATISTICS

THE *first white child* born in Indiana is believed to have been Anthony Foucher, born at Fort Ouiatenon July 22, 1741, to Mary Louise Lefebure and John Baptist Foucher. Foucher later was ordained a *Catholic priest* in Canada, the *first ordained west of the Alleghenies.*

THE *smallest Indiana baby to live* is believed to have been Ada Elizabeth Worland, born in Indianapolis in 1900 weighing 1 1/2 pounds. Her life was preserved by a makeshift incubator created by a soap box 2 feet square which was placed close to an oven and surrounded by Mason jars containing hot water. Her survival is the more remarkable because she was born at home and cared for there.

THE *smallest baby born alive* in Indiana is believed to be an infant 6 1/2 inches long, weighing 6 ounces, reportedly arriving in an Indianapolis hospital February 23, 1952. It lived 12 hours. A twin was stillborn. (*Guinness Book of World Records*)

THE *first quintuplets* born in Indiana were those delivered to Suzanne Gaither, 21, in Indiana University Hospital, Indianapolis, August 3, 1983. They were Ashlee Charlene, Joshua Frank Johnson, Renee Brook, Rhealyn Frances and Brandon Benjamin. The father was Sidney Gaither, the physician Dr. Frank Johnson. The babies also were possibly the first blacks quints in the U.S.

THE *longest-running shared birthday* is that of the male members of four generations of the Carter family in Indianapolis; all were born on February 24, without planning. They are Richard R. Carter, his son, George W. Carter, his son, Donald C. Carter, and his son, Donald Duane Carter.

THE *longest-living twins* in Indiana and probably the nation are Sudie Rigdon and Martha Messersmith, *nees* Moran, who reached 100 on March 14, 1984, at Bradner Village in Marion. They had lived in the nursing home two years. Statisticians report that the odds of identical twins both living to the age of 100 is 1 in 700 million.

SANDY ALLEN of Shelbyville, at 7 feet, 7 1/4 inches, is the *tallest woman in the world* capable of standing upright. Born in Chicago June 18, 1955, Sandy weighed 6 1/2 pounds. She was listed by the *Guinness Book of World Records* while working in the State Office Building in Indianapolis and became world famous. She underwent 2 pituitary gland operations to inhibit further growth, and now works for the Guinness Museum of World Records at Niagara Falls, Canada.

THE *first adoption by a single male* in Indiana was in 1973 when Neal Tiffany of Fort Wayne, 32, received permission to adopt Marshall, 12, on order of Marion County Probate Court Judge Edward Madinger. The Tiffanys moved to Michigan in 1982.

THE *heaviest man to die* in Indiana was Robert Earl

Hughes, who weighed 1,041 pounds when he succumbed to uremia in a mobile home at Bremen July 10, 1958, at the age of 32. Hughes was buried near Mount Sterling, Ill. He was a native of Monticello, Mo. His waist measured 122 inches, his chest 124 inches, and his upper arms 40 inches, all world-record sizes. According to records, his greatest weight was 1,069 pounds.

[SEE ALSO *Marriage*.]

W

WALKING

THE champion walker in modern times seems to have been Mrs. Addie M. Harper of Indianapolis, who walked an estimated 40,000 miles in 32 years. Mrs. Harper walked daily from her home on West Michigan Street to the Veterans Administration Hospital on Cold Spring Road, where she was a food service employee. She began the five-mile trip in 1932 because she had no car and the ride on three bus lines, including waiting, took longer than the walk.

WAR, CIVIL

THE *first military engagement* in Indiana in the Civil War was a raid across the Ohio River at Cannelton in June 1863 by a Union force trying to capture horses.

INDIANA *lost more men in the Civil War* than in any other armed conflict; 24,416 of a total in uniform of 208,367.

THE *most Hoosiers killed in a single battle* in the Civil War were the 3,000-plus who died at Chickamauga.

THE greatest cause of Hoosier casualties in the Civil War was not battle, in which 7,000-plus were killed, but *accidents and disease*, which accounted for more than 17,000 deaths.

THE *unit which lost the highest percentage of men* in the Civil War was the 19th or the Iron Brigade. 15.9 per cent of the brigade's total enrollment was killed.

THE *first Hoosier killed in the Civil War in outright combat* was W. T. Gerard of Jasper County, slain at Laurel Hill, West Virginia, July 7, 1861. Two Hoosiers were killed before Gerard, but not in combat. They were Charles Degner of Ohio County, shot while standing watch June 15, 1861, and John C. Hollenbeck of Marion County, murdered by Confederates after being captured during a scouting detail.

THE sole Hoosier *general to be killed* in the Civil War was Gen. Pleasant A. Hackleman of Brookville.

THE *last man to die* in the Civil War was Pvt. John J. Williams of Portland, killed May 13, 1865, in a skirmish which occurred when segments of the 34th Indiana Infantry were attacked at Palmetto Ranche, Tex., by Confederate cavalry. Williams, in Company B, was the last to fall in a casualty list which included 82 killed, wounded, and captured. Williams had enlisted in Indianapolis March 28, 1864, at the age of 21 and his death came after the war was technically over.

BY all odds the *worst Civil War general* from Indiana was Gen. Ambrose Burnside, born Liberty, 1824, who was unsuccessful in practically all his assignments in the war and met disaster at the Battle of Fredericksburg. He later was governor of Rhode Island and a senator from that state and his name lives in the term sideburns, given to hair growing down in front of the ears, a style he favored.

CAPT. DAVID V. BUSKIRK of Monroe County reportedly was the *tallest man in the Union Army*, standing 6 feet, 11 1/2 inches in his stocking feet. He was a member of Company F, 27th Indiana Regiment, which had 67 men standing more than 6 feet out of a roster of 101 men.

TWO Hoosiers were 9 when they enlisted in Civil War units, believed to be the *youngest to enter the military*. John W. Messick of Evansville joined September 3, 1861, and Edwin Black of Hagerstown entered service July 24, 1861. Messick joined with his father Jacob and served in the 42d Regiment of the Indiana Volunteers, leaving service October 10, 1864. Black was with the 21st Indiana Infantry Regiment (later the First Heavy Artillery Regiment) in engagements against Fort St. Philip and Fort Jackson (near New Orleans), the battle of Baton Rouge, and a skirmish at St. Charles, Pa.; he was discharged December 11, 1862. Both served as drummer boys.

THE raid by Gen. John Hunt Morgan into Indiana in July, 1863, was the *state's largest Civil War action*. With 2,000 or more men, Morgan hit Corydon, Salem, Vernon, and Versailles before leaving Indiana. Much property was destroyed, Salem was set afire, and many militia were captured by Morgan but released because he could do nothing with them and didn't wish to take them as he fled.

THE *first civilians to be sentenced to death by a military court* were Hoosiers Dr. William A. Bowles, Stephen Horsey, and Lambdin P. Milligan, tried for treason, insurrection, and giving aid to the Confederacy because of their alliance with the South. Their sentences were later declared unconstitutional because there were established Federal courts in Indiana when the military court took its action in 1864, and the Federal courts should have handled the case. The trio escaped an execution set for May 19,

1865, and later were pardoned by President Andrew Johnson.

THE *first national convention of the Grand Army of the Republic* was held in Indianapolis November 20, 1866. At it Stephen Augustus Hurlbut was elected commander-in-chief. The first GAR post had been established April 6 that year at Decatur, Ill., and the first state convention was held at Springfield, Ill., July 12.

THE Grand Army of the Republic held its *last encampment* in Indianapolis in August 1949; 17 members were alive, but less than half attended. The previous encampments had been in 1881, 1893, 1920, 1921, 1942, and 1946; a total of 12 Civil War veterans attended in 1946.

THE largest Indiana collection of Civil War *photographs taken by Matthew Brady* is that of the Soldiers and Sailors Monument Museum, Indianapolis, which has more than 1,000 pictures framed and displayed.

[SEE ALSO *Boats; Inventions; Organizations.*]

WAR, SPANISH-AMERICAN

THE *first American killed in the Spanish-American War* was Jesse K. Stork of Holland, a private with Troop A of the First Cavalry. Stork, who enlisted May 4, 1896, was shot June 28, 1898, while creeping up a stream near an outpost at Las Guasimas. He is believed to have been buried in Cuba.

WAR, WORLD

THE *first American to fire a shot* in World War I was Sgt. Alexander Arch of South Bend. He pulled the lanyard to discharge an artillery piece on the morning of October 22, 1917, near Artois in Lorraine. The first shell was part of a barrage of 24. The shell casing of that first shot was sent to president Woodrow Wilson and the artillery piece was sent to the museum of the West Point Military Academy.

CPL. JAMES BETHEL GRESHAM of Evansville became the first Indianan *killed in World War I* when he and two others died November 3, 1917, during a German raid in which 11 soldiers were captured. Gresham was buried outside Bathelemont in Lorraine, France, in ceremonies which appeared in photographs in newspapers across the U.S. Later his body was transferred to Evansville. Gresham, born in Kentucky, moved to Evansville in 1901 when he was 8, joined the Army April 21, 1914, and served with Gen. John Pershing in Mexico before his unit went to France and marched through Paris to the front.

THE *first American tank battalion*, formed in February 1918, was composed mostly of Hoosiers, about 700 members from Indiana. The 301st Heavy Tank Battalion was organized at Camp Taylor, Ky., and mechanics were trained at Purdue University. Before going to Europe, the unit trained at Camp Colt, Gettysburg.

THE *greatest Hoosier hero of World War I* was Lt. Samuel Woodfill, a career soldier born north of Madison; he was cited by Gen. John Pershing as the most heroic soldier because of his actions in 1918 near Cunel, France, in attacking a series of machine-gun nests. Woodfill later served as a pallbearer at Pershing's funeral. Woodfill died almost forgotten, was buried in Jefferson County in a grave later overgrown with weeds, and finally was interred in Arlington National Cemetery in 1955.

THE *first Air National Guard unit in the nation* was the 113th of Indiana, organized in 1921 at Kokomo by World War I veterans even before such units were authorized by law. The 113th moved to Indianapolis and was taken over by the Army at the start of World War II.

THE *first state to allow payroll deductions* for bonds in World War II was Indiana, winning approval from the U.S. Treasury Department to begin December 31, 1941. The auditor's office made deductions from the salaries of state employees. The first purchaser was Mrs. Harry G. Leslie, widow of the ex-governor, then an employee in the Bureau of Motor Vehicles.

THE *nation's first million-dollar defense bond party* was held in Indiana at the French Lick Springs Hotel August 14–15, 1942; more than $1,100,000 was subscribed by the 400 who attended and by others who sent pledges. Guests at the party, sponsored by Thomas D. Taggart, operator of the hotel, were Hollywood comics Bud Abbott and Lou Costello, who were on a bond-selling tour of the nation.

INDIANA was the *first state to have a bond rally* during World War II, when $2,017,513 was pledged during day-long activities in Indianapolis led by actress Carole Lombard, a native of Fort Wayne. Miss Lombard was killed in a plane crash while returning to Cailfornia from the 1942 rally.

THE *first bond rally in the nation sponsored by blacks* was held in August 1942 in Victory Field in Indianapolis with actress Hattie McDaniels and soprano Dorothy Maynor as guests. Organizer of the event, called Americans for Victory Day, was Indianapolis attorney Frank Beckwith; goal of the rally was $50,000 in bonds.

THE *first seizure of war material in the nation* during World War II was at Valparaiso where Federal authorities took over 200,000 pounds of scrap metal from the Frank Shumake junkyard after he repeatedly refused to sell at price-administration figures in March 1942. The scrap was shipped to the Gary steel mills.

INDIANAPOLIS was the *first city in the nation to convert abandoned railroad tracks* into steel for World War II tanks under a project which began March 11, 1942, with the taking up of Indianapolis Railways rails on Lexington Avenue at Pine Street. The rails were turned over to the National

Malleable and Steel Castings Company and thence to Marmon-Herrington Company to be made into tanks. The $67,000 paid for the rails was used by the city to repave the streets.

THE *first tri-service recruiting booth in the nation* was opened in the Claypool Hotel in Indianapolis in March 1942, providing pamphlets and leaflets with information on the Army, Navy, and Marines.

THE *first naval training school* in the U.S. to provide instruction to civilians for production of war material was built in Indianapolis at 6000 East 21st Street. Construction began in April 1942. The institution became the present-day Naval Avionics Facility.

THE *youngest Hoosier commissioned an officer* in World War II was Roscoe Remer of Evansville, 18 when he was made a second lieutenant in the Army Air Force in September 1942 after completing twin-engine flight training at Columbus, Miss.

THE *highest-ranking Hoosier killed in World War II* was Maj. Gen. Edwin D. Patrick of Tell City, chief of staff to Gen. Walter Kruger, commander of the Sixth Army. Patrick was hit while inspecting machine-gun emplacements on Luzon, Philippines. His death was March 17, 1945.

THE first all-metal lifeboats and rafts were manufactured in Kokomo, the lifeboat in December 1941 by Globe American Stove Company, and the life raft, called the "Kokomo Kid," in November 1943.

THE *first civilians in the U.S. to adopt uniforms for work* in World War II were employees of Curtiss-Wright propellor plant in Indianapolis. Stenographers, clerks, typists, and secretaries donned cadet-blue uniforms with brass buttons as a clothing conservation measurement in February 1942.

INDIANA was the *first state to establish a check system to keep reckless drivers from getting rationed tires* in late 1942.

Under the system, state police would forward tickets for careless driving to the ration board, and those who appeared there to get tires were reminded of their abuse and, in some cases, were refused tires.

THE *first female recruiter* was Mrs. Harry E. Massingill, Jr., who began work for the Navy in South Bend in late 1941. The first recruit she signed up was Jesse James Cannon, Jr., 17, of Plymouth.

INDIANA UNIVERSITY is believed to have been the *first university in the nation to establish military training for women* with the Women's Auxiliary Training Corps program begun in the fall of 1942. The WATC was similar to ROTC training.

THE *first female chairman of a World War II ration board in the nation* was Mrs. Inez M. School of Connersville, appointed to the post in Indiana upon the resignation of Fred Hackman. Mrs. School had been on the price panel of the board and was a former vice-chairman of the Democratic State Committee.

THE *first Hoosier female to join the regular Navy* was Wilma Juanita Marchal of Tell City, sworn in as a yeoman December 18, 1943, when the first six women were taken into the regular branch from the WAVES. At the time she was the *highest-ranking female member* of the Navy.

THE *first female doctor from Indiana in the armed services* in World War II was Martha L. Butler (Mrs. John Butler) of Princeton. She was commissioned a captain in March 1944 at Madigan Hospital Center, Fort Lewis, Washington.

THE *first prosecution of alleged tire rationing violators in the U.S.* during World War II was in Indianapolis where a federal court heard a case against Charles L. Hart and Russell W. Baker, officials of the LaSalle Sales Company of Boonville.

THE *first black to shoot down a Nazi plane* in World

War II was Lt. Charles B. Hall of Brazil, who downed a German Folke-Wulf 190 on July 2, 1943, while flying a P-40 in the Mediterranean Theater, and shot down two more planes before being recalled to the U.S.

THE *only Navy officer to lose a blimp in World War II* was Nelson G. Grills, Indianapolis attorney, who was a lieutenant in charge of a blimp patrolling for enemy submarines off the tip of Florida in July 1943. He found a sub which, for the first time in the war, was equipped with anti-aircraft guns; Grills's blimp was downed. The crew of 10 was rescued.

GERRY KISTERS of Bloomington was the *first soldier to receive a Medal of Honor* after he also had received a *Distinguished Service Cross* in World War II. President Franklin D. Roosevelt presented the Medal of Honor June 21, 1943, for Kisters's actions in the Sicily campaign. He had received the service cross in May 1943 from Gen. George C. Marshall, for bravery in Africa.

THE *only World War II German buzz bomb to reach Indiana* is that at Greencastle, obtained in 1946 from Army Ordnance Division in Maryland and converted into a memorial for war veterans in front of the Putnam County courthouse.

[SEE ALSO *Armaments; Boats; Holidays; Knight; Military; Sailors* and *Soldiers*.]

WAR, KOREAN

CPL. RICHARD E. MILLIS, a military photographer who began photographing Korean combat immediately after the nation was invaded, June 25, 1950, became the *first casualty from Indiana*. Born at Greensboro, he was educated in schools at Kennard and joined the Army infantry in World War II. He re-enlisted after the war, became a photographer, and was stationed in Japan when the Korean conflict began. After his death he was named Hoosier of the Year for 1950.

[SEE ALSO *Sailors and Soldiers.*]

WAR, VIETNAM

THE *most decorated Hoosier of the Vietnam war* was Marine Staff Sgt. Donald F. Myers, who was awarded two silver and two bronze stars by the United States and several medals by the Vietnamese government for his valor. Myers, who retired in 1973 because of combat-related disabilities and became a counselor with the Veterans Administration in Indianapolis, also received five Purple Hearts for wounds received in action. In 1983 Myers was commended by the VA for his action in disarming a disoriented veteran who had pulled out a loaded pistol during a talk with VA officials.

WATER

JAMES BUCHANAN EADS of Lawrenceburg became the *first native-born American to win the Albert Medal*, given June 10, 1884, for Eads's *plan to deepen the Mississippi River* with jetties. The medal, established in 1862, was in memory of Prince Albert of Britain and presented for distinguished merit in promoting arts, manufacturing, and commerce. Eads, born on the Ohio May 23, 1820, was abandoned with his family at St. Louis at the age of 13 when the ship carrying them burned. Drawn by the river, he became a student of the Mississippi. "There is not a space of 50 miles in the long stretch from New Orleans to St. Louis over some part of which I have not walked on the bed in my diving bell," he said. He worked to free the river of snags and clear it of sunken boats. He already had proposed opening the mouth of the stream by redirecting the currents when the Civil War broke out. Eads was given the job of making seven iron-clad ships so the Union could secure the river, a task he completed in the remarkable time of 100 days. His bridge across the Mississippi at St. Louis, at that time the largest arch bridge in the world, was completed in seven years, despite critics who said it couldn't be done. At last given Congressional authority to try to clear a channel at the mouth of the Mississippi, Eads succeeded by using willow mattresses to redirect the currents and rearrange sediment. This feat brought him to international attention and he traveled the world examining rivers. After his assessment of the Mersey in England he was given the Albert Medal. He died in 1887.

MADISON was the *first city in Indiana to have a municipal water system*, one of the few in the nation, when it was completed in 1849. The creators sold the system to the city in 1852. It began using wooden conduits, which soon deteriorated and were replaced by iron pipes; there were a reservoir and pumps. Pioneer accounts report that water was piped into the town from springs in the surrounding hills as early as 1814.

THE *only operating shed aqueduct* in Indiana is that on the Whitewater Canal in Metamora, a state memorial. The covered aqueduct carries boats over the river some 16 feet above the water of the stream and was constructed in 1848.

The largest harbor and the only *deep-water harbor* in Indiana is Burns Ditch, east of Gary, which opened in 1970 and handled a record 1,928,008 tons of cargo in 1984.

THE largest *river port* is Southwind Maritime Center on the Ohio River, which handled 3,538,419 tons of cargo in 1984.

THE *deepest natural lake* in the state is Tippecanoe Lake in Kosciusko County, measuring 123 feet.

THE *largest natural body of water* in Indiana is Lake Wawasee, covering 3,410 acres.

MONROE RESERVOIR, created by damming Salt Creek near Harrodsburg, is the *largest man-made lake* in Indiana. Water covers 10,750 acres; this can be expanded to 18,450 if needed for flood control.

THE *deepest man-made lake* is Brookville Reservoir, measuring 147 feet deep.

THE *largest state fish hatchery* is East Fork Hatchery, near Washington, which has 44 acres of water and can produce 10 to 40 million fish yearly, depending on species. It opened in 1983.

THE *biggest natural waterfall* in Indiana is Cataract Falls of about 35 feet in Richard Lieber State Recreation Area.

THE *longest navigable lost river* in America is in Bluespring Caverns near Bedford, which carries boats over a mile on water completely underground.

[SEE ALSO *Boats; Bridges; Structures*.]

WEATHER

INDIANA's *first radio and TV weatherman* was James C. Fidler of Muncie, who did weather stories for the *Muncie Evening Press* and weather broadcasts for WLBC when he was in high school and college, circa 1930. Later he went to Cincinnati and did weather broadcasting there. He worked many years for the Weather Bureau Reporting Service, which prepared forecasts for broadcasters. In 1952–54 he appeared on the Dave Garroway morning TV show doing the weather, but he stopped over an objection that he was violating union rules because he received no pay for the telecasts.

THE record for *cold* in Indiana is 35 degrees below zero, February 2, 1951, at Greensburg, 35 miles from the

Ohio River; this surpassed the previous low of 33 below zero at Lafayette January 2, 1887.

THE *coldest summer* was that of 1816, when ponds and rivers froze every month and an estimated 60,000 pioneers suffered bitter weather throughout the season. In May Indiana had snow or sleet on 17 days. In June there was snow, and livestock froze to death. A farmer leaving home June 17 joked that he might get lost in a snow storm; he did, and was found with both feet frozen. Similar weather afflicted the rest of the nation, too; 1816 was called "the year without a summer."

THE *most recorded annual snow* was 107 inches which fell at LaPorte near Lake Michigan in 1929; LaPorte had had 100 inches of snow in 1924.

THE *highest recorded official temperature* in Indiana is 116 degrees at Collegeville in Jasper County July 14–15, 1936. In the same period several nearby areas had a temperature equally high; Shoals recorded 114. A reading of 113 in Southern Indiana had been the record high before 1936.

THE *driest summer* in Indiana was in 1933 when 4.34 inches of rain fell in the three-month period of June, July, and August.

INDIANA'S *greatest temperature difference* occurred in Jasper County in 1936: a temperature of 116 was officially recorded July 15, followed on July 29 by frost in the northern part of the county.

IN modern times the *latest frost* (or is it the earliest?) occurred July 29, 1936, in low areas in Jasper County.

WOMEN

THE first *Pan-American conference on women* was planned by Marie Stuart Edwards in offices on the second floor over a business at Peru. She was publicity director of the American Women's Suffrage Association and became president of the Indiana Franchise League in 1917. She was the first national treasurer of the League of Women Voters. The conference was held in 1921. Mrs. Edwards, born in Lafayette in 1880, died in 1970.

WHAT may have been the *first old-age pension system in the nation* was established for widows by George Dean, an Englishman farmer of wealth near Winslow in Pike County. Under a trust established at the time of Dean's death in 1855, widows living within eight miles of Winslow got $1.50 a week, then a sum sufficient for survival. In 1926 a total of 28 widows were cared for by the trust, which died when the Social Security system began in 1935.

THE *first woman to be president of the Professional Skaters Guild of America* was Sandy Schwomeyer Lamb of Indianapolis, who served from 1983 to 1985. The guild, most of whose members are teachers of figure skating, has about 900 members.

[SEE ALSO *Industry; Mail; Museums; Newspapers; Organizations; Police; Sports; Railroads.*]

X

X - R A Y S : SEE *Medicine.*

Y I E L D : SEE *Plants.*

Y O U T H : SEE *Governors; Politics, city; Sports, swimming and tennis; War, civil.*

Z

Z O O S : SEE *Animals.*

INDEX OF NAMES

A

Arnold, Chuck, *see* Sports, racing, automobile
Arnold, Reggie, *see* Sports, football
Arnold, Ross Harper, *see* inventions
Arvin, Richard Hood, *see* Inventions
Ash, George, *see* Structures
Atkinson, George, *see* Games
Auman, Gregory, *see* Stunts
Austin, Burt, *see* Sports, football
Avery, Theodore, *see* Plants

B

Babb, Bob, *see* Sports, track and field
Bailey, George, *see* Sports, racing, automobile
Bailey R. E., *see* Sports, baseball
Baker, Jim, *see* Sports, racing, skiing
Baker, R., *see* Sports, track and field
Ballentine, Von Lee, *see* Plants
Baker, E. G. (Cannonball), *see* Speed
Baker, Rich, *see* Sports, fishing
Baker, Russell W., *see* Wars, world
Balz, Mrs. Arcada Stark, *see* Politics, state
Banas, Norm, *see* Sports, baseball
Banholzer, Carl, *see* Food and drink
Banks, D., *see* Sports, track and field
Banks, Henry, *see* Sports, racing, automobile
Bannwart, Wessel, *see* Animals
Banta, George, *see* Plants
Banvard, John, *see* Art and artists
Barbour, Paul, *see* Plants
Barker, Sarah Evans, *see* Courts
Barner, Terry, *see* Sports, fishing
Barnes, Nick, *see* Sports, football
Barnhill, Dr. John F., *see* Medicine
Barrett, Toni, *see* Stunts
Barth, Mrs. Louisa W., *see* Courts
Bashore, Sonny, *see* Sports, fishing
Barr, Guy, *see* Sports, basketball
Barz, Gerda, *see* Sports, Senior Olympics
Barz, Hans, *see* Sports, Senior Olympics
Bass, Sam, *see* Crime and criminals
Bateman, Bonnie, *see* Sports, bowling
Battaglia, Carla, *see* Sports, track and field
Baxter, Kelvin, *see* Aviation
Bays, David L., *see* Sports, fishing
Beaman, Ellsworth, *see* Plants
Bean, Walter D., *see* Education
Beard, Emma, *see* Sports, bowling

C

Green, LeBaron, *see* Sports, track and field
Greer, Joann, *see* Colleges and universities
Greiner, Arthur, *see* Sports, racing, automobile
Gresham, Cpl. James Bethel, *see* Wars, World
Greyhound, *see* Sports, racing, harness
Grills, Nelson G., *see* Wars, World
Grissom, Virgil I., *see* Astronauts
Groeninger, Constance, *see* Sports, bowling
Grondziak, Marsha, *see* Sports, track and field
Gruelle, John, *see* Dolls
Guerin, Mother Theodore, *see* Colleges and universities
Guest, Orlando, *see* Sports, football
Guinea Gold, *see* Sports, racing, harness
Gullet, Patrick, *see* Sports, track and field
Gunness, Belle, *see* Crime and criminals
Guthrie, Janet, *see* Sports, racing, automobile
Guy, Jim, *see* Sports, shooting
Guyer, Laura, *see* Stunts
Gwin, Max, *see* Art and artists

H

Haas, Carl and Paul, *see* Plants
Hackleman, Gen. Pleasant A., *see* War, Civil
Hafner, H., *see* Sports, swimming
Hagans, Jack A., *see* Sports, basketball
Hagen, Patricia, *see* Recreation
Hagerman, R. E., *see* Plants
Haines, John F., *see* Organizations
Haines, Leslie, *see* Automobiles and trucks
Hall, Lt. Charles B., *see* Wars, world
Hall, Charles Corydon, *see* Manufacturing
Hall, Gary, *see* Sports, swimming
Hall, Ricky, *see* Sports, basketball
Hallas, Bob, *see* Sports, baseball
Hallman, Walter F., *see* Games
Halloway, Susie, *see* Sports, bowling
Halstead, Charles Earl, *see* Police
Hamilton, Francis, *see* Radio
Hamilton, Henry, *see* Art and artists
Hamilton, Ted A., *see* Stunts
Hammond, George H., *see* Railroads
Hanauer, Chip, *see* Boats
Hanks, Sam, *see* Sports, racing, automobile
Hanley, Mrs. Barbara, *see* Police
Hanly, James F., *see* Governors
Hanna, Mike, *see* Sports, track and field
Hansen, Chuck, *see* Sports, football

K

L

Loviscek, Paul, *see* Sports, football
Lundquist, Steve, *see* Sports, swimming
Luphra, Amarjett, *see* Marriage
Lyman, Steve, *see* Stunts

M

MacBeth, George A., *see* Manufacturing
MacGordon, Elsie, *see* Radio
MacKenzie, Doc, *see* Sports, racing, automobile
MacLean, Arthur, *see* Archaeology
Madden, Ray, *see* Politics, U.S.
Madison, Chad, *see* Sports, track and field
Madruga, Rojer, *see* Sports, swimming
Maggioni, Vincent, *see* Sports, bicycling
Magill, Mike, *see* Sports, racing, automobile
Magner, Morris K., *see* Plants
Mahler, James L., *see* Photography
Mahorney, Gertrude, *see* Colleges and universities
Maier, Paul, *see* Plants
Majors, Eleanor, *see* Sports, track and field
Male, Tom, *see* Sports, football
Malone, Maicel, *see* Sports, track and field
Mance, Mercer M., *see* Courts
Mann, David, *see* Sports, racing, soap box
Marchal, Wilma Juanita, *see* Wars, world
Mandera, Pat, *see* Sports, track and field
Markezich, Ron, *see* Sports, track and field
Marham, Fred, *see* Sports, bicycling
Marshall, Bob, *see* Sports, wrestling
Marshall, Cy, *see* Sports, racing, automobile
Marshall, George, *see* Plants
Marshall, Humphrey, *see* Duels
Marshman, Bobby, *see* Sports, racing, automobile
Martin, A. J., *see* Animals
Martin, Kevin, *see* Sports, track and field
Martin, Mac, *see* Sports, racing, running
Martin, Mark, *see* Sports, racing, automobile
Martin, Tom, *see* Sports, track and field
Martindale, Charles, Jr., *see* Stunts
Mason, Jack, *see* Sports, racing, automobile
Massingill, Mrs. Harry E., Jr., *see* Wars, world
Mateja, Phil, *see* Sports, football
Mattice, Floyd J., *see* Radio
Mattingly, Don *see* Sports, baseball
Matze, Chris, *see* Sports, track and field
Mauer, Michaellyn, *see* Firemen
Maust, Henry, *see* Art and artists

N

Q

R

S

T